SOME STORIES

YVON CHOUINARD

LESSONS FROM THE EDGE OF BUSINESS AND SPORT

patagonia

Yvon Chouinard Some Stories
Lessons from the Edge of Business and Sport

Patagonia publishes a select list of titles on wilderness, wildlife, and
outdoor sports that inspire and restore a connection to the natural world.

Patagonia Books, Patagonia Inc.,
259 W. Santa Clara St., Ventura, CA 93001-2717

Hardcover edition
Printed in Canada on 100 percent postconsumer recycled paper

Editor – John Dutton
Art Director, Designer – Christina Speed
Production – Rafael Dunn
Creative Director – Bill Boland
Director of Books – Karla Olson

Photo Editors – Jenifer Ridgeway, Jane Sievert
Project Manager – Jennifer Patrick
Photo Archivist – Sus Corez
Creative Advisor – Jennifer Ridgeway

JACKET PHOTO FRONT: *Yvon in the Black Dihedral, North America Wall, El Capitan, Yosemite.* Tom Frost/Aurora

JACKET PHOTO BACK: *Yvon Chouinard. Ventura, California.* Tim Davis

ENDPAPERS PHOTO: *The 1972 Chouinard Equipment catalog described Lost Arrows as "horizontal pitons
incorporating simplicity of design, economy of material, high strength, and classic beauty."* Rick Ridgeway

Hardcover ISBN 978-1-938340-82-6
E-Book ISBN 978-1-938340-83-3
Library of Congress Control Number 2019930559

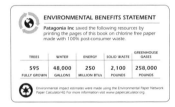

1% FOR THE PLANET MEMBER

DEDICATION

To all my friends, past and present, who were a big part of these adventures.

ACKNOWLEDGMENTS

A special thank you goes to longtime friend and Patagonia photography editor Jennifer Ridgeway, whose tireless work and creative eye made this book what it is.

Over the years I've had some badly needed help from various editors and I'd like to sincerely thank Charlie Craighead, John Dutton, Nora Gallagher, Vincent Stanley, and Dylan Tomine. Thank you also to Patagonia photo editor Jane Sievert for her work on this book.

Stories

Preface

The Golden Age of a sport is when the most innovation in technique and equipment occurs, and I've been fortunate to have lived and participated in the Golden Age of many an outdoor sport: spearfishing, falconry, fly fishing, whitewater kayaking, telemark and backcountry skiing, ice climbing, and Yosemite big-wall climbing.

I don't consider myself much of a writer, I'm more of a storyteller really. I've had a pretty rich, adventurous, and, so far, lucky life in which I've amassed quite a few stories that would be of interest to some people. That's the reason for this book.

I'm a passionate reader, but I rarely read fiction. You have to be a lot more creative to write fiction. Fashion photography is way more difficult than landscape, art more difficult than illustration. Also, I prefer to watch documentary films.

In school, I was tasked with writing an essay titled "I, Why." What a horror! I stared at my white sheet of paper for an hour trying to find a cornerstone to build on. But if you tell me to write a five-hundred-word essay on what I ate for breakfast, no problem.

I've tried to live a simple life focused neither on the past nor future, but on the present. Admitting to myself that I'm basically a simple person, I've tried to keep my words and sentences simple.

I've found that I get a lot of creative satisfaction from breaking the rules in sport and business. Plus, it's a lot easier than conforming and, in the end, leads to better stories.

OPPOSITE: *Yvon on the North America Wall, El Capitan, Yosemite. 1964.* Tom Frost/Aurora
NEXT SPREAD: *Jumaring under the Great Roof, North America Wall, Yosemite.* Tom Frost/Aurora

Lessons from the Edge

First published in Extreme Landscape: The Lure of Mountain Spaces *by Bernadette McDonald, National Geographic Society, 2002. Also, much of this material appeared in* Let My People Go Surfing: The Education of a Reluctant Businessman *by Yvon Chouinard, Penguin Books, first edition 2006, updated edition 2016.*

When I was seven, our family sold our house in the French-speaking town of Lisbon, Maine, and auctioned off all our possessions. The six of us piled into the Chrysler and drove to California. The day after we arrived in Burbank, I was enrolled in public school. Being the smallest boy in class, and unable to speak English, I did the logical thing. On the third day of school, I ran away.

I eventually went back, but ever afterward I remained at the edge of things. Before the other kids in my neighborhood were allowed to cross the street on their own, I was bicycling seven or eight miles to a lake on a private golf course, where I would hide in the willows and fish for bluegills and bass. Later I discovered Griffith Park and the Los Angeles River, where I spent every day after school gigging frogs, trapping crawdads, and hunting cottontails with my bow and arrow.

I didn't take part in any of the usual activities of high school. I remember math class was an opportunity to practice breath holding so that on the weekends, I could freedive deeper to catch the abundant abalone and lobster off the Malibu coast. A few of us misfits started a falconry club where we used falcons and hawks for hunting.

OPPOSITE: *Fifteen-year-old Yvon with an immature red-tailed hawk, Burbank, California.*
Yvon Chouinard Collection

Rappelling down to falcon aeries led to learning to climb, which led to trips to Wyoming at the age of sixteen to climb Gannett Peak, the highest mountain in the Wind River Range. Every year thereafter was spent climbing mountains, kayaking, and fishing rivers. During some of those years I slept

---

We liked the fact that climbing rocks and icefalls had no economic value for society.

---

200 nights in a sleeping bag. In fact, I resisted buying a tent until I was over forty. I preferred to sleep under the stars or, in storms, under a boulder or tucked beneath the branches of an alpine fir. I particularly liked sleeping in a hammock hanging from a rock wall on multiday climbs.

My passion for climbing mountains led to earning a living working as a blacksmith—forging pitons, ice axes, and other tools. I never intended for this craft to become a business, but every time my partner Tom Frost and I returned from the mountains, our heads were spinning with new ideas for improving the existing tools. Our guiding principle of design was a quote from the aviator and writer Antoine de Saint-Exupéry: "In anything at all, perfection is finally attained not when there is no longer anything to add, but when there is no longer anything to take away." Quality control was always foremost in our minds because if a tool failed, it could kill someone.

All winter I forged gear. For the rest of the year, I continued to lead a counterculture life on the fringes of society—living on fifty cents a day on a diet of oatmeal, potatoes, and canned cat food; camping all summer in an old incinerator in the abandoned CCC (Civilian Conservation Corps) camp in the Tetons of Wyoming. In the spring and fall I would climb the granite walls of Yosemite Valley. We were the "Valley Cong," living like guerillas in the nooks and boulders behind Camp 4.

We liked the fact that climbing rocks and icefalls had no economic value for society. We were rebels from the consumer culture of our parents. Businessmen were "grease balls" and corporations were the source of all evil. The natural world was our home. Our heroes were Muir, Thoreau, Emerson, Gaston

Grinding away at the Ventura shop. Tom Frost/Aurora

Rébuffat, and Hermann Bühl. We were living on the edges of the ecosystem—adaptable, resilient, and tough. What didn't kill us made us stronger. We also grew smarter.

I learned to appreciate simplicity. Management is the art of organizing complexity. You shouldn't try to solve complex problems with more complexity.

Of course, every winter I returned to my business, even if I didn't call it that. Later on, we applied the same philosophy of simplicity of design and reliability to the production of climbing clothing. The best products are the simplest. Our customers appreciated our "hand-forged" Stand Up Shorts, rugby shirts, and corduroy knickers. It took me twenty years of being in busi-

ness before I would admit that I was a businessman—and would probably be one for the rest of my life.

The values learned from a life in nature, from climbing and other risk sports, could also be applied to business. In the practice of Zen archery, you forget about trying to achieve the goal—that is, hitting the bull's-eye. Instead, you focus on all of the individual movements. You practice your stance, reach back, and pull an arrow out of the quiver, notching it on the string. You match your breathing to the release of the arrow. When you perfect all the elements of shooting an arrow, it can't help but go into the bull's-eye. Climbing mountains, too, is a process. How you climb a mountain is more important than getting to the top.

The process to perfection is through simplification. When TM Herbert and I made the first ascent of a route on El Capitan, which we later named the Muir Wall, we studied the route from below, calculated how many days it would take, and took just enough equipment and supplies. Ten days later, we reached the top with no water, food, or bolts left. We knew our abilities, had accurately calculated the risk, and then pulled it off. Later, climbers would solo the route, free climb it, do speed ascents. Each generation of climbers has evolved physically and mentally so that equipment becomes less necessary. When the best speed climbers do the 3,000-foot Nose route on El Capitan, they no longer need haul bags or Gore-Tex because they are down by lunch; they may do Half Dome and maybe a couple more walls before the day is over.

Living a life close to nature has also taught me about responsibility. No animal is so stupid and greedy as to foul its own nest—except the human animal. Ten years ago, the prestigious Worldwatch Institute reported, "If growth proceeds along the lines of recent decades, it is only a matter of time before global systems collapse under the pressure." Recently, in its *State of the World 2000* report, Worldwatch had this to say: "We hoped that we could begin the next century with an upbeat report, one that would show the Earth's health improving. But unfortunately, the list of trends we were concerned with then—shrinking forests, eroding soils, falling water tables,

OPPOSITE: *Tom and Dorene Frost, Tony Jessen, Dennis Hennek, Terry King, Yvon Chouinard, Merle, and Davey Agnew at the Skunkworks in Ventura, California. 1966.* Tom Frost

collapsing fisheries, and disappearing species—has since lengthened to include rising temperatures, more destructive storms, dying coral reefs, and melting glaciers."

We are destroying the very systems on which our lives depend. We continue

———

*Because we are all part of nature, we
need to look to nature for the solutions.*

———

to delude ourselves into thinking that technology is the answer. But technology is a limited tool. It creates industries, but eliminates jobs. It cures disease, but doesn't make us healthier. It frees us from some chores, but so far has led to a net loss of leisure time. There is a downside to every technological advancement. All technology has really done is to allow more of us to reside on Earth. Because we are all part of nature, we need to look to nature for the solutions.

To act responsibly, we need to make some fundamental changes. We have to work toward becoming a sustainable society. Planning and decisions need to be made on the premise that we're all going to be around for a long time. The Iroquois Nations extended their planning for seven generations into the future. Such planning would preclude natural disasters like clear-cutting the last of the old-growth forest or destroying rivers with dams that will silt up in twenty years. As a businessman, if I really believe in the rightness of such planning, then my own company, which is dependent on nonrenewable resources to make consumer goods, must also do the "right thing."

When I think of sustainability, I think back to when I was a GI in Korea. There, I saw farmers pouring night soil on paddies that had been in continuous use for 3,000 years. Each generation of farmers had left the land in as good or better condition as when they received it. Contrast this with modern agribusiness, which wastes two bushels of topsoil to produce one bushel of corn, and pumps groundwater at a rate 25 percent faster than it's being replenished. A

OPPOSITE: *Half Dome, Yosemite.* Mikey Schaefer

Camping in the Tetons. "I didn't own a tent until I was in my forties—and that's not my sissy air mattress." 1958. Ken Weeks

responsible government encourages farmers to be good stewards of the land and to practice sustainable agriculture. But why should only the farmer or the fisherman or forester have the responsibility to see that Earth remains habitable for future generations of humans and other wild things?

My business has taken a close look at its own impact on nature. We do an ongoing environmental assessment of all our business processes, including a "life cycle" analysis of our products—from material source, to manufacturing, to shipping, to consumer care, to ultimate disposal. Then, once you have taken the trouble to learn what you're really doing, you have to act upon that knowledge. We switched to 100 percent organic cotton, partnered with bluesign® to manage our dyes and chemicals used in our products, and dramatically increased the use of recycled materials in our line. We replaced paper cups with permanent ware at our offices. We use energy-efficient lightbulbs throughout our buildings. We use 100 percent postconsumer recycled paper in our catalogs, marketing materials, and for office purposes. We use reclaimed lumber and source local materials to build our retail stores as much as possible.

One of the most positive changes was to stop using conventionally grown

---

In the long run, any attempt to achieve sustainability on Earth with six billion people seems doomed to fail.

---

cotton. Cotton can be one of the most damaging crops. Twenty-five percent of the total amount of insecticide used in the world is applied to cotton, which occupy only 3 percent of the world's farmland. Before harvesting, a cotton field is treated up to twenty-five times with fertilizers, growth promoters, herbicides, pesticides, and fungicides. Then the plant has to be defoliated before being harvested. Arsenic was used for this purpose—now paraquat is used, the chemical America used to spray on its wartime enemies. Most of the chemical residue ends up in the aquifer, in workers' lungs, and, since cottonseed is a food product, in your potato chips. When we learned this in 1995, we decided that we would rather not be in business if we had to make clothing this way. Since 1996 we have not used any industrially grown cotton in our clothing.

We've made some big changes but we've made some disheartening discoveries also. One is that "sustainable manufacturing" is an oxymoron. It's impossible to manufacture something without using more material and energy than the resulting final product. For instance, modern agriculture takes 3,000 calories of fossil fuel to produce a net 1,000 calories of food. The rest is waste. If you wanted to replace the output of one Orlon mill with natural wool, you would have to raise sheep from Maine to the Mississippi. Yet Orlon is made from oil, which is not sustainable. In the long run, any attempt to achieve sustainability on Earth with six billion people seems doomed to fail. But we have to work toward that goal of sustainability, recognizing that it's an ever-receding summit. It's the process that counts.

22

These environmental assessments have educated us, and forced us to make hard choices. Each day that we act positively on those choices takes us further along the path to sustainability. Yet we are not martyrs. Every time we elect to do the right thing, it turns out to be more profitable and it strengthens our confidence that we are going to be in business for a long time. That's the lesson corporations need to learn.

But because we realize we're still net polluters, we take another step: We "tax" ourselves for using up nonrenewable resources. We reserve one percent of our total sales and use it to protect and restore our natural environment. Rather than waiting for the government to tax energy consumption and pollution, we decided to do it ourselves. Over the past fifteen years Patagonia has contributed more than $15 million to grassroots environmental organizations ($100 million by 2018).

In 2002, we decided to take this idea even further: We started an organization called One Percent for the Planet, an alliance of businesses pledging to donate one percent of their total revenue to efforts that protect and restore our natural environment. Each member company contributes to organizations of its choosing. This simplifies the decision-making process of the licensing corporation (and minimizes attendant bureaucracy) and encourages member companies to develop independent relationships with the groups they support. In return, member companies are licensed to use the One Percent for the Planet logo in their marketing.

Few believe that society's religious leaders, politicians, or corporate moguls are going to save us from the apocalyptic slide that we are on when there already exist hundreds of thousands of non-governmental organizations (NGOs) devoted to solving the world's problems. They are far more capable of doing it than multinational corporations or bureaucratic government agencies. The problem is these nonprofits are often dependent on small donations or "bake sales" to fund their good works. The intent of the One Percent for the Planet Alliance is to help fund these diverse environmental organizations so that, collectively, they can be a more powerful force. They can start the revolution.

PREVIOUS SPREAD: *"My climbing partner, Ken Weeks (lying down), and I cleaned out this incinerator and lived in it one summer in the Tetons." Jackson, Wyoming. 1958.* Lorraine Bonney

OPPOSITE: *Aid climbing on the north face of Quarter Dome, Yosemite.* Tom Frost

The one percent idea doesn't have to be limited to businesses. Any individual can do that right now—simply tax yourself. The best part is you decide where the money goes. It's taxation with direct representation, a true democracy. We can all be part of the revolution to transform the way people think and act.

The importance of environmental action is the most recent lesson that a life on the edge has taught me. All along the way, the natural world forces you to see what you might otherwise miss. Our treasure, anything of real value, comes from the Earth and sun, and it's our responsibility to protect it.

OPPOSITE: *Product testing in "full" Scottish conditions. "All along the way the natural world forces you to see what you might otherwise miss." 1969.* Doug Tompkins

Southern California Falconry Club

Minutes, Unpublished, 1953

When I was fifteen I was elected secretary of our falconry club. Writing these minutes was my first writing assignment outside of school. Obviously, I had some help.

The adults like Bob Klimes, a music teacher, Don Prentice, an all-around adventurer, and Tom Code, a biology graduate student at UCLA, treated us kids like adults. They taught us falconry and climbing. It was the most formative time of our lives.

On his ninetieth birthday in 2018, Tom Code reminded me that in 1954 he and I rappelled to a peregrine aerie in Lompoc, California. The thin, crushed eggs we found were the first evidence implicating DDT in the demise of the peregrine falcon in North America. There were no falcons east of the Mississippi River and few pairs left in the West. Tom and a few friends developed a captive breeding and release program that pulled the peregrine back from the edge of extinction. Now the peregrine falcon is a common bird all over the country.

The first meeting of the Southern California Falconry Club was held May 2, 1953, at the home of Jerry Allen, 1037 North California St., Burbank. Those in attendance were Jerry Allen, Skip Carmel, Yvon Chouinard, Robert Klimes, Ken Miller, and Warren Trobough.

The meeting was brought to order at 9:15 pm by President "pro tempore" Robert Klimes. The first line of business was to establish the frequency of meeting dates. It was voted unanimously to hold weekly meetings for the first month, and thereafter two meetings per month would follow. The next vote was on the term of office. The voting decided that the term would be for six months with four officers and for the first period starting May 1, 1953, the term would be three months with three officers; namely Robert Klimes, president; Warren Trobough, vice president; and Yvon Chouinard, secretary-treasurer.

Some of the members of the Southern California Falconry Club. "That's me on the right with a goshawk." 1956. Yvon Chouinard Collection

The next business was acceptance by vote, of the name of our club, THE SOUTHERN CALIFORNIA FALCONRY CLUB; as suggested by Warren Trobough. The dues were affixed at $3.00 per quarter payable at the beginning of each quarter, or at fifty cents per meeting. The first dues are payable to the treasurer at the next meeting May 9, 1953.

The duties decided on for the next meeting were that the president should investigate getting a charter for the club and that Skip Carmel and Jerry Allen should present information concerning the printing of cards for the club.

The remainder of the meeting was held in discussion of the proposed constitution of the club. The meeting of the club was adjourned at 11:50 pm.

ATTEST
Yvon Chouinard, Secretary   Robert Klimes, President

California Surfing and Climbing in the Fifties

Introduction to a book by Tom Adler, 2013

"On either end of the social spectrum there lies a leisure class." – Eric Beck

The most exciting time in the life span of any sport or social movement is the golden age, the first dozen years or so when innovation in the equipment and technique comes fast and furious.

It's natural that the Golden State with its diverse immigrant culture, its vast natural resources, and laid-back attitude would give birth to so many sports and social revolutions.

The fifties were the easy years in California. With full employment from the Korean War, we were enjoying all the fruits of the fossil fuel culture. Gas was a quarter a gallon, used cars could be bought for twenty-five dollars, campgrounds were free, and you could easily live off the excess fat of society. Those of us in the counter cultures of climbing and surfing were as climber Pete Sinclair said, "the last free Americans."

I've been lucky to have been part of that golden age of not only surfing and climbing but also falconry, spearfishing, whitewater kayaking, and, later on, telemark skiing.

OPPOSITE: *Surfing in the morning at Malibu and bouldering in the afternoon at Stoney Point. California. 1955.* Roger Cotton Brown

NEXT SPREAD: *Harry Daley, Tom Frost, Royal Robbins, and Yvon (left to right), Stoney Point, California. 1959.* Roger Cotton Brown

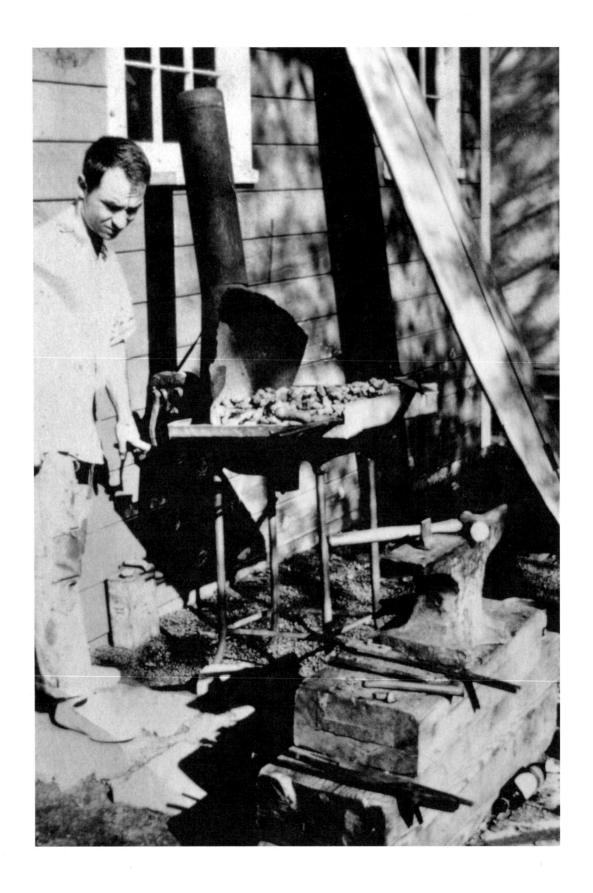

In 1954, I went down to General Veneer in Los Angeles, bought some balsa planks, and made my very first surfboard. I later traded that board for a Model A Ford engine. Tooling down Malibu Canyon from my home in Burbank, if I saw another surfer coming back from Malibu they would give me a thumbs-up if there was surf.

My first blacksmith shop was a chicken coop in my folks' backyard in Burbank. There's a photo of me hammering out my first pitons in 1957 and there's a surfboard in the background. I'd often climb for half a day at Stoney Point in Chatsworth, then go up to Rincon for the evening glass after I'd free-dive for lobsters and abalone on the coast between Zuma and the county line. I almost always got my limit of ten lobsters and five abalone.

A good deal of my shop work was portable, so I'd cruise the coast from San Diego to Big Sur, working on the beach and riding waves when the tide and the wind were just right. During those years I figured I slept on the ground 250 nights a year.

When I moved my shop to Ventura to be closer to the surf, the ultimate day was what we called a "McNab": Skiing on Pine Mountain, climbing on the Sespe Wall, playing tennis, and surfing the glass-off at C Street or Rincon. Where else in the world except New Zealand could you pull off a day like that?

OPPOSITE: *Forging pitons outside Yvon's first shop in Burbank. "I made the surfboard in the background from balsa wood and fiberglass, and eventually traded it for a Model A Ford engine." 1957.* Dan Doody

NEXT SPREAD: *Clearing storm clouds on Cathedral Rocks, Yosemite.* Glen Denny

To Dave and Ann Craft

Letter, Unpublished, 1961

In the late fifties and early sixties I supported myself by making pitons and carabiners in the winter months in California. In the early spring I would head to Yosemite Valley to climb and sell the gear out of the back of my car. Leaving my car behind I would head east and climb in the Rockies and Canada in the summer, and then catch a ride to the Shawangunks in New York in the late fall. There I would climb with my Vulgarian friends like Dave Craft and then hitchhike back to California.

From the day the doctor refused to write to the draft board about the prob- lem with my heart arrhythmia, I knew the world was caving in on me. I didn't want to leave the Shawangunks, but winter was coming and I wanted to get back to California. Anyway, whenever things get bad I feel like I have to hit the road.

In New York, I found a car-delivery agency that had an old 1952 Pontiac that needed to be delivered to New Mexico. I paid a fee of twenty-seven dollars, and they said I would collect sixty-two dollars from the owner for my expenses. If I needed to make repairs, just keep the receipts and it would be reimbursed. The car was already running rough when I left. Driving across country usually gives me a charge—the open road and all—but not this time. With the Army waiting to snuff out two of the most important years of my life, there was no joy in traveling. In Pennsylvania, I passed signs saying to

OPPOSITE: *It was either join the circus or become a climber. Chuck Pratt on the brink of Vernal Fall, Yosemite.* Glen Denny

pull over if sleepy, so I did in Ohio and woke up to a pair of cops working me over like I was an escaped felon. In Ohio, it's against the law to sleep in your car!

In Kansas, the automatic transmission crapped out. I couldn't contact the

———

The next day the judge said we were booked on the charge of vagrancy: "wandering about aimlessly with no apparent means of support."

———

agency or owner and couldn't just leave the car there because I'd get arrested for auto theft. I waited for three days to get it fixed. I drove on, collecting more repair bills for a water pump, distributor, etc. The transmission gave out again in Denver. I left the car in a garage and hitched to Boulder and joined up with Chuck Pratt, who was hanging around. He was going back to California too, so we left Boulder together. On the way back to the garage, we got ticketed for hitchhiking. The garage took all the money ($400) that I made selling pitons in the East for the repairs.

Finally, in Albuquerque we delivered the car to an old bitch who accused us of driving all over hell and gone. She refused to reimburse me for repairs because her contract said it was supposed to be delivered by October 20. I didn't even leave New York until the twenty-third! The cops came and agreed with her side of the story and gave us twenty-four hours to get out of town. We had ten dollars between us so we hitched to Grants, New Mexico, where we were thrown in jail for seventy-two hours. The jail was hideous! Puke all over the cement floor we had to sleep on. No windows, and freezing cold. Drunk Indians up all night chanting. We took a bus out of town and hitched to Gallup, where a rescue mission took us in. We listened to the sermon, ate

OPPOSITE: *Chuck Pratt (left) and Yvon testing a prototype haul bag in Camp 4, Yosemite. 1969.*
Glen Denny

real food, and slept in a bed. All the next day it snowed from 7 am to 6 pm. No one would give us a ride.

All the box cars in the freight yards were locked. An open gondola was not an option but we found an unlocked jeep on a piggyback. We crawled on the floor and ninety miles later in Winslow, Arizona, we were awoken with a flashlight beam in our faces. The railroad bull said he caught us because he saw that the windows of the jeep were frosted.

The next day the judge said we were booked on the charge of vagrancy: "wandering about aimlessly with no apparent means of support." "How do you plead?" he asked us.

I replied, "What happens if we plead innocent?"

"We are going to hold you here until you get a trial in a few weeks, and you'll need to get a lawyer," he told us.

"And if we plead guilty?"

"We will check you out with the FBI and you will have to wait in jail for that."

"OK, we plead guilty, your honor." Bam! Eighteen days in jail!

Chuck and I each had a five-foot by six-foot cell to ourselves. We were fed a bowl of oatmeal and a slice of Wonder bread in the morning and a bowl of beans and bread at night. Chuck couldn't stand oatmeal so he traded with me for my slice of bread. After a few days he got put on a work detail at the police garage cleaning grease off of motors. I worked on a garbage truck with a couple of Navajos. I was able to find some edible garbage, which helped, but Pratt came out of jail weighing 115 pounds. We had no money and "twenty-four hours to get out of Winslow."

Pratt got home to a draft notice and I got mine soon after.

OPPOSITE: *Hitchhiking to Yosemite in the 1950s was the fallback move when funds were low. Stranded on the empty reaches of US Highway 395, a climber dreams of high places while awaiting a big rig or a poultry truck … anything. Owens Valley, California.* Bob Swift

Remember That Big Storm

San Francisco, Unpublished, 1961

A wave conceived from the universal Mother Pacific,
In the cradle of storms, the Aleutians;
Traveling across the black unknown sea,
Not knowing which is the shore it seeks.
No different from its brothers,
No different from its predecessors;
When lagging, nourished by the unseen trades,
Always the dread of not reaching a goal.

Another wave thousands of miles from the land,
Born from a splitting rupture in the earth.
Of no special shape,
Of no special character,
Merging with the cold artic wave.
Together they form a majestic swell,
Which towers above the others through
Force of its combined strength and character.

Near the cold lonely Marin County shore
Great southwesterly gale winds
Pushing, forming, the already magnificent wave,
Building it higher and greater than ever;
Giving it renewed strength, greater courage.
There is now no obstacle on Earth that can stay its course.

It will arrive at its goal in
A fearless, headlong, strength-filled plunge.

OPPOSITE: *A temporary sculpture. New South Wales, Australia.* Ray Collins

The Master's Apprentice

First published in the Alpinist, *Number 14, Winter 2005*

Unlike many Yosemite climbers in the 1960s, I left the Valley every year by the Fourth of July for the Wind Rivers, the Tetons, the Canadian Rockies, and the Alps. But until the summer of 1961, when I served an alpine apprenticeship with *sensei* Fred Beckey, I felt like an amateur on hard alpine terrain. Perhaps I'm alive today because of what he taught me.

After a long spring of climbing new Valley routes, I met up with Fred in Washington, where we pulled off a fast ascent of the Liberty Ridge on Rainier. We then drove north in Fred's pink and black Thunderbird. At a "telephone" pick-up bar, I had to suffer the embarrassment of watching Fred on our table phone trying to wear down some floozy blonde sitting not twenty feet from us. We got away with our pockets full of creamer, sugar, ketchup packets, and crackers.

We continued up to Canada, where our first big objective was the 4,500-foot north face of Mount Edith Cavell. Dan Doody was going to film the climb for Bill Burrud Productions, so we got to scam a few days of room and board at the Jasper Park Hotel. Problem was, we couldn't eat in the dining room without a coat and tie. Beckey had bought a sports coat for twenty-five cents at a thrift store; we shared it, eating sequentially. The coat came down to my knees, and one of us had smeared egg yolk on the dress shirt. I felt like a complete dork eating by myself in the ritzy dining room, trying to cover up

OPPOSITE: *Master alpinist and dirtbag Fred Beckey with the Thunderbird. Webster's dictionary ascribes the word "dirtbag" to climbers. Owens Valley, California.* Eric Bjornstad Collection

Yvon, Fred Beckey, and Dan Doody before the Mount Edith Cavell climb. Alberta. Yvon Chouinard Collection

the soiled shirt with a napkin so the cute summer waitress wouldn't notice. For years afterward I would have nightmares featuring giant yellow blobs.

The park warden wouldn't sign us out to do a "suicide wall"; he didn't want to be responsible for some Eiger-like tragedy played out in front of the tourists at the teahouse below the face. We went anyway, under the cover of darkness. Rocks, melting away from the summit snowfield, were bombarding part of the wall, so we stopped whenever we found a protected place to belay. Near one stance under a small overhang, the rockfall was almost continuous, and neither I nor Fred was eager to encounter it. Finally, Doody shamed me into venturing out by offering to lead the pitch himself.

The summit icefield was rotten granular ice; Fred and I had to cut hundreds of steps with our Kuno Rainier axes. Back at the parking lot we found a note from the warden stuck on the T-bird saying: "Good show, boys."

"Fred and I on the last climb we did together, the Sespe Wall." Ojai, California. 2010. Jeff Johnson

From Jasper Park, we rode a freightcar to the Selkirks, where the un-climbed, 2,500-foot north face of Mount Sir Donald was the attraction. We were prepared for a Matterhorn-north-face kind of mixed climb, but the quartzite was horizontally banded, making small but solid holds. Concerned about rockfall, we moved fast, climbing mostly unroped and knocking the beautiful face off in five hours.

A few days later the T-Bird was forging creeks and driving over deadfall on the barely existing road into the Bugaboos. Those days you had to have an ax and shovel to have any chance of getting there.

NEXT SPREAD: *Beckey-Chouinard Route. The route goes up the sunlit buttress right of center on the South Howser Tower, British Columbia.* Marc Piché

At this point I had been climbing for two months with Fred. After a quick but cold and wet climb of Pigeons Spire's Northwest Face, we were stuck in a two-man tent for five days of bad weather. I can hibernate as well as anyone, but finally all the little quirks that make Beckey an interesting character started to get to me. For example, we had only one book to share, and Fred would tear

---

The master had given a very impressionable twenty-two-year-old a lesson in "light-and-fast"—or was it "quick-and-dirty"?—alpinism.

---

out each page after he read it. I'd ask him please not to do that until I'd read it, but he would forget and the pages would disappear.

The South Howser Tower had only one route on it at the time, and the peak hadn't seen a second ascent in twenty years. One of my climbing heroes, Emilio Comici, once wrote that he wanted to find a climb by spilling a drop of water from the top and then following the line it made. Well, the east face of the South Tower was blessed with a corner and crack system that offered the possibility of just such a straightforward climb. However, as Fred wrote later, "a direct route up this face had its problems—an overhanging *bergschrund*, steep ice, and a 900-foot slabby, steep rock wall with narrow clefts and ice patches." Getting to the start of the intended line was a complicated mixture of steep ice and intricate traversing to avoid the biggest part of the *bergschrund* and reach our crack system. From then on, we found it a strenuous but most enjoyable rock climb.

The west side of the Howser Towers was terra incognita to the climbing world in those days—only an airplane lets you view part of the Bugaboos. Beckey, Herb Stanley, and John Rupley had gone around a bit in 1959, discovering the back side of the South Tower and, in fact, climbing two pitches on its elegant west buttress, but they were not prepared to go farther.

After our east face climb, we spent a long, rainy, and terribly arduous day going around the entire Howser massif. We returned to camp knowing that we wanted to climb this west buttress. Fred later described it in the *AAJ (American Alpine Journal)*: "Its clean line, obvious exposure, and lack of any transverse ledges outlined it as the most spectacular route on the western Howser wall. And, above all, the most exciting part of it to a rock-climbing alpinist was the evident fact that there was only one route, no veering—just one line up the sweeping buttress."

I've prided myself on my ability to assess an unclimbed wall accurately from the ground, knowing how long it would take, what sort of equipment and food was needed—no more, no less. I guessed two and a half days to do the nearly 2,500 feet of rock. It turned out to be a dream climb. We were in great shape, the granite was perfect, the weather flawless. At the first bivouac, Fred pulled out his sports coat, stuffed the lining with crumpled-up pages from our Louis L'Amour novel, and in the morning burned the whole thing to make tea, adding the creamer and sugar for extended calories. The master had given a very impressionable twenty-two-year-old a lesson in "light-and-fast"—or was it "quick-and-dirty"?—alpinism.

I returned to the Howsers in 1965 with Doug Tompkins, Jock Lang, and Eric Rayson. Our objective was a complete traverse from north to south of all the towers. Having just knocked over big walls in the Valley like the N.A. and Muir, I overconfidently predicted that we would do the traverse in a day and a half, and we took just enough food for such.

As we crossed the Bugaboo Glacier unroped, I dropped into a bottomless crevasse up to my armpits. The climb—much more difficult and involved than I had predicted—took us two and a half days. Obviously, I still had a lot to learn before I became a real alpinist.

The North Wall of Mount Edith Cavell

First published in the American Alpine Journal, *1962*

This was one of the first big alpine climbs done in the Canadian Rockies. When we tried to sign out for the climb, the warden refused because in his opinion it was a "suicide climb." When we returned to the car after the climb there was a note from him saying, "Good work, boys."

Mount Edith Cavell, in Jasper National Park, rises on its north side a full 4,000 feet above its base. Even in normal years the cliffs are plastered with ice and snow. For Dan Doody and me it stood as the symbol of our ideal—a technical climb in alpine conditions with objective dangers. Having discovered the wall independently, we had both fallen under its spell. We came with Ken Weeks in 1960 to climb it, but it rained and snowed every day. Also, we made the mistake of looking at the wall too often. It is not a good thing to look at great walls for too long a time.

But winter restored our confidence. We made our plans for the summer and collected together the best equipment that we could find for this, our greatest climb. I even made some special pitons with no taper for the stratified rocks.

We arrived in Jasper in early July with Fred Beckey along to take the place of Ken Weeks, who had since joined the army. Driving up to the teahouse

OPPOSITE: *Mount Edith Cavell. The route goes up the angel icefall then left directly to the summit. Alberta.* John Scurlock

at the base of the wall, I could see that the face was very dry because of the abnormally hot May and June. However, the weather now was very poor and we had to wait out the rainstorms in the Jasper Park Lodge. Every morning at 3 am, I would rise and look outside only to see storm clouds. Finally, on July 19, the weather bureau predicted clearing weather for the next day, followed by a new front the following day. If we got an early start and moved very fast, we might possibly climb the face in one day and beat the storm.

The next morning, I awoke with a thumping heart and ran outside to find the sky still overcast and the weather very warm. Disgusted, I did not bother to wake the others. But then at 7 am, Doody stormed into my room asking, "What the hell is going on! Why didn't you wake me?" The sky had turned perfectly clear. We woke up Beckey and decided to climb, even though the late start ruined our hopes of doing the wall in one day.

Shouldering our very heavy loads, we quickly walked from the tea house along the glacier to the base of the face. Doody's pack was especially heavy as he had a great deal of movie camera equipment. (This was to limit his leading on the climb.) He was planning to make a film about the climb for television. Without hesitating, we crossed the simple *bergschrund* and started up the easy rocks. It felt good to be moving fast on the enjoyable, steep face on good holds, not worrying about ropes and pitons. We quickly passed a few cairns that Beckey and I had built on a previous reconnaissance. There was not even a hint of rockfall, and the climbing was mostly fourth class and easy fifth. We stayed unroped to save time on the lower third of the wall as it was threatened by the ice cliff of the left arm of the Angel Glacier. In a short time, we were at the base of this 150-foot cliff. Spotting a gap through it, Beckey led up and over in grand style in three pitches, using no ice pitons. I felt relieved to get above the cliff and on the flat, safe Angel Glacier. Later the entire ice cliff collapsed, covering our route completely.

We trudged up the glacier to the base of the upper wall where we were greeted by the constant rumbling of rockfall. The route we had picked out from below followed a zig-zag system of ledges and cracks up the center of the face, but it was there where most of the rocks were falling. As we looked over to an alternate route on the left, a volley came down, peppering the snow like

OPPOSITE: *The bivouac on Mount Edith Cavell, Alberta.* Dan Doody

54

machine-gun fire and dashing our hopes for that route. Only one possibility was left—to go up the very center of the face via the vertical rock rib which stood out a little way from the wall, in the hopes it would be free from rockfall.

Beckey crossed the difficult *bergschrund* and sped up the first pitch, a difficult vertical system of jam cracks. He moved very fast knowing that his belayers

———

... I heard a roar and automatically pulled my head in like a turtle to let a sheet of snow and small rocks shoot over ...

———

were in constant danger of rockfall. The next 1,000 feet of climbing was moderate to difficult on very steep rocks, just loose enough to keep us alert and to make us distribute our weight over more than one or two points. Because of rockfall, every belay spot had to be under an overhang. To save time, pitons were hardly used except as anchors. The belayer kept his eyes and ears open for rocks. One place in particular stands out. After an extremely rotten and difficult pitch, Beckey was belaying me up when Doody yelled, "Rock!" I quickly ducked and a rock the size of a grapefruit hit where my head had been. This was one of the "high flyers" that were dislodging from 500 to 1,000 feet up. Doody had the same experience when he came up. We all huddled under a steep wall. Beckey and I were jumpy, but Doody was very calm and quiet.

The next lead was mine and, after several false starts, I managed to get the courage to leave the "womb" and go onto the "shooting gallery." I came down several times and finally left my pack since I could not make the move over a tricky, unprotected overhang. I finally got over it and moved onto the easier rocks as fast as I could. Doody took the next lead and went for 120 feet without any protection in very fast time. When I tried to follow, I couldn't quite make it and had to use a pull from above. It had been a fine lead by Dan. Above the last pitch of the vertical section of the buttress, the angle eased off, offering no overhang to belay from. All that I could find was a four-foot boulder, which my head stuck out a couple of inches from. As I was bringing Beckey up, I heard a roar and automatically pulled my head in like a turtle to let a sheet of snow and small rocks shoot over, leaving all the area around me white.

It was easier above and the rockfall eased somewhat, but unfortunately the rock became more and more rotten. Beckey led for the rest of the day since he was climbing in top form. He led pitch after pitch of moderately difficult rock, paralleling a couloir down which avalanches of rock and snow plunged every few minutes. We knew would have to cross this couloir and dreaded the thought.

At 10 pm we reached the spot at which we would cross. Beckey led up and placed a poor piton, then dropped back down and crossed the verglas-covered gully, a magnificent lead over steep, rotten rock. He stopped only long enough to brush the snow off the handholds and look for the route. When I came across, I realized how great a lead this was. I then led another pitch before Doody was brought up. Beckey went up one final pitch and found a place to bivouac, the first that we saw on the entire face that was large enough to sit down and yet afforded protection from the ever-present avalanches and rock-fall. We each had a two by three-foot ledge to ourselves. It was about midnight and, having gone all day without food or water, we were very happy to stop at last.

Fast-approaching heavy clouds soon showed that it would storm in the morning. But a retreat from here would be impossible, and we felt that the worst of the wall was below us. Having accomplished so much that day, we felt confident that we could handle anything this terrible wall could offer. It was a warm night and I slept well—one of the best bivouacs that I have ever had.

In the morning, I looked down between my legs at the Angel Glacier 2,000 feet below, peered up to a completely overcast sky, saw Doody to my left, a black blob on his little ledge, and twenty feet up to my right, Beckey, who was just waking up. I felt very good and very happy to be alive, so good in fact that I started singing—quite a contrast to the day before. A feeling of calmness came over me, accompanied by great confidence: I felt invincible!

It began to rain just as we started climbing. It was easy climbing on low-angle rock and we moved at a steady, deliberate pace. We were not going to let ourselves be forced to move fast by fear. A far cry from yesterday! It be-gan to hail and we could hardly hear each other above the noise of the wind and thunder. Lightning was hitting the summit 800 feet above us. Clouds moved back and forth unveiling ghastly views of the ice-plastered wall to the right and left of us.

In about three hours we reached the summit ice slope. It looked very steep but not long, possibly two pitches to the summit rocks. But it would take 500 feet of step-cutting before we were to reach them! The ice was in terrible shape. Since it was granular and kept sliding, I had to chop steps all the way. The higher up we got the worse the ice became, and the slope continued to steepen. Through breaks in the clouds, Doody and Beckey appeared below me, huddled against the slope trying to avoid the ice chips. Below them the wall dropped sheer and Eiger-like for 3,500 feet. Lulls in the storm gave hopes that it would stop, but hail and snow kept us soaked through for the rest of the day. Freezing feet made me chop a little faster, but I had to make bigger steps for my weaker legs. With only a few ice pitons, we had to keep the leads fairly short. My left foot had lost all feeling.

After an interminable amount of time, we reached the summit rocks only a little way from the top. But the face was not going to give in so easily. The next 300 feet took everything I had to lead. On horizontal bands of the loosest shale, pitches had to be short because of the lack of piton cracks. Each move was a desperate effort to keep from sliding down the wet slabs. Doody belayed perfectly calmly, never complaining of countless rocks dislodged onto him. The last pitch put me eighty feet above Doody on extreme rocks with no protection. I got above a small band of dirt and there I was, with my hands on the summit! I tried to pull myself up but could not. My feet slid continually and my fingers dug deeper into the dirt, but I could not move. I looked across fifty feet to the summit pole and then down 4,000 feet to the ground. Oh God, what a place to get it! I was afraid for the first time during that day. With frantic eyes, I spotted a two-foot long patch of hard snow ten feet to my right. I very cautiously eased over. It felt solid, so I pulled up, mantled, and was up. Never have I felt so happy as that day on the summit with my friends.

Even though we encountered a great deal of objective danger, I feel there are times when this wall is perfectly safe. When we climbed the wall, it was in very poor condition. Future parties should try to climb it in cool weather, perhaps the first week of July, when the summit ice slope would be in better shape, avoiding the rockfall caused by the summit icefields avalanching and flushing rocks. Since retreat from high up the face would be next to impossible, enough gear should be taken along to last three days even though in good

Sorting it out at the trailhead in the Wind Rivers, Wyoming. Fred Beckey Collection

conditions, a two-man party could climb the wall in one day. The summit rocks should be avoided by climbing the sixty-degree ice to the left. Speed is the biggest safety factor on nearly any great wall, so it is better to go unroped as much as possible. No more than ten pitons need to be taken, two of which should be knifeblades.

Route summary: First ascent of the north face, Mount Edith Cavell, Canadian Rockies; 11,033 feet; July 20–21, 1961; Fred Beckey, Yvon Chouinard, Daniel Doody.

Quarter Dome, North Face

Unpublished, 1962

The 2,000-foot high North Face of Quarter Dome ranks among the most aesthetic rock climbs in North America. It has all the qualities that make a great, classic route: The lines are smooth, graceful, and logical—as Antoine de Saint-Exupéry said, "partaking of the simplicity and elementary curve of the human breast or shoulder." The rock is flawlessly perfect, making for truly enjoyable climbing. And it's not too easy nor too difficult, with just enough artificial climbing to force one to bivouac.

The Quarter Domes are located three miles up the Tenaya Canyon, which is just a continuation of the Yosemite Valley. The Domes are hidden from the casual tourist by a curve in the canyon, and it was not until 1961 that I first saw the north face of East Quarter Dome. I had gone up Tenaya Canyon to look over a possible line on the virgin south wall of Mount Watkins, but it was the graceful beauty of the Quarter Domes that really caught my eye. I vowed then to come back and fulfill a climb on the north face of the east one.

September 12, 1962, found Tom Frost and myself hiking up the trailess canyon in the misty morning light. We were filled with anxious anticipation because at any moment, maybe at a bend in the river or a clearing in the tall trees, we would view our objective. Neither of us had ever seen the Quarter Dome up close, and we had no idea if there was even any possibility of a route on the north side.

Finally, the wall came into view closer than I had expected, steeper and smoother and much larger than I had remembered, and far more mysterious

OPPOSITE: *Tom Frost on Quarter Dome, Yosemite.* Yvon Chouinard

and beautiful. We filled our water bottles at the creek and then bushwhacked our way up the hillside to its base. Throwing off our heavy packs we canvassed the wall for a possible line. There were three feasible ways to start, but higher up, things looked very doubtful. We were able to piece together only one vague-looking route which started by going up the face of a flying buttress to a large ledge. At its end there was a doubtful traverse to a flake system that looked even more doubtful. The flakes appeared to end at some very steep, blank-looking slabs which were capped with overhangs.

Not only was there the usual awe and sense of inferiority we mere humans feel when standing under these great cathedral-like walls, but there was also the fear of the unknown. Looking up 1,500 feet to the cracks, chimneys, and overhangs, we wondered, *How thin is that flake? Do we dare to chimney behind it? How do we get from the end of the arch to the other? Can we pass those overhangs?* I was pessimistic and afraid. But inspired by Tom's confidence that a logical and continuous route existed, we uncoiled the ropes and sorted the hardware.

I belayed Tom from the top of a ramp on the left side of the flying buttress, where he hand-traversed a horizontal crack to the right, then went up a perfectly sized chimney to the center of the buttress. After he hauled up his pack, I swung mine onto my shoulders, removed my anchor, and followed.

We stayed in the center of the buttress for several hundred feet, doing mostly enjoyable free climbing. The granite was superb. Since the wall is at a higher elevation than the Valley, it lacked the glacier polish which curtails the amount of free climbing one can do in the Valley.

We gained height very rapidly and soon found ourselves at the long, "doubtful traverse" that we had looked at with such apprehension from 500 feet below. With no hesitation, we walked across it with our hands in our pockets and stopped at the base of the flake system where, with another sigh of relief, we discovered that the flakes were much thicker than they had appeared from below. We climbed these flakes for a few hundred feet to a fine sandy ledge where we cleared off a nice, flat spot to spend the night. It had been an easy day and it was still early, but neither of us had been feeling too sharp, so we decided to take advantage of the gracious accommodations and call it a day.

The next morning we followed our platform to its left terminus and reached the main system of flakes and arches, which we would follow for the next thousand feet. The climbing from here on consisted of chimneying behind these huge flakes until progress was stopped by an overhang in a chimney. Tom placed a piton upside down and proceeded to nail across and up to where this flake turned into a long, graceful arch.

At the 1,500-foot level the flakes and arches merged into the wall, and what was left were perfect, clean cracks in an otherwise blank wall. It was all

———

Not only was there the usual awe and sense of inferiority we mere humans feel when standing under these great cathedral-like walls, but there was also the fear of the unknown.

———

artificial climbing, but what nailing! We were in a series of ascending arches and cracks that were truly an artificial climber's dream. Tom took the first one—a 140-foot, bottomless crack which ranged from one-inch angles to knife blades. There were several more A1 cracks like this where you had to hit the pitons with only three blows for them to be bombproof.

We had several tension traverses and pendulums switching from crack to crack, which made the second's job a bit complicated. We did not want to leave the pendulum pitons behind because we needed every one we had for the long nail-ups. Frost, with his remarkable engineering mind, pulled off two clever tricks. One time he inserted a piton in a slot with his fingers and lowered himself down to my level, where I could pull him across. Then he merely flicked his descending rope, and down came the piton and carabiner. The other time he chipped off a flake the size of a dime, wrapped a sling around it and stuffed it into a crack. He then lowered himself to where he could pendulum. We pulled the rope through, leaving only a tiny white nylon "flower" sticking out of the dark granite.

With the arches above us and flakes below, we looked up to see only over-hangs and to the sides and below nothing but smooth unbroken gray shields. Some of the belays were hanging because of the lack of ledges. The exposure was complete.

Not being able to see over the overhangs, the route-finding was confusing and, at one point, we lost the way for a pitch. A bolt had to be placed to connect two cracks together—the only blemish we left on the wall.

It was nearly dark when we realized that we would not make the summit that day, even though we were only one rope-length away. I climbed half of what turned out to be the most difficult pitch of the climb—a horizontal arch with a bottoming crack—so I anchored the rope to as many pitons as possible and rappelled down to Tom, who was on the only ledge in the last 500 feet of the wall. It was a lousy bivouac ledge, sloping and only a foot wide. We had to tie ourselves in tightly to keep from slipping off. The wind blew all night and it was very cold at this altitude, so we did not sleep very well.

In the morning we devoured the last few crumbs of food and, after stretching out our stiffened limbs and "gobbied" fingers, we set up the last pitch. Tom took the lead and continued putting knife blades and RURPs under the arch until he found a vertical crack, which he nailed for a few feet, then free climbed over a couple of overhangs to the summit.

It was a beautiful morning with the sun coming up over the Eastern Sierra. Tom pulled out a piece of jerky that he had been slyly saving, and we shared our reward. After bouldering around on an erratic rock on the top, we shouldered our packs and walked down through the still-dark and peaceful Sierra forest.

Note: The climb is a Grade 5 and is long and sustained, but the difficulty never exceeds F7 and A2 except for one short pitch of A3. This makes it a perfect climb for a less-than-expert climber who wants to do a big climb, yet is not capable of doing the extreme pitches usually found on big walls.

OPPOSITE: *A nice bivy ledge on Quarter Dome, Yosemite. 1962.* Tom Frost/Aurora

NEXT SPREAD: *The great rocks of Yosemite Valley (left to right): El Capitan, Clouds Rest in the far distance, Half Dome, Sentinel Rock, the three Cathedral Rocks with Bridalveil Fall beneath them, and the Leaning Tower.* Glen Denny

Modern Yosemite Climbing

First published in the American Alpine Journal, *1963*

It's embarrassing reading this essay now. Its bombastic statements are from a young climber pretty full of himself. Nevertheless, its prediction of Yosemite techniques being used on big walls all over the world was not overstated.

Yosemite climbing is the least known and understood in the world and yet one of the most important schools of rock climbing in the world today. Its philosophies, equipment, and techniques have been developed almost independently of the rest of the climbing world. In the short period of thirty years, it has achieved a standard of safety, difficulty, and techniques comparable to the best European schools.

Climbers throughout the world have recently been expressing interest in Yosemite and its climbs, although they know little about it. Even most American climbers are unaware of what is happening in their own country. Yosemite climbers in the past have rarely left the Valley to climb in other areas, and conversely few climbers from other regions ever come to Yosemite; also, very little has ever been published about Yosemite. Climb after climb, each as important as any done elsewhere, has gone completely unrecorded. One of the greatest rock climbs ever done, the 1961 ascent of the Salathé Wall, received four sentences in the *American Alpine Journal.*

Just why is Yosemite climbing so different? Why does it have techniques, ethics, and equipment all of its own? The basic reason lies in the nature

OPPOSITE: *The sort-out before a big-wall climb during the "iron age" in Yosemite.* Royal Robbins

of the rock itself. Nowhere else in the world is the rock so exfoliated, so glacier-polished, and so devoid of handholds. All the climbing lines follow vertical crack systems. Every piton crack, every handhold is a vertical one. Special techniques and equipment have evolved through absolute necessity.

Special Problems. Since Yosemite has characteristics all of its own, it also has its special problems and difficulties. Because the Valley lies at an altitude of only 4,000 feet, the cliffs are often covered with trees and bushes, and the cracks are usually filled with dirt and grass, making it more difficult, time-consuming, and uncomfortable for the ascent party.

Situated in the center of sunny California, the threat of stormy weather is not serious; however, when an occasional storm does hit, usually in the spring or fall, it can be serious because most climbers are not prepared mentally, physically, or materially for it. American mountaineers have tended to belittle the climbing in Yosemite because it lacks the storms of the high mountains, but personally I have never suffered so much from the weather as I have in Yosemite.

Bad weather in the Valley means hot weather. The usual climbing temperature is eighty-five to ninety degrees during the day and fifty degrees at night. Temperatures above one hundred degrees are common. During June

ABOVE: *Climbers Eric Rayson, Yvon Chouinard, Chuck Pratt, TM Herbert, and unknown (left to right) scope a route. Yosemite Valley.* Royal Robbins

OPPOSITE: *Yvon on the West Face of Sentinel Rock, Yosemite.* Royal Robbins

Pioneer Yosemite climber and blacksmith John Salathé discusses the finer aspects of piton design with Yvon. The brand for his Peninsula Wrought Iron Works was a "Diamond P," which was the inspiration for the Chouinard Equipment "Diamond C." Tom Frost

and July of 1961 there were fifteen consecutive days with temperatures above ninety-five degrees! It is usually too hot to do much climbing from late July to the first of September. The heat poses a related problem, that of carrying great loads up the walls. The *minimum* water that must be taken on the big climbs is one and a half quarts per man a day. Water, food, and bivouac equipment, combined with the usual forty-five pitons and thirty-five carabiners, make a considerably heavier load than one carried on a comparable climb in the high mountains. On a two or three-day climb, the second man climbs with a fairly heavy pack, while the leader hauls up another. The latter always has two ropes, one to climb with and the other to haul up extra pitons or the pack.

Safety. Even when the standard of extreme difficulty has been achieved, safety has not been disregarded. The most important reason for this is, of course, the American's love of safety and security and his innate fear of death, all of which has caused revolutionary innovations in belaying and equipment. Pitons are used far more numerously for protection than in Europe. Objective danger is also less in Yosemite than anywhere in the world. There is little danger of natural rockfall or loose rock—the rock is so smooth and steep and has few ledges, a fall usually only helps to build one's confidence. Bad storms are also rare.

Free climbing. Not only is every piton crack vertical, but nearly every handhold

---

John Salathé was the first to realize the need for a piton for climbing on granite.

---

is a vertical one. Laybacking, jamming, chimneying, pinch-holds, and friction climbing are the usual techniques. Face climbing, such as one finds in the Tetons or the Rockies, is a rarity.

Most people who have ever climbed in the Valley are under the impression that the rock is similar to what's found in Chamonix or the Bugaboos. But that is not so; they are completely different types of rock. Yosemite granite does not fracture in angular blocks as does the granite of the French Alps or even the rest of the Sierra Nevada. The Valley is actually a series of exfoliation domes that have been cut in half by a river and glaciers. This means that most of the climbing is on flakes, be they small and thin, or large like dihedrals. Pitons are placed almost always behind a flake or in a vertical inside corner. This vertical-crack climbing takes not only a great deal of technique but also enormous strength. Yosemite climbers develop certain characteristic muscles as a direct result of using vertical holds.

There is undoubtedly more chimney climbing in Yosemite than in any other area in the world. Chimneys range from those that require one-arm and one-leg techniques to others that have chockstones bigger than a house, from perfect "Rébuffat" styles to flaring, bomb-bay, horizontal "horror" chimneys, and from short slots to some that are over 1,000 feet high. Also characteristic of the Valley is friction climbing on glacier-polished slabs. There are climbs in the Valley that have hundreds of feet of this. Very difficult moves have been made on these slabs, using friction, fingernail holds, and edging on tiny flakes. These must be treated as if one were only a few feet off the ground because

1   2

the second one loses confidence, even for a moment, hands sweat, legs shake, feet slip—and one is out in space.

All the techniques of free climbing were established not in Yosemite but at Tahquitz Rock in Southern California. From the 1930s to the present day, it has been the training ground for nearly every prominent Valley climber. This magnificent rock has over seventy routes on massive, exfoliated granite, similar to Yosemite's except for its lack of glacial polish and dirt in the cracks. This means that a move will go free at Tahquitz whereas in Yosemite, it would normally require direct aid. Because of its accessibility, compactness, and sound piton cracks, Tahquitz offers ideal conditions for pushing free climbing to its limits. Most of the routes were first done with direct aid but, over a period of time, nearly every route has been done free. It was the first area to have class 5.9 climbs and continues to have the greatest concentration of class 5.8, 5.9, and 5.10 routes in the country.

Early Climbing Hardware

1. *Penninsula Iron Works piton forged by John Salathé.*

2. *1957 Jerry Gallwas piton used on the North Face of Half Dome.*

3. *The first piton forged by Yvon Chouinard, 4130 steel, 1957.*

4. *1958 Angle piton forged by Yvon Chouinard.*

5. *1958 "Longwear" piton forged by Dick Long.*

6. *1958 "Stove Leg" piton used on the first ascent of El Capitan and made by Bill 'Dolt' Feuerer.*

All photos Patagonia archives.

3

4

5

6

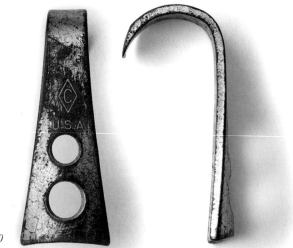

Early Climbing Hardware

7. *1960 RURP (Realized Ultimate Reality Piton).*

8. *1958 Knifeblade piton.*

9. *Hand-forged "Lost Arrow" piton, 1957–1962.*

10. *Chouinard Equipment "Cliffhanger," 1966.*

All photos Patagonia archives.

When one finds a layback or a friction pitch at Tahquitz, it is a textbook-type pitch; a layback requires pure layback technique, a friction pitch requires pure friction technique. Nothing else will do. One can develop granite-climbing techniques here far better than in Yosemite or anywhere else. I cannot impress enough on climbers from other areas that they should climb at Tahquitz before going to Yosemite. Every spring even the native climbers spend a week at Tahquitz getting in shape for the Valley walls.

Artificial Climbing. Because most piton cracks are vertical and there are few ceilings, the double-rope technique, standard throughout the rest of the world, is never used in Yosemite. Nor is tension used except on overhanging rock. Instead, only one rope is run through all of the pitons, and large numbers of runners are used in order to eliminate the rope drag. The use of one rope has greatly increased the efficiency, simplicity, and speed of artificial climbing.

Stirrups (slings) made of one-inch-wide nylon webbing have taken the place of step stirrups. There are many reasons for this: 1) The slings grip the sides and cleats of the climbers' heelless *kletterschuhe* and give a much greater feeling of security and comfort, especially when belaying in slings for a long period of time. 2) The slings can be used for runners around large blocks, bushes, or trees. 3) In an emergency, they can be cut up and used for rappel slings. 4) They can be carried more neatly on the person or pack. 5) They can be used for prusiking more efficiently. The only additional things needed are three small loops of 1/4-inch or 5/16-inch cord. 6) They make no noise so that the belayer can hear the little familiar sounds that help him to understand, without looking up, what the leader is doing and to anticipate the belay signals. 7) They allow one to "sit" in one's slings, thus saving a great deal of energy. 8) There is less chance of dropping them either when a piton pulls out or through carelessness. As far as I can tell, they have no disadvantages over step stirrups. Possibly the reason why they have not been adopted by Europeans is that they are unable to obtain the flat nylon webbing needed for their construction.

Each climber carries three 3-step slings. The leader never leaves them in place but moves them up from piton to piton. A carabiner is kept on each sling and is never removed. On low-angle rock, only one sling is used; on steeper rock, two are used, one foot placed in each. On overhanging rock, a third sling is used to clip into the next piton. When cleaning out a pitch, two or even three slings are often clipped together to reach pitons that are far apart.

The actual technique is done thus: A piton is placed, a carabiner is clipped in, the rope is inserted, and finally the slings are clipped onto this carabiner.

On doubtful pitons, the slings are clipped in *before* the rope is inserted; the climber steps up and tests the piton and *then* inserts the rope. This leaves less slack in the rope if the piton should pull out. Of course, a carabiner must be used whose gate can still be opened while the carabiner supports body weight.

Equipment. The first pitons were developed for use in the Dolomites in limestone, where a piton is expected to flow into a very irregular crack or hole and fill all the tiny internal pits and irregularities, and have such great holding power that it can never be taken out. It was generally considered that only a piton of very malleable steel or iron had the qualities to fulfill these requirements. All European pitons today are still being made this way, whether they are going to be used in limestone or not.

John Salathé was the first to realize the need of a piton for climbing on granite. During his attempts on the Lost Arrow, he saw that he needed a stiffer, tougher piton that could be driven into solid veins of rotten granite without buckling, that was lighter than an iron piton, that had greater holding power, and yet could be taken out faster and more easily and be used over and over again. Out of old Model A Ford axles, he forged some beautiful horizontals, which to this day are almost revered by those lucky enough to own them.

The alloy-steel piton is based on a theory radically different from that of the iron piton. It is not expected to follow cracks but rather to act like a spring, pressing against the sides. It has been proven to have greater holding power in granite and similar rock because it can be driven harder and deeper without buckling into the typical smooth cracks so that it is actually tighter. The entire length of the piton is stiff, so the head does not bend when removed, thus making it possible to do a several-day, 300-piton climb without leaving a single piton in place. The invention of the alloy-steel piton is as important to rock climbing as is the new ice screw to ice climbing.

In the early 1950s a new piton was invented by another famous Yosemite climber, Charles Wilts, which helped as much as anything to set such a high standard of artificial climbing. This piton, with a blade the size of a postage stamp, was appropriately called the "knifeblade." It was the first piton to be made of chrome-molybdenum aircraft steel and could be used in very thin cracks where no other piton could possibly enter. Although originally made for artificial climbing, it was soon found that these pins often had even greater holding power than angle pitons. In 1957, Jerry Gallwas forged some regular horizontals out of chrome-molybdenum steel (SAE 4130) for the 1957 ascent of Half Dome; some of these have been used over a hundred times and are still in use.

Yosemite, as in any granitic area, has many wide piton cracks. Wooden wedges were never much used because these large cracks are usually filled with dirt. Several people made large angle pitons, some up to four inches wide, using various materials. Some were fashioned from aluminum channel, angle iron, and cut-off stove legs, like those made by William Feuerer for the 1950 ascent of El Capitan.

All of these pitons were made by individuals in home workshops and available only to personal friends. Salathé sold a few, but most climbers thought his price of fifty-five cents was too expensive! In 1958 the author started to make this newer type of equipment on a commercial basis. He developed a new aluminum carabiner, stronger than existing steel models, which had a gate that could still be opened under a climber's weight and shaped to be used in combination with the Bedayn carabiner in the Yosemite method of artificial climbing. Ringless alloy-steel angle pitons were invented that were superior in every way to existing models. The larger angle pitons were made of heat-treated alloy aluminum to save weight. A full line of horizontals of alloy-steel was developed, ranging from a knife blade to a wedge.

Abortive attempts on Kat Pinnacle's west face showed the need for a piton that would go into tiny bottoming cracks (a crack where the piton hits bottom before being fully inserted), which even knife blades failed to enter. From this need came the RURP. This Realized Ultimate Reality Piton helped to usher in A5 climbing and was instrumental in allowing tens of existing bolts to be passed up and chopped out. These diminutive pins are far from being just novelties but have become an absolute necessity on nearly all of the newer climbs.

The importance of this new equipment can best be emphasized by saying that since 1958, every major rock climb in North America has used the author's equipment. The future of rock-climbing equipment lies in the use of the lighter steel and aluminum alloys. Weight is now the major problem to be overcome.

Ethics and Philosophies. The most obvious split between European and Yosemite rock-climbing philosophies is whether to leave pitons in or not. In Europe they are left in place. In Yosemite, even if a climb has been done a hundred times, the pitons are still removed. I believe that nearly everyone, whether European or American, agrees that if practical, a route should not remain pitoned. It is entirely practical in Yosemite to take the pitons out. With the pitons removed and with no guidebook to show the way, a third or succeeding ascent of a route is as difficult as was the second. It is conceivable that a climber who is capable of doing the Bonatti Pillar on the Petit Dru with all the pitons in place might not be able to climb the north face of Half Dome, although both climbs unpitoned are of equal difficulty.

In the Alps, climbing is not called artificial until a stirrup is used. Free climbing in California means that artificial aid of any sort is not used, whether it be a sling around a knob of rock, a piton for a handhold, foothold, or to rest on. After a piton is placed for safety, it may not be used for aid in climbing without changing the classification of the climb.

Especially on short climbs, free climbing is forced to its limits. Guidebooks list not only the first ascents of a route but also the first free ascent. Some climbers feel that it is more of an honor to do the first free ascent than the actual first.

Nowhere else, except on the sandstone climbs of the Southwest, is the need for expansion bolts more pronounced than in the Valley. However, this does not mean that they have been indiscriminately used. Climbers have gone to extremes to avoid placing them, except for an anchor, where the ethics are less stringent. The usual attitude toward bolts is that they should only be carried by the better climbers because only they know when a bolt *must* be placed. If a bolt is put in and a later party feels it unnecessary, then it is chopped out. Lack of equipment, foul weather, or a less-than-expert leader is never an excuse for a bolt.

It has become popular in other parts of North America, especially in the Northwest, to lay fixed ropes up a climb to avoid having to bivouac or take a chance with the weather. These ropes create an umbilical cord to where you can quickly retreat if things get tough. This manifests Americans love of security and shows that the climber should not be there in the first place. The only routes now being done with fixed ropes in Yosemite are those that take so long on the first ascent that they could not be done in any other way; such are the multiday routes on El Capitan.

Perhaps I have given the reader the impression that I feel that Yosemite is the only place to climb and that its philosophies and ethics are the last word. Personally, I would rather climb in the high mountains. I have always abhorred the tremendous heat, the dirt-filled cracks, the ant-covered, foul-smelling trees and bushes that cover the cliffs, the filth and noise of Camp 4 (the climbers' campground), and worst of all, the multitudes of tourists who abound during the weekends and summer months. Out of the nearly 300 routes in the Valley, there are less than 50 which I should care to do or repeat. The climbing as a whole is not very esthetic or enjoyable; it is merely difficult. During the last couple of

Yvon and climbing/business partner Tom Frost in Yosemite. Tom Frost Collection

years there has been an aura of unfriendliness and competition between climbers, leaving a bitter taste in the mouth. Like every disease, it was initially spread by a few, and now it has reached a point where practically no one is blameless.

The native climbers are a proud bunch of individuals; they are proud of their valley and its climbs and standards. An outsider is not welcomed or accepted until he proves that he is equal to the better climbs and climbers. He is constantly on trial to prove himself. When he is climbing, he is closely watched to see that he does a free pitch free, that he does not place more than the required number of pitons in an artificial pitch, and that he does the climb speedily. Climbers have left the Valley saying that they will never return because of the way they were treated by the native climbers. These problems will, in time, resolve themselves as the Yosemite climbers move afield and see that there is no room or need for competition or enmity in the mountains.

There have been times when I have felt ashamed to be a Yosemite climber, and there are times when I feel as if I truly hate the place; but then there are times when I would rather be there more than anywhere else in the world. If at times I hate the place, it is probably because I love it so. It is a strange, passionate love that I feel for this Valley. More than just a climbing area, it is a way of life.

The Future of Yosemite Climbing. Nearly all of the great classical lines in Yosemite have been ascended. All of the faces have been climbed by at least one route. This does not mean that there are no new routes left, because there are countless new lines on the cliffs that lie between the great formations. Some will be as difficult as any yet done, but that is all they will be. They will offer very little esthetic pleasure. The rock is often poor, the cliffs covered with bushes, and the cracks filled with dirt and moss; blank areas will require bolts. As a line becomes less logical and direct, the esthetic beauty of the climbing also diminishes.

To do a winter climb for the sake of making the first winter ascent is senseless. Winter conditions can be better than in the summer. To do a route under actual winter conditions means climbing immediately after the storm, which is nearly impossible and suicidal. Because the rock is so smooth, ice will not adhere to it except during and directly after a storm. To climb then means having to clear off all the verglas on the holds because the ice is too thin and badly anchored to climb on directly. To clean off all the verglas is a slow process. At Yosemite's low altitude, the hot California sun early in the morning loosens great sheets of ice and sends them crashing down.

Solo climbing will not be practical until the routes are pitoned. Otherwise, because of the great amounts of direct aid, a two-man party can climb faster and more efficiently on the big climbs. I doubt that the big walls will be pitoned for a long time to come. Besides, at present, solo climbing is against the law.

Climbing for speed records will probably become more popular, a mania which has just begun. Climbers climb not just to see how fast and efficiently they can do it, but far worse, to see how much faster and more efficient they are than a party that did the same climb a few days before. The climb becomes secondary, no more important than a racetrack. Man is pitted against man.

OPPOSITE: *Warren Harding and Bob Swift on the Lost Arrow Spire, Yosemite. 1962.* Glen Denny

The future of Yosemite climbing lies not in Yosemite, but in using the new techniques in the great granite ranges of the world. A certain number of great ascents have already been done in other areas as a direct result of Yosemite climbers and techniques, notably the north face of Mount Conness in the Sierra Nevada, the west face of the South Tower of Howser Spire in the Bugaboos, the two routes on the Diamond on Longs Peak in Colorado, the Totem Pole and Spider Rock in Arizona, the north face of East Temple in the Wind Rivers, the northwest corner of the Petit Dru (voie Americaine), and the first American ascent of the Walker Spur of the Grandes Jorasses in the French Alps. Although these ascents are as fine and as difficult as any in their respective areas, they are merely the beginning of a totally new school of American climbing, that is to say technical climbing under alpine conditions. The opportunities here are limitless. I have personally seen in the Wind River Range and the Bugaboos untouched walls that are as difficult and as beautiful as any ever done in the history of alpinism. In the Wind Rivers alone, there are opportunities for fifty Grade VI climbs. The western faces of the Howser Spires in the Bugaboos are from 3,000 to 5,000 feet high. The Coast Ranges, the Logan Mountains, the innumerable ranges of Alaska, the Andes, the Baltoro Himalaya all have walls that defy the imagination.

Who will make the first ascents of these breathtaking rock faces? From the Americas, the climbers can come only from Yosemite. The way it now is, no one can climb enough in the high mountains to get in shape to do a Grade VI climb, either in the mountains or in Yosemite. These extraordinary climbs will be done by dedicated climbers who are in superb mental and physical condition from climbing all year round; who are used to climbing on granite, doing much artificial climbing and putting in and taking out their own pitons; who are familiar with the problems of living for a long time on these walls, hauling up great loads, standing in slings, sleeping in hammocks for days at a time; and who have the desire and perseverance needed to withstand the intense suffering, which is a prerequisite for the creation of any great work of art. Yosemite Valley will, in the near future, be the training ground for a new generation of super alpinists who will venture forth to the high mountains of the world to do the most esthetic and difficult walls on the face of the Earth.

OPPOSITE: *Yvon and Mike Covington on the Cookie Cliff, Yosemite.* Yvon Chouinard Collection

Sentinel Rock:
A New Direct North Wall Route

First published in the American Alpine Journal, *1963*

Sentinel Rock has probably meant more to Yosemite climbers than any other rock formation in the Valley. It is the peak that climbers in Camp 4 see first in the early morning, when it is dark gray and frightful, and the last they see in the late afternoon, when it turns all shades of gold. More than any other formation it shows the fantastic changes of light and shadows which so characterize this "valley of light." One can stand on the valley floor and watch the rays of sun expose hidden dihedrals, cracks, ledges, and chimneys and make them disappear again with the passing of shadows. It is in the late afternoon, when it is glowing with warm yellow light, that it is the most awesome, beautiful, and alluring. It is a common sight at this time to see a climber quietly looking up, perhaps thinking he would like to be up there. John Salathé must have been captivated by its beauty when he picked it to be the second of his two great climbs in Yosemite.

When I returned to the Valley in June with thoughts of a new direct route on the north wall, I learned that a direct had been finished just the day before. Tom Frost and Royal Robbins had completed a magnificent three-day ascent, using over 200 pitons and no expansion bolts. Though greatly disappointed, I felt there were possibilities for two other new direct lines on the north wall. TM Herbert and I decided to try a new line between the old North Face route and the new direct one.

OPPOSITE: *Sentinel Rock beckons to the aspiring climber, Yosemite.* Tom Frost

The next day we carried loads of equipment, water, and food to the base, expecting to start climbing the following day. But for the whole week it rained and snowed. We could not even climb an easy route, as all our gear was up at the base. When the weather finally cleared, we climbed in the early morning light up the Tree Ledge Traverse to the base of the actual wall. The traverse

---

Time and again, Herbert would be completely stopped, only to find as the last resort a small crack hidden in a niche or behind a clump of dirt or a bush.

---

is a system of ascending, sand-covered ledges with uncomfortable, unroped moves here and there. One always feels relieved to get to the start of the real climbing.

The first section of the wall ascends a chimney behind a 400-foot-high slab. After two easy pitches, the third turned out to be a long, awkward, poorly protected chimney. Above it we traversed left and then went up the face of the slab, placing a direct-aid piton from a very difficult position. From the ledge on the top of the slab, the wall soared upward with unbelievable steepness. Herbert nailed up for twenty feet, traversed a few feet to the right, and started placing a varied assortment of pitons in what proved to be one of the most difficult leads on the wall. The artificial climbing was slow and awkward; a piton here, one over there, no real system to follow.

Time and again, Herbert would be completely stopped, only to find as the last resort a small crack hidden in a niche or behind a clump of dirt or a bush. On the next lead, I nailed up some easy slabs, then up an overhanging corner from the middle of which I dropped back down and swung over to the right to a steep step, which I nailed to the next belay point. We exchanged hardware and hauling lines, and Herbert started off. First, a few delicate moves to

OPPOSITE: *A carabiner brake used in the 1960s for descending a rope.* Tom Frost/Aurora

the left, then a piton placed upside down, then twelve more, all upside down, took him 130 feet to a foothold at the base of an inside corner. As at each of the last three belay points, an expansion bolt was necessary for an anchor. In gathering darkness, we rappelled down to the ledge on the top of the slab for a bivouac.

The next morning after prusiking up the ropes, I started placing large angle pitons in the overhang inside the corner. After a while, I switched over to some small cracks on the right wall of the corner. Everything seemed awkward and I had trouble standing up high on my stirrups. Looking down, I saw that the hauling line was hanging out from Herbert. About eighty feet up, I traversed to the right to a fine flat edge. Herbert ran out of rope on the next lead, an easy class 3 and 4 pitch. I then nailed a thin vertical flake until I reached a roof where I placed a piton, which let me drop down and pendulum to the left. I climbed up using large holds to a wide, easy crack, which I nailed for twenty feet. From its top, I traversed left and dropped into a prominent large dihedral. Belaying from a chimney, I watched Herbert tackle the next pitch. After placing two three-inch angles in the corner, he laybacked over on an overhanging bulge, where he inserted a long horizontal piton on the left wall of the dihedral.

From here it was solid nailing up a good crack in the inside corner. He passed a small overhang but took a ten-foot fall from the second one. Immediately back up, he put in a bolt instead of a piton. Placing a couple more pitons for anchors and belaying in stirrups, he hauled up the packs, tied them off, and put me on belay. Belaying in slings is so common now on the big Yosemite climbs that you rarely think twice about it—except when you clean out a pitch and have only three or four pitons left between you and the belayer. Each succeeding piton removed makes you feel less secure. Finally, when both of us and two heavy packs were hanging from two of three anchor pitons, I did not hesitate to hurriedly start up the next pitch.

I placed a few insecure pitons in a dirt-filled crack of the corner and moved over two awkward overhangs to find myself under the large overhang which capped the dihedral. I could tell at once that we were in trouble. The overhang was formed by layers of flakes three to five inches thick, which resounded with hollow Afro-Cuban sounds under hammer blows. To nail these would be madness; if one broke and fell, it would shoot down and guillotine the belayer. Suspended from a bolt, I peered over the overhang to see that the nearest good crack was twenty-five feet diagonally up and to the right. With only four bolts left, I was doubtful that we could reach it. I could not even try because I knew that we would need all four of the bolts to retreat. What folly! All that work for nothing! I stood in my stirrups for half an hour, swearing and cursing my stupidity for not bringing more bolts along. It really hurt to have to

———

I could tell at once that we were in trouble. The overhang was formed by layers of flakes three to five inches thick, which resounded with hollow Afro-Cuban sounds under hammer blows.

———

retreat from so high, but because it was crazy to stay there, we started down.

The retreat called for a rappel, then a tension traverse from the end of which we placed a bolt or a piton to rappel again; otherwise we would have ended in midair under the overhang. This we did all the way down the wall. That day, however, we only made two rappels and got back to the flat edge, where we spent the night. We reached the Valley floor by noon the next day.

Back we came in September. We hurried up the first eight pitches to bivouac high for an early start in the morning, barely making it up to the ledge before dark. The next day we reached our high point at noon. All the way up, I had been amazed at how difficult the climbing was. Though I was in better shape than in the spring, it seemed harder than I had remembered it.

From the high point, I placed a knife blade, a bolt, a two-inch angle, and another bolt—all the while diagonaling up to the right and going over a couple of flakes. It was awkward and tiring to place the bolts over the side on the steep wall where I was never in balance. Four bolts and three pitons higher, I reached the vertical crack, which I nailed for twenty-five feet before I stopped to belay. Before bringing Herbert up, I climbed up a few feet of his pitch and placed his first four pitons. When belaying in stirrups, it helps to start the next lead before bringing your second so that he can quickly pass you with a minimum of confusion. While belaying, I amused myself by dropping pieces of moss and dirt and watching them sail out into the void. What beautiful exposure! Just like a Dolomite wall.

The next pitch followed a dirt-filled bottoming crack. Before a piton could be placed, the dirt had to be cleaned out with the point of the hammer. Updrafts caught the lighter pieces of dust and wafted them into Herbert's eyes. Every time he moved, a small cloud moved with him. Nearly all the pitons entered the crack only a short way and had to be tied off with a hero loop. He did a fine job leading the pitch as I could tell when taking out the pitons; they offered no resistance at all.

It was getting dark as I quickly ascended the next pitch—a chimney narrowing to a one-and-a-half-inch, direct-aid crack. After I reached a small ledge, I went left until my rope ran out. Herbert then led over a difficult bulge, fought his way through a class-7 bush and climbed a deep chimney to a ledge big enough to bivouac on. After the long, hard day, we stopped there in the dark. Close to the top with the difficulties over, I slept well.

The next morning, we climbed a fine free pitch up vertical holds and jam cracks. Another short scramble and we were on the summit, absorbing the warm rays of the benevolent sun, purified and happy; happy that for a few hours we had been free and happy to take some of this freedom back with us.

Route summary: New direct route on north wall of Sentinel Rock; Yosemite Valley, California; September 1962; Yvon Chouinard, TM Herbert.

OPPOSITE: *TM Herbert performing in Camp 4, Yosemite. "TM used to tell funny stories on climbs—trying to make you lose concentration and fall off—and once back in camp he would tell people you couldn't follow his brilliant leads." 1969.* Glen Denny

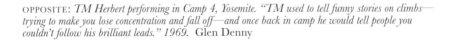

Personal Notes from the North America Wall

El Capitan, Yosemite, Unpublished, 1964

OCTOBER 21

1st Pitch: In the afternoon, Tom Frost and I hike to the base of the wall and I nail the first pitch. Tom cleans while Chuck Pratt, Royal Robbins, and some friends pack up the food and water to the base. The first pitch is surprisingly easy but very steep.

We come down and have a campfire with our friends. The night is warm for late October, but I can't sleep. This is the most nervous I've been before a climb. This wall is Royal's idea; I've never even glassed the route and have no idea where it goes—if at all. These guys have been on two routes on El Cap. I haven't and I've just gotten out of the Army and am not in great shape.

In the morning as the sun hits the top of the Wall of the Morning Light, I see a peregrine falcon all lit up by the sun go into a stoop above us and it disappears into the shadow. *My God*, I think, *this is a metaphor for us blasting up to who knows what.*

2nd Pitch: Tom methodically nails his way up, placing pitons in poor cracks. Looking down from the belay I watch the others below preparing the bags to haul up as soon as Tom and I move higher. A sharp tug on the rope tells me Tom has taken a small fall. A tiny flake has broken under his fifi hook.

OPPOSITE: *Called the North America Wall due to the dark rock outline. El Capitan, Yosemite.* Tom Frost

3rd Pitch: Toughest nailing I've ever done. Absolutely vertical with badly bottoming cracks. Nearly every piton just barely goes in and has to be tied off. Others are nested two or three together looking like steel flowers. I take a small fall when a crack breaks off.

4th Pitch: Another difficult pitch for Tom. Ties off pitons by driving the hero loops into the cracks with the pitons, then ties into the loops thus avoiding any leverage at all. Very clever. We get to a small ledge at dusk. Royal and Chuck haul up the 200 pounds of gear in four duffel bags. The ledge is only sixteen inches wide and can only fit three so I hang my hammock above. Not a good setup. We eat salami, cheese, bread, and drink our allocated one and a half quarts of water each.

OCTOBER 23

5th Pitch: Chuck and Royal's turn to climb while Tom and I haul. Chuck free climbs to a large ceiling then nails under it to the right. It's very warm and we are really thirsty and tired.

8th Pitch: Royal leads, nailing a dihedral and another crack to Calaveras Ledge. Good bivouac.

OCTOBER 24

11th Pitch: I chimney behind a thick flake to Big Sur Ledge. It feels so cool in the chimney I hate to leave. Tom and I eat lunch and flake out on the ledge. It's so hot you can't touch the rock. It's just too hot to climb. The ledge is covered with flicker feathers—peregrine meal. I feel fairly good today, but thirsty.

12th Pitch: After it cools off Tom leads up, places a bolt and we lower him down. He has to pendulum off to the left but it's so steep he just hangs midair. We pull him in on the haul line then let him go. After two tries he grabs a

OPPOSITE: *Yvon checking out the view from the Big Sur Ledge on the first ascent of the North America Wall on El Capitan, Yosemite. 1964.* Tom Frost/Aurora

handhold and slams in a piton and continues to nail up a six-inch expanding flake. Dangerous stuff. He places a bolt, rappels off and we pull him back in.

Pitches 13 to 15: Royal and Chuck continue to traverse left to the base of the black overhanging dihedral that we have been dreading. They return to Big Sur Ledge in the dark via an intricate system of fixed ropes. We pull them in from the void.

OCTOBER 26

16th Pitch: Tom and I prusik up the fixed ropes, let ourselves down, then up again until we reach our mates' high point in the dihedral. I lead up. Really scary up here. The wall itself overhangs and the dihedral leans out at a wild angle. The exposure is unbelievable.

17th Pitch: Tom does a fantastic job of nailing this dangerous pitch and makes it to the Great Roof. Pratt comes up and hangs a few feet below me and waits to haul. I clean the pitch in absolute darkness. I use only feel and the light of the occasional spark from the hammer. My fingers are swollen like little sausages, and my wrists ache from hammering. The Great Roof is a twenty-five-foot ceiling. The wall overhangs the base so much there's not much probability of retreat from here. By midnight we have set up our hammocks one above the other.

OCTOBER 27

Pitches 18 and 19: I open my eyes to the wildest sight imaginable. It looks like a tenement house on a work day: hammocks every which way, blue parkas, hauling ropes splayed out, shoes all hanging in a haphazard fashion from anchors.

A TV news helicopter flies by and later I learn we are on the nightly news

OPPOSITE: *Tom Frost (on top), Royal Robbins, and Yvon (peeking out of the bottom) bivouacking under the Great Roof on El Capitan. "My parents knew I was a climber but didn't know what that meant until one day on the evening TV news they watched a helicopter scan the face of El Capitan and zero in on these crazy guys sleeping in hammocks 2,000 feet off the ground." Yosemite.* Chuck Pratt

where my parents discover for the first time that when I've been saying that I climb, it doesn't mean hiking up hills.

There's a semblance of a crack leading out under the roof and thankfully it's Pratt's turn to lead. We stay and belay from our hammocks and watch the ropes going farther out. The piton placements are bad. Mostly placed in a quartz band. We can't see Chuck anymore, just hear him moaning. Royal really dreads following and has to replace a couple of pitons that have fallen out.

Tom and I are left to clean house, and we wait to go up and haul. When it's time, we have to let ourselves out until the rope is vertical and then prusick up. We can hear Royal's hammer beats transmitted through the rock. He is having a hard time on the next pitch. Looks like bad weather coming in.

20th Pitch: Royal has a wild look in his eyes. He is heading to the barn! He makes short work of a long pitch and he reaches a cave (Cyclops Eye) which is tucked under a big overhang. The rest of us go up in the dark.

Rained and snowed all night but we stayed dry in our cave. There's a curtain of water falling twenty feet out from us.

OCTOBER 28

21st Pitch: A moderate free pitch.

22nd Pitch: Tom does a great job with difficult aid climbing with bottoming pitons.

23rd Pitch: Tom and I feel lousy today. Tired and running out of energy. Two meals a day of one square inch of salami, a tiny square of cheese, and a handful of gorp is just not enough. I deal with an expanding flake and a dangerous block that's threatening to fall and crush everyone below. We retreat to the Cyclops where Royal and Chuck have had a rest day. It's very cold. Rain and snow all night with blowing wind in all directions.

OPPOSITE: *Tom Frost pendulums toward the Black Dihedral, North America Wall, Yosemite.* Yvon Chouinard

OCTOBER 29, 8TH DAY

24th Pitch: Cold, dreary day with snow all over the rim on the Valley, twelve inches on top. Chuck leads a very difficult pitch over loose flakes.

25th Pitch: Getting dark, so Royal goes for it. He yells to tie in another rope, then another and stretches out the pitch to 200 feet. We all go up to the best bivouac spot yet. The Igloo is protected from the elements and has a flat sandy floor.

OCTOBER 30

26th Pitch: It was a cold night but a fine bivouac. I mark that this is my fiftieth bivouac on a wall. Clear beautiful weather. We find a few branches and make a fire, brew tea, and eat the last of our food.

I lead up an easy free pitch. I feel great! We are going to make it. Tom says he feels like taking it easy today and just takes photos. But we all know he is just being good-hearted in letting us get to the top first.

27th Pitch: Royal takes his place and leads a difficult free and aid pitch. He puts in some bad placements to go over an arch, steps off a RURP to do a strenuous pull-up.

28th Pitch: Fourth class to a tree and third class to the top. I drop some ropes for the others and they follow up.

OPPOSITE: *Chuck Pratt nailing on the Great Roof, El Capitan, Yosemite.* Tom Frost

Muir Wall, El Capitan

First published in the American Alpine Journal, *1965*

Just beyond this glorious flood the El Capitan rock, regarded by many as the most sublime feature of the valley, is seen through the pine groves, standing forward beyond the general line of the wall in most imposing grandeur, a type of permanence. It is 3,300 feet high, a plain, severely simple, glacier-sculptured face of granite, the end of one of the most compact and enduring of the mountain ridges, unrivaled in height and breadth and flawless strength.
— *John Muir,* The Yosemite

More than any other mountain or formation, El Capitan has been responsible for the changing philosophy and the rising standards of American climbing. I speak not only of rock climbing but of ice as well, for new standards of ice climbing are being established by Yosemite-trained "rock specialists."

The new philosophy is characterized by small expeditions going into remote areas and trying new and extremely difficult routes with a minimum of equipment, no support parties nor fixed ropes to the ground; living for days and weeks at a time on the climb and leaving no signs of their presence behind. This purer form of climbing takes more of a complete effort, more personal adjustment, and involves more risk, but being more idealistic, the rewards are greater.

Probably the basis for this type of climbing was established by the naturalist John Muir. He used to roam the Sierra for weeks, eating only bread and

OPPOSITE: *The Muir Wall Route marked on a photo of El Capitan, Yosemite. The circles denote bivy spots.* Ed Cooper

whatever he could pick off the land, sleeping under boulders in only his old army overcoat, and rejoicing with the summer storms. He chose to accept nature as it was without trying to force himself onto the mountains but rather to live with them, to adjust himself to the rigors of this sort of life.

It was a vigorous life indeed, but his writings tell us of his communion with nature and his profound mystical experiences. Scientists will explain that when the body is weakened by fasting, the senses become more acute and receptive. This partly explains Muir's mysticism but does not explain how, even though he was essentially fasting, he still managed to keep his prodigious strength. The answer to this is simple: he was fully adjusted to his environment and to eating less food.

This same attitude was later accepted by John Salathé and 'Axe' Nelson, who trained their bodies to do with very little water in anticipation of their 1947 Lost Arrow climb. Their five-day ascent with only one pint of water per man per day is still the most remarkable achievement in American climbing.

The nine-day first ascent of the North America Wall in 1964 (A.A.J., 1965 14:2, pp. 331–338) was not only the first one-push first ascent of an El Capitan climb, but also a major breakthrough in other ways. We learned that our minds and bodies never stopped adjusting to the situation. We were able to live and work and sleep in comparative comfort in a vertical environment. When the food and water ran low, we found that we could obtain an enormous amount of energy from eating just ten raisins. We reached the summit feeling as if we could go on for another ten days. No longer would we ever be afraid of spending so many days on a climb, whether it was a Yosemite wall or a long Alaskan ridge.

After this climb, we asked ourselves the inevitable question, "What next?" The answer was obvious … another first ascent on El Cap in one push with two men instead of four. This would not only double the workload and responsibility, but would also considerably decrease the safety factor.

It is the unknown that frightens brave men and there are plenty of unknown factors in trying a new route on this great wall. In the spring of 1965, after studying our proposed route for two years, calculating our equipment down to the last piton and cup of water, and weighing the consequences of

OPPOSITE: *TM Herbert on the Muir Wall, Yosemite.* Yvon Chouinard

a failure high up on the face, TM Herbert and I felt at last ready for the big push.

Our proposed line started to the left of the Salathé Wall route, ascended some inside corners and arches, crossed the Mammoth Terraces and continued more or less up, keeping to the left of the south face or 'Nose' route.

June 14: In the cool early morning, we walked to where we had left our duffel bags and equipment the day before. The climb begins at the 'Moby Dick' slab, a popular two-pitch climb of F9 severity. From the ledge at the top, we dropped down en rapel for twenty feet to the left and began nailing up. The pitons held well but they were awkward to place in the inside corner that leaned left. There was gardening of dirt and grass before a piton could be placed and as usual, belays in slings. We had to place two bolts in order to reach a sixty-foot-long horizontal flake and from these we hung our hammocks and had a secure, restful sleep.

June 15: I completed the traverse placing the pitons very carefully so that the flake would not expand. Then TM continued on, alternating pitons and bolts in a dangerous-looking loose arch. After reaching a trough-like groove, the climbing became easier and we rapidly gained height. Toward sundown, TM pendulumed to a large ledge where we would spend the night. Somehow our hauling system got fouled and many a terse word was exchanged and much-needed water spent in perspiration before we were able to lift our two, fifty-pound bags onto the ledge. The strain of the climbing, the terrible California sun, and that ever-present fear and uncertainty were all working away, and were reflected in us.

We had a fine ledge where we could lie out at full length and use our hauling bags for extra warmth. Besides, in the morning there would be no problem in having to repack the bags while hanging from pitons. The single fact that we had a ledge put us back into an elated mood and we joked and talked until we fell asleep.

June 16: As we had expected, the third day turned out to be mostly moderate free climbing up the right side of the 'Heart.' In the late afternoon, we reached another fine ledge a pitch above the enormous Mammoth Terraces.

OPPOSITE: *Yvon high up on the Muir Wall, Yosemite.* TM Herbert

The last lead was done in the rain as the weather had quickly turned from oppressive heat to a fine drizzle. When it began to pour in earnest we crouched in our cagoules and waited. During a brief break, TM started nailing the next day's lead, while I belayed and collected water that was running down the rock. It had a bright green color and tasted so foul that we decided to keep it only as a reserve for the last day.

June 17: For the first half of the day we followed a single crack and then switched to another, which we followed until we were forced to quit climbing early when the intermittent rain settled into a downpour. Since we were obviously in for a nasty bivouac, we prepared for it as best we could. We even tried to hang our hammocks above us as a shield against the torrents of rain. It never stopped all night and the cold was intense, as in a high mountain storm. Soaked through, we huddled together to keep warm. TM had a particularly bad night, shivering so violently that he could hardly speak. When he did he sounded almost delirious. We were despondent and, for the moment, had lost our vision and our courage. Yet we kept any thought of retreat to ourselves.

June 18: The returning light restored our courage. A perfect crack in an overhanging corner allowed us to gain height rapidly while the overhanging wall shielded us from the rain. At the top of the corner, Herbert began placing bolts across a blank area, doing a fantastic job of stretching out the distance between them. We hoped this traverse would lead us to the 'Grey Bands' from where we would reach the beginning of the upper part of our route. After resting from the exhausting work of placing eleven bolts, all horizontally, he dropped down, went around a corner, and began to layback up vertical flakes. Losing voice-contact with me, he painstakingly backed down until he could belay from the top of a very shaky flake. It was a tremendous effort and certainly saved the day. I just had time to finish the next pitch and to reach the Grey Bands before dark. We rappelled down to a good ledge and fumbled around in the dark to set up our bivouac. My down jacket was hopelessly soaked from the constant rain and so TM gave me his sweater, which had to do for the rest of the climb.

June 19: The cold gray dawn revealed an appalling sight. Barring us from the summit were 1,000 feet of wild, overhanging wall capped by a 30-foot ceiling. A quick inventory showed two days' worth of food and water and only nine expansion bolts. There was no going down from here. The only practical retreat would be to traverse the Grey Bands for the 400 feet to the Nose Route, of which we knew we could climb up to the top in two or two-and-a-half days. Aside from the uncertainty of the way ahead and our short supplies, we were physically and mentally exhausted from the strain of the climbing and the cold, wet bivouacs. *Should we retreat or go on?* Here was that line that has to be crossed of which Herzog speaks so eloquently in Annapurna. The cost of a failure can be dear, but the values to be gained from a success can be so marvelous as often to change a person's whole life.

After all, why were we here but to gain these personal values? Down below there were only ten people who even knew we were up here. Even if we were successful, there would be no crowds of hero worshippers, no newspaper reports. Thank goodness American climbing has not yet progressed to that sorry state.

Our decision made, TM led upward. At this point the route becomes vague in my mind. The artificial climbing blends into the free. The corners, dihedrals, jam-cracks, bulges, are all indistinguishable parts of the great, overhanging wall. The pitches never end, and one day merges into another. I recall only bits and pieces. A horrible flaring chimney sticks in my mind, and the most difficult pendulum in my life. Always the overhangs and bulges keep us from knowing exactly where to go.

And I remember a wonderful peregrine falcon aerie deep back in a chimney; soft white pieces of down stuck to the crystals of grey granite.

June 20: The view below our hammocks was terrific—2,500 feet between us and the ground. But that was another life and we began to discover our own world. We now felt at home. Bivouacking in hammocks was completely natural. Nothing felt strange about our vertical world. With the more-receptive senses, we now appreciated everything around us. Each individual crystal in the granite stood out in bold relief. The varied shapes of the clouds never ceased to attract our attention. For the first time, we noticed tiny bugs that were all over the walls, so tiny they were barely noticeable. While belaying, I stared at one for fifteen minutes, watching him move and admiring his brilliant red color.

How could one ever be bored with so many good things to see and feel! This unity with our joyous surroundings, this ultra-penetrating perception gave us a feeling of contentment that we had not had for years. It reminded TM of his childhood days when the family all came together on the porch of his home to sit and watch the setting sun.

The climbing continued to be extreme and, in our now very weakened state, strenuous pitches took us hours to lead. TM was normally a fairly conservative climber, but now he was climbing brilliantly. He attacked the most difficult pitch of the climb, an overhanging series of loose flakes, with absolute confidence; he placed pitons behind the gigantic loose blocks that could break off at any moment, never hesitating and never doubting his ability.

June 21: Awakening on the eighth day, we promptly devoured the last few bites of food and the last of our water. Four bolts were left; 400 feet to go, and always that summit overhang weighing on our minds. It was going to be close. When the cracks were good, they were all one size; we had to constantly drop down and clean our own pitches in order to use the same pitons higher up. Often the cracks were bottoming, which meant having to put pitons back-to-back and tying them off with only the tips holding. The slow progress was extremely frustrating. The rain continued to fall in a silvery curtain that stayed a good twenty-five feet away from us. Hanging from pitons under an overhang we placed our last bolt, hung by a "cliff hanger" on a tiny flake, and barely reached a good crack to our left.

Our friends on top urged us on with promises of champagne, roast chicken, beer, and fresh fruit. The summit overhang still barred us from the top, as we insanely tried one blind crack after another. Finally, with the help of a light from above, we placed the last piton. We took a few halting steps on the horizontal and abandoned ourselves to a gastronomic orgy.

Looking back up at our route late one afternoon when a bluish haze covered the west side of El Capitan, it seemed to have lost a bit of its frightfulness but appeared even more aloof and mysterious than before. It is far too deep-rooted to be affected by the mere presence of man. But we had been changed. We had absorbed some of its strength and serenity.

Route summary: First ascent of Muir Wall, El Capitan, Yosemite Valley, California; June 14–21, 1965; Rating–NCCS VI, F9, A4; Gear–350–500 pitons, 30 bolts; Yvon Chouinard, TM Herbert.

OPPOSITE: *Out of water, out of food, out of bolts—coming up the last pitch of the Muir Wall, Yosemite.* TM Herbert

To Malinda Pennoyer from Fitz Roy Base Camp

Letter, Unpublished, November 1968

Hi Kid,

Sending this letter from base camp. It will be taken down by the horse driver who brought up the last of our gear. Fitz Roy sticks up above us 9,000 feet. It's an incredible place! The pampas lays at our feet with the same lovely beauty of the Wyoming prairies, except here there are ostriches and guanacos and condors and armadillos and all sorts of other weird animals. Our base camp is on the edge of a small stream back in a bunch of trees. Not much sun gets through, but it's away from the terrible wind.

Two days ago, Doug and I went up to where we will have our next camp in an ice cave. What a hard day! Had to gain 4,000 feet of elevation through three feet of new, powder snow. Perhaps we are here a bit too early. We are all suffering from aches and pains from working too hard on the first few days. Walked twenty-five miles the first day I got here just to see the other side of the mountain. Looks like we will have to repeat the original French route and not try anything new. It will be a job just doing that and making a movie. Looks like a month of tough work ahead.

Been away from civilization for only a week and a half and already my crotch smells like a vulture's breath and my teeth have a film of yellow scale on them. Been letting myself go I'm afraid. I'll be a real wild man after a month!

OPPOSITE: *Ellen Malinda Pennoyer in Camp 4, Yosemite.* Chouinard Family Collection

These are truly the greatest mountains in the world, I'm happy to have seen them and I'll be thankful if we can get up the Fitz. One thing is for sure, though, this is the first and last expedition I go on. The work involved just to do a couple of thousand feet of real climbing is unbelievable! Today it's about thirty degrees at our base camp which is only at 2,500 feet elevation, a super strong wind is blowing, and we have to carry loads up 3,000 feet of hillside, snow slope, across frozen lakes, and dump them somewhere. It's going to be a drag. Sure would rather be in hot, steamy Fresno with you! This may be the last letter for a while. Hope all is well and I miss you more than ever. Much love.

PS: Could you call Susie collect and tell her all is well for Doug.

Fun Hogs

First published in 180° South *by Yvon Chouinard, Doug Tompkins, Chris Malloy, and Jeff Johnson, Patagonia Books, 2010*

You never know how an adventure will influence the rest of your life. In 1968, when Doug Tompkins proposed that we drive from California to Patagonia—in those days a name as remote and alluring as Timbuktu—neither of us could have known it would be the most important trip either of us would ever take. The goal was to put up a new route on an obscure tusk of granite called Cerro Fitz Roy and have some fun along the way. The experience led to an unlikely fate for a couple of dirtbags: We became philanthropists.

Doug owned a small outdoor store in San Francisco, where he had a few sleeping bags and tents sewn in the back room; I had a blacksmith shop in Ventura where we forged pitons and machined carabiners for a market that needed no research—we and our friends were the customers.

It took Doug and me only a couple of weeks to turn our work over to others, talk Dick Dorworth and Lito Tejada-Flores into driving down with us (English climber Chris Jones would hook up with us later), and secure a van—a high-mileage 1965 Ford Econoline. I built a sleeping platform in the back, and then we shoehorned in four pairs of skis, eight climbing ropes, racks of carabiners and pitons, camping gear, cold-weather clothing, warm-weather clothing, wetsuits, and fishing rods. We tied two surfboards on the roof. We

OPPOSITE: *Fitz Roy's southeastern side. The Italian Col is the notch on the left. Snow slopes lead up to the base of the 1952 French route. The California Route goes left on hidden snow slopes to reach the foot of the southwest buttress, seen in profile on the left-hand skyline. Patagonia.* Chris Jones

took along the banner Doug's wife, Susie, made for us to fly from Fitz Roy's summit; its big block letters read: "VIVA LOS FUN HOGS."

We all had complementary talents. Because I had taken auto mechanics in high school, I was appointed team mechanic. Doug and I were the most experi-

---

We were sleeping on the ground around the van when an army patrol woke us, a sixteen-year-old kid pointing his machine gun from my head to Dick's.

---

enced climbers; Doug and Dick were expert skiers. I was a surfer, and Lito was a climber and photographer to whom we assigned the task of documenting the trip with a wind-up 16-mm Bolex we bought secondhand. Lito had never before made a movie or even shot with a movie camera. We were living up to Doug's credo, borrowed from Napoleon, "Commit first, then figure it out."

Only a week after leaving Ventura, we were surfing the breaks outside Mazatlán. South of Mexico City the pavement gave way to a dirt road that, except for a few concrete stretches through capital cities and a gap in Panama, would continue to Patagonia. Once we crossed into Guatemala, however, we confronted a challenge greater than a dirt highway. We were sleeping on the ground around the van when an army patrol woke us, a sixteen-year-old kid pointing his machine gun from my head to Dick's. We managed to convince them we weren't CIA agents, just tourists on a surf trip, then made a beeline for the border of Costa Rica, which had the only sane government in the region—and great surf breaks.

We had to scuttle our plan to stay there for a while when the volcano above our break erupted. So much ash fell between sets that the decks of our surfboards turned black—and it was almost impossible to breathe.

OPPOSITE: *The 1965 Ford Econoline van heading south (screen grab from the film* Mountain of Storms). Lito Tejada-Flores

We drove south to Panama to ride breaks that probably had never been surfed before, and then, to get around the roadless Darién Gap, drove our van on board a Spanish freighter bound for Cartagena, Colombia. Dick, famous for his night driving skills—and aided by cassette tapes of Joplin, Dylan, and Hendrix, and a few other means—power-drove all the way to Ecuador, where I knew of a surf spot Mike Doyle had discovered.

All this time Lito filmed our adventure with the wind-up Bolex. Doug had talked me into sharing the costs of the camera and film with him. He was convinced that once home, we—the "producers"—could sell the film to make enough to pay for the trip and then some. (When we got back, we spent more money editing the footage into a one-hour film, *Mountain of Storms*, which made it into a few specialty film festivals but was never distributed.)

We surfed in Ecuador, then sold our boards in Peru. In Chile, we pulled out the skis and skinned up and skied down Llaima, a big volcano outside Temuco, and farther south, Osorno, sometimes called the Fuji of South America.

Just south of Puerto Montt the highway came to an end, blocked by deep fjords and the great tidal glaciers descending from the continental ice caps. We loaded the van on small ferries and crossed sapphire-blue lakes framed by beech forests and snow-capped volcanoes, off-loaded the van, and drove the short distance to the next lake crossing. In Argentina, on the leeward side of the Andes, the landscape changed suddenly from temperate rain forest to open steppes. The Econoline, seasoned by over 12,000 miles of hard driving, barreled down the celebrated Route 40, the dirt road that connects northern to southern Patagonia.

Miles later we left Route 40 and followed a road more like a horse track around Lago Viedma, one of a series of large, glacially carved lakes in the southern Andes. This was the worst road any of us had encountered, and we didn't see another vehicle for 180 miles. Then the trail petered out entirely. In those years only a footbridge crossed the Río de las Vueltas, so we parked the Econoline and talked some army soldiers into helping us carry our gear to base camp. The only other humans in the region were the gaucho Rojo,

OPPOSITE: *Carrying loads into the Valle del Río de las Vueltas. At the time, there was no bridge for cars going across. Argentina.* Chris Jones

and the widow Sepulveda and her sons, who ran a sheep station three days by horse from Lago del Desierto.

At that point, we had been on the road for nearly four months; it would take us another two months to climb Fitz Roy. The peak had been summited

———

I spent a total of thirty-one days
confined to a snow cave.

———

only twice, first by the iconoclastic Frenchman Lionel Terray, who wrote that Fitz Roy was one of two climbs he had no desire to repeat. Terray built his reputation on ascents of peaks that were obscure to laymen but considered classics by climbers for their beauty or the difficulty of their routes. He understood that how you reached the summit was more important than the feat itself. His approach appealed to those of us who had cut our teeth on first ascents of Yosemite's high walls, where you got to the top only to realize there wasn't anything there. Terray said it all when he titled his autobiography *Conquistadors of the Useless*.

Once at the base of Fitz Roy, between brief breaks in the scudding clouds, we could trace a line of ascent (now called the Ruta de los Californianos) that would be hard but doable. Then the weather changed.

Because the Andes rise so suddenly out of the Southern Ocean, the storms that blow in the latitudes of the Howling Fifties collide with the peaks like a train hitting a huge wall. The winds of Patagonia are so strong you feel you can bite into them.

Our tents were no match for such winds, so we had to dig snow caves, including one at the base of the final rock ridge leading to the summit that became our high camp. In the sixty days it took us to reach the summit, we had only five days of weather clear enough to climb. The rest of the time we waited.

I spent a total of thirty-one days confined to a snow cave. I had skewered my knee with my ice ax while cutting ice for the stove. So while the others left periodically to go down and rustle a sheep to augment our meager food reserves, I stayed on my back staring at a gloomy ceiling of ice melting inches

Inside the second ice cave: "canned food, cooking gear, and one of our trusty steel shovels (purchased in a hardware store on the drive down) used for digging ice caves. Without the steel shovels, we probably would not have been able to do the climb. The hard ice would have chewed up any US-made snow shovels of the time." Cerro Fitz Roy. Chris Jones

above my face. Every time we started the stove to cook, the walls dripped onto our down sleeping bags, which became useless wet lumps as a result. We were perpetually cold and hungry. I turned thirty years old inside that cave; it was a low point in my life. But because it honed me to handle adversity, it was a high point too.

When the weather finally broke, we knew we had to move fast. Doug and I led the pitches and, at the top of each one, fixed a rope that Lito would then use to ascend, filming us as we started the next pitch. Dick and Chris followed, carrying our gear. We were very efficient and before sunset, we reached the top and posed while Lito filmed us holding Susie's banner.

The feeling of jubilation on the summit of any tough climb is tempered by the awareness that you still have to get down. We couldn't get back to the

ice cave before dark, and after twenty-one hours straight of climbing and rappelling we were forced to bivouac. The wind returned and it was a miserable night, but as Doug Scott, another climbing friend, once said about a bivouac high on Everest, the quality of the survival was good.

———

Appreciate something for long enough and you learn to love it. And anytime you love something, you also want to care for it and safeguard it.

———

Doug has said that spending so much of our formative years in close proximity to the beauty of nature allowed an appreciation for it to enter our bones. Appreciate something for long enough and you learn to love it. And anytime you love something, you also want to care for it and safeguard it.

In the mid-1980s I returned to the base of Fitz Roy with my friends Rick Ridgeway and Tom Brokaw. At the trailhead, we stepped out of our van to begin the trek. In the grassy fields, where only fifteen years earlier Rojo's sheep grazed, lay a maze of survey markers, each with a pennant of orange tape indicating that as the location of a new street, a new restaurant, a new hotel. A few months later the town of El Chaltén was under construction.

By then my business had grown. So had Doug's. While he was away on our long road trip, Susie started a small line of boutique women's dresses called Plain Jane that she and Doug later developed into a billion-dollar company called Esprit.

My wife, Malinda, and I also went into the rag trade, after importing some rugby shirts from Scotland that took off and threatened to make enough profit to support the climbing business. The clothes, like the gear, had to be

OPPOSITE: *Yvon leads across a thin crack. "Tense moments pass as the thin mist swirl around us, and the route ahead is not entirely obvious." Cerro Fitz Roy.* Chris Jones

129

strong, long lasting, and perform perfectly for the use intended. We introduced clean lines, bold colors, and light, technical layering to outdoor clothing—and named our new company Patagonia.

Doug and I wanted to give back to what we cared about most. By the mid-1980s, Patagonia, the company, had started to give 1 percent of its sales to grassroots organizations to help save a patch of land here or a stretch of river there. Around the same time, recognizing the environmental damage that business does, Esprit introduced its pioneer "eco-collection" of women's wear made with natural fibers and dyes and organically grown cotton.

In 1990, I decided to take the senior management of my company off-site for an examination of our goals and responsibilities. We loaded our backpacks, and Patagonia-the-company journeyed to Patagonia-the-place. The experience was seminal. Coming out of that trip, and during the sessions that followed our return, we wrote the company mission statement that's still used to guide our decisions: "Build the best product, cause no unnecessary harm, and use business to inspire and implement solutions to the environmental crisis."

A bit later on, we did an analysis of the environmental impacts of our four main clothing fibers. On learning that conventional cotton accounted for 25 percent of all the insecticides used in world agriculture, we decided to go organic—even though there wasn't enough organic cotton available then to supply our needs. In the first decade of the 2000s we introduced the first closed-loop recycling program in the clothing industry, and most recently we created a website where our customers can examine the environmental consequences of the clothing they buy from us, both the good and the bad.

During the past twenty years there have been a few times when, frustrated with the business, I've thought about selling it, putting the money into a foundation, and using it to affect environmental change and protection. Each time, though, I've decided that the better strategy was to keep the company and use it as a model for responsible business.

That wasn't true for Doug, however. In the late 1980s, after he and Susie divorced, he sold his half of Esprit and put the money into his own foundation. At first he followed the same strategy we had at Patagonia,

OPPOSITE: *December 20, 1968, 8 pm, Funhogs (left to right): Dick Dorworth, Doug Tompkins, and Yvon on the summit of Fitz Roy. "Our Funhog banner was loosely translated for the locals as 'Sporting Porks.'" Cerro Fitz Roy.* Chris Jones

making grants to small, front-line environmental groups. But then he hatched a plan for an entirely different model. Land in Patagonia was cheap, but also threatened by development—as we had seen with El Chaltén at the base of Fitz Roy—and by oil and gas development and overgrazing on the *estancias*. What if he used his foundation's resources to buy these threatened lands and protect them?

Doug flew his small Cessna to southern Chile and Argentina to check out *estancias* that might be for sale. He bought several parcels, including a farm on the edge of a fjord that would become home to him and his second wife, former Patagonia CEO Kristine McDivitt. He then began acquiring contiguous properties that eventually he would combine into Pumalín Park—at nearly 800,000 acres—the largest privately held park in the world.

Kris joined Doug in his work on conservation projects across Patagonia, including a new effort of her own called Conservación Patagónica. Her goal was to attract the support of philanthropists to help acquire large properties that would then be returned to the people of Chile or Argentina. Her first project was on the Atlantic coast just north of the Straits of Magellan. Today, Monte Leon is Argentina's first and only maritime national park, protecting twenty-six miles of wild coastline, home to a vital seal rookery as well as a penguin colony of about half a million birds. Her current project is to create Patagonia National Park, centered around the magnificent Valle Chacabuco which cuts transversally through the Andes, providing habitat for overlap species from both the wet windward as well as the dry leeward biomes.

This project is, in a sense, all in the family. Patagonia, the company, has contributed money as well as subsidized some of our employees to do volunteer work removing fences and eradicating non-native plants.

Our company has become an attractive place to work for anyone who cares about the fate of the planet, and this, in turn, has made it easy to recruit good employees. It's also an appealing company to the outdoor athletes who test and promote our products. We attract some of the top climbers, surfers, and skiers in the world, not so much the most competitive, but those who relate to the soul of the sport—climbers who are more into the quality of the

OPPOSITE: *Doug Tompkins descending from the first ascent of Ruta de los Californianos in 1968. Cerro Fitz Roy.* Chris Jones

route than gaining the summit, and surfers more interested in an undiscovered wave on a remote coastline than another contest prize.

That is certainly the case with one of our key surf ambassadors, Chris Malloy. Before he decided to look me up, and then come to work for us, Chris began his own pilgrimage trying to understand his growing disillusionment with the life of a professional competitive surfer. He was living in Hawai'i, wrestling with those questions, when a close friend and North Shore lifeguard named Jeff Johnson showed him a copy of an obscure film about a bunch of friends back in the 1960s who bought a funky Ford van and drove it all the way from California to a place called Patagonia.

Chris and his friends were kind enough to include Doug and me in their revisit of our adventure—and to take advantage of some typically nonstop Patagonia rain to ply us with questions on how we came to value what we do and how we set down our road. The photos and stories in *180° South* give you the perspectives of two generations of climbers and surfers who have come into contact with the wild and had their lives changed forever. It is the nature of nature that you can't come to know it from a book, but you can get a glimpse here. Even that much will make you want to act—and live for it.

Doug and Kris Tompkins, through their foundation the Tompkins Conservation and with the financial help from many philanthropists, have helped conserve 13 million acres in Chile and Argentina as of 2018. This wild habitat is secured in a dozen new national parks and other protected areas. And their work continues.

OPPOSITE: *Less than two years after her husband, Doug Tompkins, died in a kayaking accident, Kris Tompkins realizes their joint dream: the signing on March 15, 2017, of the initial protocol with Chilean President Michelle Bachelet to create what will be named the Pumalín National Park – Douglas R. Tompkins.* Jimmy Chin

NEXT SPREAD: *Doug Tompkins flies his beloved Husky over the backcountry of Pumalín in 2008. Starting in 1991, it would take Doug, and later his wife Kris, twenty-six years of focused, strategic work to make Pumalín an actual national park, and one of the largest conservation victories by private individuals in history.* Scott Soens

Thoughts on Climbing
in the Kaisergebirge

Unpublished, 1971

Partner: Peter Habeler, about twenty-eight years old, five foot eight, good-looking, super confident. One of the new generation of Austrian guides.

Fleischbank, Southeast Wall, First Ascent: Wiessner/Rossi: An all-time classic. Kor would love it. Nice free climbing on fabulous grey limestone. Just like Mount Louis in the Canadian Rockies. Rup, rup, rup the sound of an oblong high flyer. Two parties are up ahead. I'm breaking the first rule of helmetless climbing. Always be first on a route. I'm nervous. We rope up.

First pitch goes okay. Steep, really steep. A hard pitch to the start of the famous tension traverse. Got to remember to keep the leads short; this isn't the Valley. Pitons everywhere! The whole climb can be done free but why act like a bad guest? I play their game and grab every peg and pull up. We pass up a beautiful Swiss girl with a guide, the guide is blond, five foot eight, good looking, etc. She only speaks German so I can't even say hello. Besides, with my Pancho Villa mustache and baggy knickers I must look pretty funny.

Rossi's overhang is all pegged up, the hard friction pitch has little steps chopped into the rock. Expansion bolts right next to a perfect one-hundred-foot jam crack. A beautiful pitch totally compromised with the bolts. The summit is a field of pop tops, bottles, toilet paper, and trash. I clean a twenty-foot radius. They tell me not to bother as the shit is endless. I feel guilty. We see two chamois goats.

On the way to the hut, there are steel cables and steps hewn into the rock. The Egger Steil trail was built by the Egger brewery on the condition that the hut would always serve their beer. The hut sleeps 300 under down comforters

and sheets. Sausages, potatoes, and sauerkraut—and beer.

Predigtstuhl, Direct West Face: Dodgy third class to the base. I wish Peter would give me a belay. First pitch is already vertical, I could do it free but why bother. Limestone is perfect rock for nuts. Fantastic old pitons of all kinds. You could clean the route and have an A1 piton museum.

Steep good climbing, stemming.

Belay thoughts: Old Austrian climbers and the greatest of them all, Mattias Rebbitsh. Old Cassin pitons with broken rings. Wood blocks with rotten cord. No tied-off pegs here. You pound the tips of these soft pegs in as far as they'll go, then pound the piton down. No testing, just clip in and hope. Pierre Alain carabiners that won't open under a load. Metal stirrups that are noisy, clumsy goddamn things. Fifis hooks get snagged on everything. What am I doing here? Hanging on shit gear, useless locking carabiners. My arms are pumped. This is not my game.

ABOVE: *Peter Habeler on the Fleischbank, Austria.* Yvon Chouinard

NEXT SPREAD: *Peter Habeler leading a steep pitch on the Predigtstuhl, Austria. Peter and Reinhold Messner were the first to climb Mount Everest without oxygen, in 1978.* Yvon Chouinard

Chouinard Ⓒ Equipment

Coonyard Mouths Off

First published in Ascent, *1972*

"Today's climber ... carries his courage in his rucksack. ... Faith in equipment has replaced faith in oneself." – Reinhold Messner

Mountaineering is very much in vogue in America. What was once a way of life that only attracted the oddball individual is now a healthy, upstanding, recreational pastime enjoyed by thousands of average Joes. The climbing scene has become a fad and the common man is bringing the Art down to his own level of values and competence.

Living in California, I can see previews of coming attractions in America. I saw the Peace and Love movement turn to Violence and Hate even before it got to other parts of the country. Now there are bad vibrations in the overpopulated surfing scene and even worse vibrations with the climbing craze. The same problems which prevented us from realizing the Great American Dream are now facing mountaineering. Just as man continues to disrupt the natural order of things, so mountaineering has become increasingly technical, decreasingly difficult, much too crowded, and far less adventuresome. The purity, uncertainty, naturalness, and soul of the sport are rapidly being changed.

Having been passionately committed to climbing for seventeen years, and with a business directly related to climbing and its problems, I feel a heavy

OPPOSITE: *This T-shirt graphic was designed by Mike Rogers over beers with Yvon in the early 1980s. "I was lamenting the increasing popularity of 'hangdogging' (a climber who rests while suspended by their climbing rope)." Only a handful of these shirts were made to give out at an American Alpine Club meeting.* Mike Rogers

responsibility to make known my apprehension over what climbing is becoming.

Bolts. After the Wall of the Early Morning Light fiasco, there was a considerable increase in the sale of bolts in the climbing shops in Southern California. A kid buys a bolt kit before he even knows how to use a runner! Yet Reinhold Messner became one of the world's greatest alpinists without ever having drilled a single hole.

It's no longer enough to say that only the expert climbers should be allowed to place bolts. We've said that all along and it's not working! Even the 'Mad Bolter' surely considers himself an expert.

On the big-wall climbs of the 1960s, bolts had their place. They made it possible to ascend the great routes on El Capitan and Half Dome. This era is gone and yet bolts are being used in ever greater numbers to force illogical routes up blank faces. This permits the average Joe to do climbs that are normally over his head, and they allow the experts to do incredibly hard climbs without having to stick their necks out. Bolts are even used for no apparent reason, like the one I once saw next to an eight-foot circumference ponderosa pine.

I believe we have reached the point where the only hope is to completely degrade bolting. We must refuse to recognize it as a legitimate means of climbing. If you are in sympathy, you must stop using bolts. Disparage others who do. Moreover, tell your local climbing shop that you are not buying anything from them until they stop selling bolts, or at the very least remove them from the front counter.

The Lost Arrow Tip is as dead as the Hudson River. It is no longer a climb. The Nose of El Cap to Sickle Ledge is a disgusting experience. You now use half-inch angles where the pioneers used RURPs. Bashies have been welded into piton holes, leaving the rock once again smooth and flush, except for the rotten sling sticking out. Cracks are deteriorating, flakes are broken off, trees are being girdled by rappel ropes. Even the quartz-hard Shawangunks in New York are suffering from the onslaught of too many climbers. It can't go on like this. And it won't. The Park Service has already closed three climbs in Yosemite because of deterioration of the rock.

We once thought that America had the highest standard of rock climbing in the world because we removed our pitons and left the climbs "clean." This policy worked fine when there were just a handful of us, and it's still a good way to climb a big virgin Alaskan wall. But in the Valley or the Gunks, it is now a selfish, destructive ethic.

I'd like to offer a few immediate solutions. Stay off climbs which you don't intend to finish. Don't climb to Sickle Ledge unless you plan to do the entire Nose route. Stay off climbs that are obviously over your head—otherwise you will just be placing more pitons than necessary for protection. Don't use artifi-

———

... Reinhold Messner became one of the world's greatest alpinists without ever having drilled a single hole.

———

cial aid on free climbs. These actions would certainly help solve the problem, but the final answer is to leave *necessary* pitons in place on all climbs, artificial and free.

The fixed-piton idea would appear at first to be a degeneration of artificial climbing standards, and it will probably end up being so. However, we could start playing the chock-and-natural-protection-game instead of the piton game and thus perhaps even *raise* the existing standards. For instance, I believe that it's possible to climb El Cap using only chocks and a few thin pitons (these could be fixed).

The chock solution is dependent on everyone *using* nuts, not just carrying them around for looks, but really trusting them. Nuts and runners can be used in place of pitons on free climbs 95 percent of the time in Yosemite. I spent five days there last spring, climbing every day, and never placed a piton. I don't even carry a hammer in the Tetons anymore. This system of necessary fixed pitons and using natural protection will only work if the guidebook writers cooperate. The "all-clean" (no pitons necessary) routes should be mentioned to avoid extra piton placement and removal. The new Shawangunk guide will contain this information, plus the names of the party doing the first *clean* ascent.

Responsibility. I prefer to climb without wearing a hard hat. I won't argue the safety issue pro or con—it's just that my head feels freer and more receptive to the good things happening all around when I climb. I believe that the wearing of a crash helmet should be a matter of personal choice. However, in some climbing areas, like Devil's Tower, Wyoming, it has become government policy.

The same thing is true with solo climbing in some National Parks. We have no one other than ourselves to blame for these restrictive policies. We have allowed the overstressing of the safety aspects of crash helmets in the American Alpine Club Accident Reports, which insurance companies read. It won't be long before your life insurance will cover you only when wearing a crash helmet. It already applies to motorcyclists, to gardeners working along freeways, and to students in climbing schools.

We have also allowed the Park Service to feel directly responsible for climbing rescues to the extent that either rangers are on the rescue teams or the Park Service pays your friends to rescue you! Since Big Uncle has become responsible for our safety, he feels the obligation to legislate on matters that should be a personal choice.

The responsibility for rescues should be with the climbers themselves, and should be handled on a voluntary, nonpaying, noncharge basis. Helicopter costs could be paid for by an American Alpine Club insurance policy as in France, or by a rescue-fund kitty, as in Britain.

The increasing frequency of rescues on big climbs goes to show that many climbers are showing an irresponsible attitude by attempting big walls before they are really equal to the problems involved. During the spring of 1971, there were over thirty attempts on El Capitan, with only four successful climbs! One of the failures involved climbers who had merely gotten wet, sat down and waited for a rescue while another party (on another route) continued on.

Population. One day last summer, sixty-five people stood on the summit of the Grand Teton. These people had camped either on the Lower Saddle or in Garnet Canyon. This means that there were probably one hundred persons camping in the area, a timberline environment which is not capable of supporting more than ten groups without suffering severe damage to the fragile meadows, trees, and wildflowers.

Already, the State of California is requiring reservations and is limiting the number of people allowed to go into a wilderness area. This will also happen in the Tetons and the climber will be the one to suffer. The Alps are able to support far greater numbers of climbers than we are because of their hut systems.

OPPOSITE: *"Experiencing firsthand how the pitons I forged were damaging the rocks we climbed, we began making and selling removable climbing protection, like these Hexentrics and Stoppers." Yvon in Yosemite. 1973.* Tom Frost

I agree that huts encourage even more people to go into the mountains, but the huts need not be as elaborate as those in the Alps. In any case, a hut on the Lower Saddle and another in the meadows of Garnet Canyon, plus a ban on open fires and tent camping, is the only way we can preserve the environment and still allow more than a few parties a day to climb in these areas.

Should a hut system be adopted, I only hope that the builders will have more esthetic sense than to build a wooden A-frame at Boulder Camp in the Bugaboos (as the Canadians intend to do). To build anything but a rock hut there is like putting a Spanish Adobe on the coast of Maine.

Go back, Jo Jo. A party now starts up El Capitan with the confidence of knowing that if anything happens they will be rescued within a day or so from any point on the wall. The fear of the unknown, the fear of being unequal to the wall, of flaming out 1,500 feet from nowhere can still be a real fear, but the outcome is now a certainty.

We have our topo to make sure we won't come up against any unforeseen difficulties. Let's take our jumars so that we'll only have to climb every other pitch and thus save our strength for leading because that's where it's at. Don't forget the chalk for that 5.9 friction and a few bolts, mashies, bashies, and a space blanket for security. And a hundred moms and dads down in the meadow ready to get that rescue going just as soon as you yell for it—maybe even before! When you come up to the A5 RURP traverse, just smash in a few tied-off one and a half-inch angles, plug up that hole with a mashie and you're up. In the bar remember to tell your friends that El Cap is a piece of cake— nothing over A3 and 5.8. Then go back to Iowa and quit climbing because you've done the ultimate.

I'm trying to say that maybe Yosemite and El Capitan are not the ultimates. It was a spaced-out adventure once, when the odds were more stacked against you, but it's not such a big deal anymore. George Lowe thought that his winter ascent of the north face of the Grand Teton was a far more difficult climb than the Salathé Wall. If you want to experience the same adventure and the same difficulties that the El Cap pioneers had, then you've got to go somewhere else, where there are virgin walls, where you are going to feel the same loneliness of being five days from the bottom and five days from the top.

OPPOSITE: *A Realized Ultimate Reality Piton "RURP."* Tom Frost

The Bavarian climber Willo Welzenbach was the greatest climber of the post–World War I period. He was a complete alpinist, equally adept on rock and ice. In 1925, he put up over twenty new routes in the Alps. He made the first ascents of six of the greatest north walls of the Bernese Oberland. His routes were characterized by their logic, audacity, and beauty. Objective dangers, foul weather, bad conditions, and rotten rock—these were not absolute obstacles for him. Caught on a wall many times by bad weather, he would wait out the storm, then continue to the summit.

All of his climbs were done in impeccable style, without fixed ropes, bolts, crash helmets, topos, radios, or even down gear! These were climbs encompassing all the techniques and difficulties of grand alpinism: steep ice, hard free-climbing, avalanches, rockfalls, storms, and most of all, fear of the unknown.

This was the golden age of climbing; this was the pinnacle of the art, perhaps never to be equaled again. Since Welzenbach, Gervasutti, and Salathé, more difficult climbs have been made, but generally as a direct result of better equipment and consequent use of that equipment.

We are entering a new era of climbing—an era that may well be characterized by incredible advances in equipment, by the overcoming of great difficulties, with even greater technological wizardry, and by the rendering of the mountains to a low, though democratic, mean.

Or it could be the start of more spiritual climbing, where we assault the mountains with less equipment and with more awareness, more experience, and more courage.

OPPOSITE: *Cloud shadows on El Capitan, Yosemite.* Glen Denny

Das Tent

First published in Outside *magazine, June 1986*

Sometimes the adventure you get is not the adventure you went for.

The roar of the wind came from far above. At times, it was only a sound, and we stared blankly upward, waiting. It came as a louder, more urgent shriek, and we braced our feet and hands against the poles just as the wind, like a pile hammer, hit the tent. The sides bowed in, and the force increased: sixty, then seventy, then eighty knots. Ice spears started flying, and the tent took several direct hits. Ninety, one hundred knots, and we pushed on the poles as if our lives depended on it. The roar, the howling wind devils, the flying ice blocks, all rose in a mad cacophony, then climaxed in several bullwhip pops that shuddered and shook the tent. Then it was quiet again, but not silent; there was still that dull roar, 4,000 feet above our heads.

Doug Tompkins and I have never liked tents much. In our early climbing days in the Wind Rivers and the Canadian Rockies, we prided ourselves on always finding a dry cave among the boulders, or shelter under the low branches of an alpine fir. Once, on Fitz Roy, we spent thirty-one days in ice caves because there wasn't a tent that could stand up to the Patagonian winds. Even in the Karakoram we carried shovels instead of tents.

We were given this tent on an expedition to Bhutan last year: a small two-person model that has nine poles and weighs almost fifteen pounds. We joked about how heavy it was, and how you would have to be a big, strapping Rainier guide to ever carry it into the mountains. We did appreciate that it

OPPOSITE: *The tent. Ellsworth Mountains, Antarctica. 1986.* Doug Tompkins

looked strong and secure, sort of like a limpet, and that it would probably be a good tent for the Poles, where you could sledge it around.

People told us the weather had been bad that spring in Antarctica. Our plane, a Twin Otter, had to overnight on Tierra del Fuego because of fog at King George Island. We spent another night at Palmer Station on Adelaide Island and waited at Rothera for the clouds to clear. Still another night was spent on the ice near Siple Station before we finally reached the base of the Ellsworth Mountains at seventy-eight degrees south. The six others in our party headed off to climb Mount Vinson. Tompkins and I sledged up to the cirque under the peaks of Epperly and Shinn. We set up the tent into what we guessed was the prevailing wind and anchored it with dead-men, ice axes, and poles from the sledge. We fitted the guylines with heavy shock cord.

The climb on the 5,000-foot West Face of Shinn was mostly in a couloir. We climbed unroped to save time, and were tired by the time we reached the ice cliffs at the top. Then we turned right, across and up steep, hard ice. We had to force ourselves to concentrate on each move; a slip here would have been terminal.

Above the face the wind was blowing a steady forty knots, with stronger gusts out of the east. The temperature was about minus ten or twenty degrees Fahrenheit. We put on neoprene face masks and goggles and changed from gloves to mittens. Our goggles weren't working because spindrift had blown in through the foam separating the double lenses. Shinn is only 15,750 feet, but when you add 3,000 feet for the high latitude, it becomes a grind. The final thousand feet on the summit spire were a real effort.

We made the top, descended the south side of Shinn, and, at about midnight, visited Camp II of the Vinson group for a brew. We returned to our tent at 4:30 am. We'd been out for nineteen and a half hours. We slept until noon, and at 12:30 pm, on December 8, the first gust hit.

There had been no warning of this storm. Or if there was, we didn't recognize it. After the first gust, it was dead silent for five minutes, then another wind devil, and soon, a roar that came from the col between Shinn and Epperly.

It wasn't until several hours into the storm that there was a significant change in the altimeter. By 6 pm it had gained 350 feet, the most change either of us had seen on altimeters before. We put on all our clothes and climbed into our

OPPOSITE: *The 5,000-foot west face of Mount Shinn, Antarctica.* Doug Tompkins

sleeping bags. We leaned our packs up against the tent walls facing the wind, then lay down with our feet on the packs to brace the poles. When the gusts came, we pushed against the packs and the poles as hard as we could. When the winds rose to more than eighty knots, they tore off chunks of the crusted snow

---

One party in the Himalaya was blown off an ice slope and saved themselves only by self-arresting with their ice axes through the floor of the tent.

---

cover and hurled them at the tent. Flat on our backs with our feet propped up against the tent walls, watching shadows of the ice blocks flying by, we imagined the tent to be something like a space capsule passing through a meteorite storm.

We both knew the power of the wind. In 1972, in the Torre del Paine in Chile, we had stood on a hill leaned into a steady eighty-knot wind. We'd watched the big gusts coming across Lago Nordenskjökl, and just before they hit, we would jump up into them, spreading our arms and cagoules, and just for a minute we would hover like harriers before we fell off and slammed into the ground. And Tompkins had once done a weeklong solo walk around Lago Argentino, near Fitz Roy, to the Paine in 1979. He was hit by hundred-knot winds out in the desert, and shingle rocks were hurled at him at incredible speeds, pounding his legs until he found shelter behind some calafate bushes. The difference here was that the temperature was below zero.

Through the night of the eighth the storm raged. Each of us stared at our patch of tent wall, imagining that any moment it would tear open and that suddenly there would be nothing but white, and then the tent would explode. Seams stretched to the point where we could see light through the seam holes. We thought of the seamstress who'd made the tent. Maybe she'd been having a bad day, or it was a Friday afternoon and she was anxious to go home, and maybe hadn't bothered to backstitch that one critical seam. We lay there telling stories about other climbers in tents caught out in huge storms high up on Denali or Everest. Some were blown clear off the ridges and never seen again.

One party in the Himalaya was blown off an ice slope and saved themselves only by self-arresting with their ice axes through the floor of the tent. At least we had no cliff to fly off of, but by now we were sure that the cirque and col above us were creating some sort of Venturi effect that focused the wind right on the tent.

At 3 am on the ninth, the altimeter pegged a 650-foot gain. By this time, we had wrapped ourselves in another bivouac tent, and were prepared for the worst. In between gusts, we wondered whether the Beaujolais nouveau had arrived in California yet, and we talked about food because we had nothing to eat or drink except Baci chocolate kisses. Each one had a little message inside about love and kisses, and we joked about what the next one would say: "Kiss your asses goodbye." Black humor helped, but we knew this wasn't very funny. We had both survived many close calls in thirty years of being in the mountains: bad falls, avalanches, lightning. These things happen quickly, and then they're over. But we had never experienced a storm like this. Perhaps there were times during that storm on Fitz Roy that were as bad, but we had been secure under three feet of ice.

That evening the wind died down a bit, and Tompkins went outside and cut some snow blocks to shore things up. It was a token effort, though, because they were going to be quickly eroded by the wind when it took up again. A gust hit him while he was curled up in a ball, and it skidded him like a hockey puck for thirty feet. We slept for three hours, and then melted two cups of snow on a little solid-fuel bivouac stove. We were afraid to use our white-gas stove for fear the tent would tear apart while it was on.

The storm grew again and raged through the next day. The second pole bent in at 3 pm, and the fly developed some serious rips. We were exhausted from dehydration, from lack of sleep and food, and from holding up the tent. We thought of digging a snow cave through the tent floor, but there was no way to get rid of the snow, and anyway, we couldn't leave our positions.

Finally, another lull came, and both of us went outside for some serious ice-wall building. We cooked, brewed some tea, and slept for ten hours. When the sky cleared on the eleventh, we were whipped. We had planned on doing some more serious climbing, but by then we'd had enough of the Antarctic summer.

NEXT SPREAD: *"Conquerors of the Useless," Antarctica.* Yvon Chouinard

Letter to Ken Wilson

First published in the magazine Ken edited: Mountain, *London, England, March 23, 1973*

Dear Ken,

An article on the Torre, huh? Well, to tell you the truth, I know sweet bugger all about the Torre. Sure, I went there last February to climb that insolent motha but we were never allowed to even lay a finger on its flanks. It's like I shook hands with Raquel Welch and the drooling world wants to know—what was she like, what was she like? It's going to be a tough climb, I can tell you that much.

I spent a week with Doug Tompkins trying to get around the backside by way of the Paso Viento and the ice cap. The west wind was so insistent that at our turnback point, we literally could not have taken another forward step, so we jibed back to one of Mauri's caves on the moraine. After traveling 10,000 miles by air, truck, and foot to be in the great Patagonian wilderness, and then coming upon a garbage dump of Italian bikini underpants and old Bluet fuel bottles—well, you pretty quickly come back to reality.

At the same time that we were on this one-step forward, two-step back "Nixon trek," Robbins and Jack Miller were trying to find a new approach to the north side of the Fitz. They tried to push up that horrible icefall at the head of the Torre glacier, but they gave up, freaked out partly by the danger and partly by just being overawed by the area. Another case of "reality-itis."

We all ended up back at Rojo's *estancia* about the time the weather got really nasty. Tied up to the sheep fence there was Tompkins' little Cessna 210 which he had flown down from California; so every chance we got we would fly up for a look-see at the peaks. I've flown quite a bit in small planes, but I

OPPOSITE: *Cerro Torre unveils itself. Patagonia.* Mikey Schaefer

161

never have enjoyed it very much. My enthusiasm has never been enough to overcome the fear and inevitable nausea.

That morning was clear and windless. We never flew higher than thirty feet off the deck, like a harrier coursing the marsh or a hand running over the contours of a lover's body … up over rounded hills, across flat plains, down walled canyons, chasing ostriches and guanacos. Over a swamp, a thousand pink flamingos exploded into flight. Dylan in the headphones putting it all together. Now I finally know what it's all about.

It was frightening flying around the Torre. Freezing level was 14,000 feet and chunks of ice were breaking off the west side and not hitting the face for thousands of feet. A huge avalanche had made a mess of Bonatti's Col of Hope Route. From Mauri's high point there remains a thousand feet of vertical and overhanging hoarfrost; after that it's a piece of cake. It's the same with the southeast ridge of Maestri and that other climber—what was his name again? Well, all they had left was a little meringue of 200 feet or so. I'd heard that it's supposed to blow away one of these days and sure enough a great forty-foot overhang fell off one day—from the side, not the top. Around the west side there was no snow on the lower portion but the upper part was frosty and completely encircled with those gigantic overhanging hongos. A suicide climb for sure in those conditions. To top it all, the "50-degree slabs" above the "Col of Conquest" looked more like 75 degrees from the air and they *were* crackless.

Well, after flying around the tower about four times, I was green from airsickness, Royal was grossed out, and Tompkins had white knuckles on the wheel. We bugged out.

Down south in the Paine area it was no better. They were clocking winds of 180 kilometers per hour at the lake—300 feet above the level of the sea. Out of boredom I had gone up a hill above camp to try out various flight attitudes in my cagoule. You know how an anorak flaps away in a stiff wind? Well, when it *really* blows, it stops flapping and just hugs your body all over. Anyway, I'd lean into this steady hundred-mile-an-hour wind and wait for the gusts. You could see them coming across Lago Nordenskjöld because they filled up with water; so just before a big one would hit I'd jump into it and rise and hover like a kestrel—just for a moment of course—then it would slam me down on my ass.

For almost two weeks Royal was down and out, trying to pass kidney stones. He couldn't eat and wouldn't take medicine, but he was determined to have battle with this disease-pain business, *Il y a des autres Annapurna.* …

The weather never let up for the two weeks we were in the Paine area—not enough to even pack a load into the mountains. The three of us just sat around eating way too much lamb and chocolate puddings and getting terribly unfit. Robbins, in his agony, was looking more and more like Ezra Pound so we packed it in.

Well, that's the story of the trip. I have no plans to ever do any climbing there again. Although sometimes I imagine that on our last flight over the Cerro Torre, I saw a difficult but possible pass between the Cerro Standarht and the Aguja Bifida that takes you right around to the west side. The lower section is clean and dry, it's cold and still, and the ice up high is like styrofoam. There's a break in the great mushroom and I dream that I'm there pulling up over the top … but then I can just as easily see myself stuffed to the gills with roast lamb and Chilean wine, standing waist-deep in the Río Serrano with no thoughts in my head about those terrible mountains, and hooked onto a twenty-five-pound brown trout fresh from the sea. Lose your dreams and you lose your mind.

Cheers, Yvon

ABOVE: *Yvon rolls out a cast on Lago Fagnano, Tierra del Fuego.* Doug Tompkins

NEXT SPREAD: *Flamingos, which live up to fifty years in the wild, find safe harbor and ample food in Patagonia Park's shallow lakes.* Linde Waidhofer

On Tump Lines

First published in the Chouinard Equipment Catalog, 1980

Tump line: (Algonquin origin) A sling formed by a strap slung over the forehead or chest used for carrying a pack on the back or in hauling loads.

At the Ski Show last year I walked by the booth of one of the largest pack manufacturers, and a salesman/designer fellow insisted I come in and look over his new pack design. It was obvious that he was terribly proud of it. We spent twenty full minutes going over its sophisticated load-distribution features and anatomically "S"-curved frame welded with tungsten/inert gas and its wonderful bag made of 420-denier super K-Koted urethane eight-ounce parapack nylon held together with eighteen stiches per inch of cotton-wrapped Dacron thread. Finally, after reaching a fever pitch of enthusiasm and exhausting every aerospace term he knew, he stepped back beaming proudly. As his eyes gradually returned to their respective sockets he asked, "Well, Mr. Chouinard, how do you like it?" I shrugged. "It looks like you've put a lot of thought into this thing," I said, "and it certainly looks and feels good with all this display foam in it. But I'm afraid I'm going to disappoint you. I carry all my loads with a tump line now. And with one of those, it doesn't matter what you have on your back—a Fearsome Astro Loader like this or a sack of potatoes."

OPPOSITE: *Yvon and his lifelong climbing partner, Doug Tompkins, scouting conservation projects in Patagonia. "Doug had sold his share of Esprit and just got the idea of buying ranches in Chile and Argentina that had been overgrazed, and restoring them as protected areas and parks." 1991.* Rick Ridgeway

That riled him a bit, but he didn't know how I'd reached my tump-line conclusion. In 1968, while in the jungles of Colombia, I injured my neck while diving into a shallow river. Shortly after that face-plant, the muscles on one side of my neck atrophied, which has since caused me classic back problems such as nagging lower back pain and various muscle spasms. I've seen orthopedists and chiropractors and I've read every book I can on back problems. The consensus is this: most back problems are caused by a weak back or stomach muscles. Great. So how do I exercise muscles that have nerve damage? (And I can't stand to do any sort of exercise for exercise's sake anyway.)

Well, my back problems got progressively worse until an expedition to Nepal in 1978. There I noticed how the local people all had huge fillets of muscle running down both sides of their spinal columns. They spent their lives carrying awkward loads in excess of one hundred pounds over high passes. And they were doing all that carrying with just a crude, plaited bamboo tump line. I immediately saw the solution to my problem. As long as I had to carry a pack I might as well be exercising my back at the same time! Besides, I've never been able to fully utilize modern packs anyway. Hip-suspension packs only work on the flats with my small hips. Whenever I try to go even slightly uphill, my hips feel like they are going out of joint. Carrying heavy loads with just shoulder straps leaves me with very sore shoulders and back pain at the end of the day. And I can't breathe with sternum straps.

For the next forty-six days, I used what is probably the oldest, most widespread method of load carrying—the tump line. I "jerry-rigged" a sling with one-inch webbing that went down the side of my pack and around the bottom. On the first day, out in the jungle near Biratnagar, I found I could carry only fifteen pounds for an hour before my neck felt like it was ready to go into a spasm. After two weeks, I was carrying about thirty pounds for three or four hours a day. Finally, up near Makalu, winter set in. All the passes were covered with deep snow and I was breaking trail all day with a fifty-pound load supported by my crude tump line. My back problems had disappeared. For three months after the expedition I suffered no back pain at all. It finally started bothering me again, despite my active lifestyle of surfing, tennis, climbing, and swimming. But on another expedition to Ecuador I used the tump line

OPPOSITE: *"Try stuffing this in your backpack." Mustang District, Nepal.* Yvon Chouinard

again—with the same good results. Since then, I've been on several more expeditions and climbing trips and I've carried every load over twenty-five pounds with the tump line. Knowing what I know now, I would never go back to conventional packs—with or without my back problems.

But it's not just me. On a recent expedition to Tibet, I turned on a few friends to the tump line idea and whether they had back problems or not, they felt less tired at the end of the day. The biggest advantage, they noted, was at high altitudes where lung expansion is totally unrestricted. You can breathe with a smoother rhythm and breathe more deeply without shoulder straps.

The rig I now use is very simple. It's a two-inch wide piece of soft webbing that goes over the head and narrows down to three-quarter-inch webbing with an adjustment strap. This goes along the sides of any soft or frame pack and then around the bottom. I like the strap to go across the top of my forehead so I can press forward and build up my neck muscles, although for minimum effort it should be slightly more on top of the head. I use shoulder straps to carry about 20 percent of the load on flat or uphill stretches and tighten them to carry most of the load for downhill bits. Otherwise, the jarring effect of going down a steep slope is too much for my weak knees and neck muscles. Also, shoulder straps stabilize the load from side-swaying.

When you first try out a tump line, remember that it will take a while to get used to. You can't go directly from the aerospace age to primitive times and ideas without adapting yourself. You will need time to replace dependence on 6061-T351 Paralux frames with your own muscles and body dynamics. Take it slowly and build up to it. The more painful and difficult it is at first tells you how weak your back really is. Eventually, those muscles will get stronger. And your enjoyment of load carrying will increase, especially if you take pleasure in being out of step with the technological age.

OPPOSITE: *"The first ranch we explored was under the great peak of San Lorenzo, Argentina. Doug would go on to buy this 40,000-acre ranch and donate it to expand the Perito Moreno National Park."* *1991.* Rick Ridgeway

All That Glitters Isn't Gold

First published in the Climbing *magazine, Letters to the Editor, unknown year*

Dear Editor,

I must disagree with Marc Twight's conclusion that corporate sponsorship is the key to raising the standards of American alpine climbing (Perspective, *Climbing*, No. 108).

I also don't believe in promoting nationalistic efforts in climbing. In a conversation I had with Gaston Rébuffat a few years ago, he blamed Maurice Herzog for starting the commercialization and nationalism of climbing when he forced Lachenal to photograph him on top of Annapurna with the tri-color and a Michelin banner. All Lachenal really wanted to do was get out of there before he froze his feet.

Nationalism continued through the 1960s and 1970s with climbers claiming the first British ascent of the Eiger, the first American ascent of Everest, etc. Nationalistic second (or third, or fourth) ascents are not first ascents; they are mere rationalization for a lack of boldness and creativity in the first place. I, for one, couldn't care less about seeing American climbers raising the Stars and Stripes on foreign peaks.

Consider the history of war. In the Stone Age it was family against family, clan against tribe, then city against city, state against state, and finally country against country. Then along came the cosmonauts and satellite photos of this small delicate ball, and suddenly we realized that it can no longer be Old Glory vs. the Evil Empire. Perhaps one reason for this country's apathy in supporting our athletes is that we are finally starting to see ourselves as citizens of one world.

Sponsorship of climbers by the outdoor industry is a no-win situation for the climber in the long run. Being paid to climb forces one to compromise one's values; it encourages the alpine climber to seek routes that make good press, and it can force an otherwise wonderfully eccentric sport climber to act out a role in order to be more sellable to the media. It can often pit one friend against another. I don't even think it's good business for the sponsor. I mean, who really cares that Joe Blow used a particular pack on Everest?

I think most climbers are smart enough to see through the guise of product endorsement. No person can stay on top of the climbing game for very long, so eventually there are switched allegiances and, often, badmouthing on both sides. I enjoyed being at the Snowbird contest and being able to root for *every* climber, regardless of what shoe they were wearing or their nationality.

Sponsorship would best be solicited from outside sources, leaving the climbing industry to give away their extra profits or promotional monies in a way that benefits the entire community, not just put a few individuals on the dole.

If someone feels they need money in order to become a better climber, may I suggest a few solutions:
• Solo climb, it's a lot cheaper.
• Live with a supportive mom and dad, or get a working girlfriend or husband.
• Move to France. Greg LeMond has done more than okay by being on a French team.
• Hit on the mainstream American companies like Coors, Coleman, or Dupont.
• Get a job.

Yvon Chouinard
Ventura, California

NEXT SPREAD: *Headlamps trace through the night sky at Khumbu base camp on Mount Everest, Nepal.* Jake Norton/Aurora

Coonyard Mouths Off, Part II: Affairs of the States

First published in Climbing *magazine, Number 100, February/March 1987*

"There is a spontaneous and light-hearted quality in a sport which vanishes as the sport matures." – *Sir Arnold Lunn*

Between 1915 and 1932, the Swiss guide Hans Lauper knocked off eighteen major first ascents in the Alps, including the north faces of the Monch, Jungfrau, and Kamm, and the east face of the Eiger. During the 1930s most of the great north faces in the Alps were climbed, including the "last great problem," the Eigerwand, in 1938.

In 1947, John Salathé and Anton Nelson, wearing sneakers and driving pitons directly into decomposed granite, climbed the Lost Arrow Chimney. They placed expansion bolts on the smooth summit knob.

In 1957, the first Grade VI in North America was put up on the North Face of Half Dome. If you found a Vibram track on any trail in America, you knew it was made by a climber, who was a friend of a friend of a friend.

By 1960, gas was twenty-five cents a gallon and for fifty bucks you could get a decent car. With a couple of hundred dollars more you could spend April to November climbing all over the country. This was the beginning of the age of specialization. You climbed and that was it. Robbins was the only one we knew who also skied, and we never really trusted him because of that.

OPPOSITE: *Piton scars on Serenity Crack, Yosemite.* Dean Fidelman

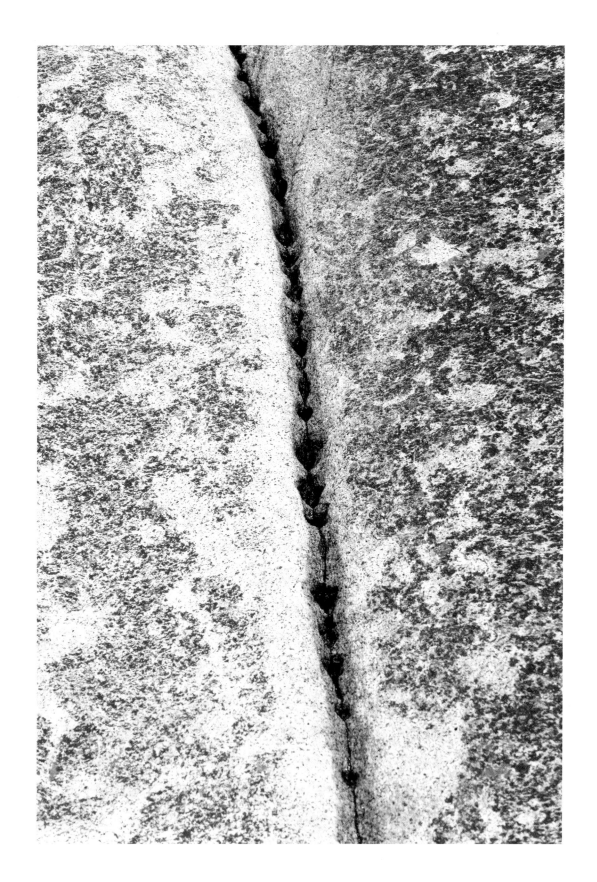

In Yosemite, you climbed cracks or you were a face climber. The first 5.10s were put up beginning in 1960, and by the end of the decade it was possible to effect a rescue on El Cap from the top.

In November 1964, finding fifteen inches of snow on the summit after making the first ascent of the North America Wall, Robbins, Pratt, Frost, and I threw off a duffel bag and watched helplessly as someone jumped out of a car, ran to the base of the wall, and made off with all our down jackets and bivouac gear.

In May 1970, *Climbing* No. 1 was hot off the press, definitely slanted toward Colorado climbing; but the Northwest had *Off Belay*, Southern California had *Summit*, and the Gunks had the *Vulgarian Digest*. The free standard was now 5.11, and the Dawn Wall was marathoned in twenty-nine days for the ultimate in big-wall living. They blew it, though—two days more and they could have inked a big promo deal with Baskin-Robbins with their thirty-one flavors of ice cream.

More and more people were getting into climbing and backpacking, but you couldn't leave your gear at the base of a wall or even in your tent any more. The *Wall Street Journal* advised corporate America to invest in the "high growth" specialty outdoor industry. The Park Service was busy setting up reservation systems for backcountry use. The Yosemite Master plan was being formulated to eliminate automobiles in the Valley by the year 1990.

In 1972, the Chouinard Equipment Catalog came out with the "Whole Natural Art of Protection," and almost overnight the game changed, most of America switching over to natural protection. People attempted to de-piton routes in Europe, like the Walker Spur but democracy wouldn't allow it; the lowest common denominator prevailed, and within weeks they were pegged up again.

Sometime around 1973 the rate of growth in outdoor sports peaked. Some companies diversified into soft goods, some didn't even see the change until it was too late. Gas prices shot upward and suddenly there was less fat in the system to support those on the bottom end of the social spectrum. The draft card burners of the 1960s were getting older, having kids, and looking to upgrade their lifestyles.

Enter the 1980s. You can't "out-rebel" your parents—they were the wigged-out, drug-crazed hippies of the 1960s—so change the rules. Drive them crazy by going to law school. Join the Boy Scouts, don't take any risks, and, above all, it's very uncool to be passionate about anything. Instead of marathon weekend drives to the Valley, you jog around the block every day and put in a nice ten-miler on the weekend, with maybe a little session of Nautilus or aerobics here and there. The heroes are Eastwood and Stallone, who both chickened out of going to the Cannes Film Festival for fear of being terrorized.

It's the "me-now" generation, and narcissism is the game. You can't even get your picture in the British climbing mags without your shirt off (and I've never seen a day in the Isles when I've even wanted to take off my sweater). Pink hair, pierced noses, lycra with codpieces, it's all good fun and doesn't hurt anybody. After all, we used to wear all white on the walls.

But the mountains are strangely empty. Backpackers are now car camping, and the only ones you see in the woods are redneck survivalists who jump out of the trees to scare the shit out of you before they "camo" back into the bushes. The only people in the Winds are kids or executives, sent there to wrest some sort of character building or moral out of confronting the wilderness.

The Valley now has a video store and the Merced is open for commercial boating. Many of the environmental gains of the 1960s are wiped out by an overzealous Secretary of the Interior (James Watt) who believes that "Jesus wants us to drill for oil in the wilderness."

The dominant environmental policy of the 1980s is that we should drill all our oil, cut down the forests, and dam the rivers right now. Go for the short-term goals, and let the future generations worry about deforestation, acid rain-killed forests, cleaning up dead rivers, and bringing back extinct species. Like Vietnam, we may have to destroy the Earth in order to save it.

Climbers are polarized into socio-geographical areas: Eldorado, Joshua Tree, Hueco Tanks. In the Tetons, they are all on the Grand, sometimes a hundred a day on the top, but the other peaks are empty. Everest is in vogue with overachieving attorneys, doctors, and businessmen. Oh, there are still a few geeks around like Stump and Lowe doing risky alpine climbing, but the system doesn't recognize, understand, or reward this kind of abnormal behavior. Which is why they do it, I guess.

Ice climbing is dead—the tools are so efficient anyone can climb vertical ice on their first day. So, what do you do the next day? Sport rock climbing is the rage, but it has as much spiritual relationship to the mountains as modern agriculture has to the earth—the dirt holds the chemicals and plants in place so they don't fall to the middle of the Earth.

It's tough making a name in climbing today. So, you climbed the Nose and Half Dome in one day? Didn't even make the sports page in the *Fresno Bee*. You can try and follow Bachar but there's too good a chance of getting snuffed. It's a lot easier to be an asshole. Make a name by being "controversial." Piss off the locals and they won't forget who you are. Infamy is better than no recognition at all.

On the positive, there is less specialization. Climbers ski, kayakers climb—the unbalanced ones are the specialists who have only one trick, the 5.13 climbers who can only look forward to a self-destructing body with its muscle tears and inflamed ligaments.

Now, for 1987 and beyond. The recent elections sent a clear message to those turkeys in Washington. The people would rather have clean rivers and be able to drink out of the tap than have MX missiles. The freshmen in some schools are now considerably more liberal than the sophomores. Reagan and his lamer-than-lame, trickle-down economy is in deep shit. The mood is changing.

Risk sports which thrive only during politically liberal times may be on their way back. There could be a resurgence in the geek sports like alpine climbing, backcountry skiing, and whitewater kayaking. Alpine touring is coming on especially strong.

Americans have no background in true winter climbing. The Europeans had winter ascents of all their north faces back in the 1950s and 1960s, while our best alpine climb, the North Face of the Grand Teton, has had only one winter ascent. American climbers in the Himalaya have a real gap in their experience because they've missed out on this winter-climbing stage. Our mountains are not as accessible as the Alps, and perhaps this new interest in backcountry skiing will give access to the thousands of American mountains awaiting first winter ascents.

Hangdogging, chipping holds, placing bolts on rappel, climbing competitions—the great debate continues. Who is right and who is wrong? I say it's pretty simple. There are ethics and there is style. Ethics are so you don't screw

OPPOSITE: *Barefoot with only jammed knots for protection, Herbert Richter belays Bernd Arnold on the Westwand on the Meurerturm in the Schrammsteine, Germany. 1973.* Steve Roper

181

it up for the next guy, and style is so you don't delude yourself into thinking you're so hot. Here's all you need to know about ethics:

The Climber's Bill of Rights: You have the right to climb anywhere in any style you wish, as long as it doesn't alter the medium or infringe on the next

———

... bad ethics in the name of raising the standards or making American rock climbers more internationally competitive is twisted zeal.

———

person's experience. It's simple. You use chalk, place a bolt, leave fixed pro, shit on El Cap Tower, it's all bad ethics. I don't care if Everest is climbed by an expedition of a hundred Rotary Club members all sucking O from base camp, as long as the mountain is not altered and it doesn't bother the other groups on the mountain.

Style is another story, and it's mostly a matter of degree. We need to establish a cornerstone.

Let's call it Perfect Climbing Style. A naked human free soloing a new route on sight. If you put on shoes you get docked one point; use chalk, one to three points depending on the climb, the heat, and the humidity; previewing or reading a guide book, another point; placing one piece of pro, another point, and so on into infinity. The farther you get away from this Perfect Style, the less proud you should be of yourself. With this criteria, the best climber in the world today is probably Bernd Arnold of Dresden, with his nearly bare feet, no chalk, and long runouts.

Is climbing, as a passion and as a sport, better off now than it was in the past? We can do harder climbs now in faster times—techniques are more refined and equipment more sophisticated—but are we really any better off?

On the plus side, we have the free climber soloing rock that was unclimbable ten years ago, the alpine climber in Europe who is so incredibly competent and fit that he needs to knock off three or four big north faces to feel like he's had a good day, and climbers applying alpine techniques to

Alaskan and Himalayan walls. There is still a lot of room in these games for adventure, spontaneity, soul, and art.

On the negative side, we have the ice climber hacking his way up the Black Ice Couloir with his three tools, the El Cap climber with his full-rack of chocks, full racks of pitons, and a full rack of Friends, and the specialist sport climber who chooses to become better and better at less and less. I'd say we are small winners.

As a sport matures, it doesn't necessarily get better. Look at alpine skiing. In the 1936 Olympics they painted your skis to make sure you used the same pair in the slalom as in the downhill. Now you can't tell the winners without the aid of electronic timers accurate to the millisecond. The specialists are the ones who take the soul out of any sport.

It's a great thing to run a marathon. You train a bit, maybe change your diet, give up smoking, and you knock it off in three-plus hours. If you want to do one in two-plus hours, you have to kiss off sex, your job, your friends, all the "nonessentials," and devote your entire life to the effort.

I say the last 10 percent of the way to perfection takes so much of your life that it isn't worth the effort. This overzealous attitude is what creates religious fanatics, body Nazis, and athletes who are exceedingly dull to converse with, unless you want to talk about their particular specialty or their bodies.

Specialization, when indulged in by true geniuses like Mozart, Babe Ruth, or Bernd Arnold, can create great art that elevates mankind above the lowly beasts. But you and I can evolve more quickly by putting that energy into more than one direction.

It's unrealistic to think we can go back to what climbing was in the 1930s, but we do need to constantly change the rules of the game to keep the sport evolving. When basketball players are all over seven feet tall, you need to raise the height of the basket. When the thrill is gone from alpine skiing, you just free up the heels and reinvent the telemark turn. Any activity, whether sport, business, or love, needs constant change, even revolution to keep it from degenerating.

Hangdoggers think they are the revolutionaries who are going to save climbing. But bad ethics in the name of raising the standards or making American rock climbers more internationally competitive is twisted zeal. Remember, these are really the arch-conservatives of the 1980s, because they want to minimize the risk factor in climbing at the expense of the rock. They

are the superpatriots who believe American climbers shouldn't be second to anyone. And like James Watt, they are the ones who believe the old Christian ethic of having dominion over the beasts and fishes (and rocks).

In the greater scope of things, how important is it that Americans climb 5.14? The grading system has to be flawed anyway, when an out-of-shape, forty-eight-year-old surfer can now do some 5.11a's, when in 1960 he could barely do 5.10a's—and that was when he was in his prime and could do one-arm pull-ups! At this rate, he will be a 5.13 climber when he's ninety!

It's bloody tough to beat anyone at their own game. Climbing and similar individual sports like solo, around-the-world sailing are a strong European tradition. They have much more accessible rock, many more climbers, and greater public acceptance of the sport. The Europeans don't have the National Safety Council and insurance companies not allowing them to take risks. It's crazy for us to think we can beat them at their own game. Do you see the French sending over a team to play in the Super Bowl?

I say change the rules! Let's play our own game. In America, we have one thing going for us that the Europeans used to have, but they've already used it up. We still have a bit of wilderness left, a few grizzlies, a couple of condors, and some still-virgin mountains and rocks. We also have a strong tradition, going back to Thoreau, Muir, and Bob Marshall, of loving and wanting to preserve wilderness.

Are we going to allow a few "me-now" hangdoggers to be the spokesmen for American climbing? Are we willing to compromise our ethics and style, all for the sake of raising the standards? If so, the climbers coming after us will have to grind off our chipped holds, plug up our bolt holes, and wash away our chalk marks in order to raise their own standards. It seems to me that climbing would be better off if we just learned to hold back a bit, and take an attitude of "each climb has its times."

OPPOSITE: *Another misguided attempt to keep America's borders safe. It's a 5.7 splinter crack to a mantle. Maybe 5.9 with huaraches. US/Mexico border.* Gary Coronado, *Los Angeles Times* (used with permission)

Salsipuedes

First published in the Scottish Mountaineering Club Journal, *Volume 30, 1972*

First winter ascent of Raven's Gully Direct in Glencoe, Scotland.

We were walking over the avalanche debris of the Great Gully on our way to Crowberry when an ominous croak split the silence. Two black ravens swooped over the Buachaille. Cunningham's words echoed in my head.

"Raven's the hardest climb in the Coe and you should do it if it's in good nick."

We soloed up the perfect styrofoam, all the way to the first giant chockstone which we mounted with a mere couple of grunts. More perfect snow. When the next block offered resistance, it was promptly overkilled with "cunning rope manoeuvres." Authorization was Ian Clough's *Guide*, "Speed is the critical factor … there is no need for an artificial code of rules. …" Right on.

Up next, another barricade, with a dank belay cave. Leaning over the roof was a pillar ladder of meringue which collapsed with the tail man. We were already one pitch above it when we spotted Hamish's barefoot exit going to the left. (Hamish MacInnes took off his boots and led out this traverse in his wool socks which stuck to the verglas-covered rock.) Going back meant having to lose out to the last motha chock. Anyhow, it was pretty nice being in the slit, and higher up looked even darker and quieter.

Escape from the gully was now defined in a fading shaft of light coming over a great stone stuck between two icy walls. The *verglas* was too thick for boots and too thin for crampons while the distance between the walls was a

OPPOSITE: *Mixed climbing in the "dank cave." Ben Nevis, Scotland.* Doug Tompkins

bridge—or more. The game was to maximize your body and scratch up as high as you could before your legs gave. At least there was a nice soft snow bottom to the chimney. Spread eagling with his crampons, Doug managed ten feet before he jumped. Trying a Nureyev split, I did fifteen and lost it. Doug got to twenty. And at thirty feet the tip of a knifeblade held for a tie-on just before my legs accordioned. The thin ray of light was growing faint as I was winched up to the peg for one last effort. Taking a wee rest in a sling, I swore that next time I came back to the Scottish winter I'd be better fit for climbing rock! The next thirty feet of the stone was indeed a shaky endeavor.

All that was left now was a slot that Hamish had slept under on his solo summer climb. Tompkins attacked the thin ice and powder snow with tied-off screws and delicate body English. After what seemed like an hour, a long *"Ahooya!"*

We weren't on top, but we were out.

OPPOSITE: *The 'Fox of Glencoe,' Hamish MacInnes, tunnels up through the cornice on Ben Nevis.*
Yvon Chouinard

Excerpts from *Climbing Ice*

First published in Climbing Ice *by Yvon Chouinard, Sierra Club Books, Random House, Inc., 1982*

"In France, we say that the third time is always lucky." So we were greeted by the guardien of the Argentière *refuge* in the Mont Blanc massif. Layton Kor and I had been here two other times in futile attempts to do the north face of the Aiguille Verte, and always the weather had turned us back. It had been a disastrous summer weatherwise. None of the big classic mixed routes had been done except for the Walker Spur of the Grandes Jorasses, climbed with eight bivouacs by a slightly more than enthusiastic Japanese contingent. Though it was already the beginning of September and Kor and I had been climbing all summer, neither of us had yet bagged one of the big ice climbs for which the Alps are so famous. Pressed for time now, we were willing to stick our necks out a little if given reasonable conditions.

I hardly had time to lay down my rucksack before Layton stepped out of the hut with an armload of bottles of beer. Sitting on the terrace, we watched the alpine glow leave the tops of some of the greatest ice climbs on Earth. The Triolet, incredibly steep and dangerous-looking with its hanging séracs; Les Courtes, 3,000 feet of ice and ice-covered rock; les Droites, the most difficult ice climb in the Alps, whose first ascent took five days and whose third ascent was only done this year. (The first 800 feet are 55 degrees to 66 degrees ice over unclimbable rock slabs, where belay is impossible because of the thinness of the ice.) And last to lose its golden crown of glow, the second highest in the French Alps, the Aiguille Verte

OPPOSITE: *Layton Kor preparing for a cold rock climb in Leysin, Switzerland.* Yvon Chouinard

and its Couturier Couloir, the least difficult of the great north walls of the Argentiére basin.

The Verte was our goal—but the sky was too blue and conditions too good; with the sun hardly down, it was already below freezing. No, we could always do the Verte. We should go for something really big; maybe the Courtes. The *guardien's* son mentioned that the North Face Direct had been done only six times before, a testimonial to its difficulty when one considers that a fearsome climb like the Triolet has probably been done a hundred times.

Midnight. I toss and turn in bed, my eyes wide open. I can't sleep, and get more and more angry because I have to sleep. There is only another hour before we have to leave. Kor is having the same trouble and so in a fit of anger we grab our gear and bolt out of the door into the moonlight. The glacier crossing is no problem with such a bright moon. At the *rimaye* we eat an early breakfast—or is it a late supper? We rope up forty feet apart and move together. Kor goes first with his headlamp, ice ax, ice dagger, and crampons, the tools of the ice climber. My world is a twenty-foot square of fifty-degree white ice; beyond is darkness. Above, another light moves at the same speed. Stick in the dagger, plant the pick of the ax, kick in one crampon, then the next—the German technique, efficient but extremely tiring on the legs and not nearly so sophisticated or varied as the French. Five hundred feet of fifty-degree hard snow goes quickly when you move together.

It is three o'clock and bitterly cold and we gloat over our new double boots. Since the snow turns to ice and steepens considerably, we start to belay. Two pitches of fifty-five-degree to sixty-degree ice are scaled partly by chopping steps and partly by front-pointing. Two more fantastic leads of sixty-plus degrees are done all on our front points with piton belays. The dawn reveals wild exposure. The beginning fifty-degree slope looks like a ramp compared to what we are on. We continue to belay and place ice pitons because the exposure is so awesome and our legs are so tired. Occasional pieces of ice come zooming by and so I fix a line from my waist belt to the ice piton that I am using for a dagger. Should I see a rock or hunk of ice coming, I can quickly drive in the piton.

We have to cope with three kinds of conditions now: hard snow, water ice, and powder snow, which change every twenty feet. By now both of us

OPPOSITE: *Yvon on the North Face of Les Courtes, France.* Layton Kor

192

are disenchanted with the German front-point technique and vow to learn the French method before we try another climb like this. Switching leads is no longer practical because by the time you arrive at the leader's stance, your legs are too tired to lead on; one man leads for three pitches or so and then we switch. Lack of sleep, severe dehydration, and the altitude have us moving like snails. On the summit, I am completely exhausted. On the descent Layton belays me down all the ticklish spots. There is obvious avalanche danger, and in fact two people were killed on these same slopes a few days before, but we have no choice but to go down. At nightfall, we reach the Couvercle Refuge; it's all over; it had been a hard day's night.

1966

After this climb, I went straight to the Charlet factory and asked them to make me an ice ax with a curved pick and deep teeth. Thus, making a tool you could swing above and pull down on without it popping out like the existing axes, which were made for cutting steps.

During the late fifties and early sixties the impecunious British and American climbers in Chamonix stayed at the Biolay campsite. It was close to the train station, the center of town, and, of course, the Bar National. Though the camping was free, it was a desperate place to live. There were no toilet facilities or potable water, and when it rained (and of course that was the only time we were in camp), the place turned into a field of mud and stinking garbage. None of the French climbers would go near the place; most of them preferred the Hotel de Paris.

The daily routine was to sleep as late as possible, wolf down some porridge, and pad through the muck into town and the bakery. Afternoons were spent in the Bar National or, if it wasn't raining, sitting on park benches watching the unapproachable French birds walk by. Then it was back to the 'Nash' for an evening of drink. A stagger back to the Biolay woods completed the day's activities.

One morning, during a fifteen-day stretch of rain and snow, morale was at an all-time low. I was morosely walking over to get some water when I stopped

OPPOSITE: *Les Courtes, France.* René Robert

in my tracks. A beautiful girl, stripped to her underwear, was washing in the stream. I could hardly believe my eyes, for the only women who hung around the Biolay in those days were usually as wretched as we were.

Since there was no avoiding at least a "good morning," we struck up a con-

---

The French call this route the "Englishman's Bedroom" because so many British climbers come straight onto it from an apprenticeship ... on small crags and end up having to bivouac.

---

versation. With a heavy Austrian accent she mentioned that she was here to climb but had been unable to find a partner. The next day dawned with blue skies, and off we went up to a hut. The following morning, we set off for the Voie des Plaques on the Aiguille de Requin. The English guidebook deems it a classic and states that it's a good introduction to Alpine climbing. It's not difficult going (mainly low-angle slabs with an occasional section of Grade IV), but it is nearly a thousand meters long and involves a glacier approach. The French call this route the "Englishman's Bedroom" because so many British climbers come straight onto it from an apprenticeship of twenty-meter leads on small crags and end up having to bivouac.

When we reached the base of the wall, there were four other parties already on the climb, and they were yelling out belay signals and dropping stones on each other. Annalee and I tied-in together and shortened the rope to about fifteen meters. I picked a line off to the left of the others to avoid the rockfall, and we started up. Annalee had never done any leading, and though we climbed together, I went first, picking the route and making certain that I was never directly above her so that I could see how she was doing. I kept flipping the rope behind blocks, and once in a while I'd leave a runner over a horn. Whenever I felt that there was a section that might give her any trouble, I'd brace myself and give her a belay. By moving together we quickly outdistanced the others and were soon dropping rocks on them!

Five hours after leaving the hut we were on the summit, having a cozy lunch in the warm sun. Down below on the slabs we could just make out the tiny dots of the others as they methodically belayed every inch of the way up. It was obvious they were in for a cold night.

Chuckling to ourselves, we took off down a gully on the west side, made a rappel, made another, and another, and … good God, had we screwed up! I hadn't bothered to check out the descent route! I had already left in all my slings and had used up my swami belt for rappel anchors. Now I began cutting up the nylon drawstrings on my pack. Next to go were my bootlaces. Then part of the rope. Well, we just made it back to the hut before nightfall. We weren't as smug as we'd been on the top, but it was certainly warmer for us than it was for the others.

When I was seventeen, I completely rebuilt a 1940 Ford two-door sedan and drove it from California to the Wind River Mountains of Wyoming. Across the Mojave Desert my old Ford and I purred past brand-new Buicks and Cadillacs that were pulled off to the side with their hoods up and motors steaming.

When I drove up to Pinedale, Don Prentice was waiting for me. He was the one who had initiated me into climbing by teaching me rappelling for the purpose of obtaining falcons and hawks for falconry. My only climbing experience thus far was innumerable rappels, hand-over-hand climbing down a rope to falcons' aeries, and a lot of scrambling on the sandstone rocks near Los Angeles.

From our camp at the head of the Green River we all went out early in the morning to find a way up Gannett Peak, the highest point in Wyoming. The others climbed up a rock gully, but I struck off by myself up the west face. For most of the day I wound my way up chimneys, gullies, and short but steep rock cliffs. This was my first mountain, and I had no idea that they were so big!

The last cliff gave way to a long snow slope leading to the 'gooseneck' and the summit. I was relieved to get off the face, as it had occurred to me that I could never get down the same way. The snow was hard with a soft, slippery surface the way it gets on an afternoon in early June. I had no ice ax and my Sears-Roebuck work boots were smooth-soled and couldn't get a purchase on the snow. To the west a thunderstorm was brewing, and suddenly I felt very small and very alone; I decided to go down.

The descent began with an exposed traverse across a snowslope just above a 300-meter cliff; then the way led down an even steeper snow gully to the talus below. I began to carefully kick steps across, trying to stay in balance. But as I became scared, my body would unconsciously lean in too far and my worthless boots would slip out of their steps. Several times I was stopped just short of falling by digging my fingers like claws into the slope.

That day I learned quite a lot about the insidious effects of fear and about plunging my heels down with vigor and depending on balance and on my legs for security. Most of all, this outing taught me that a confident attitude can often substitute for equipment and experience.

Climbing that first mountain over twenty years ago instilled a passion in me for climbing on snow and ice that continues to this day. I have noticed that most climbers are a product of their first few climbs. A person who learns his climbing on small but difficult crags may take up big-wall climbing or become an alpinist, but his first love will always be free climbing on the crags. I have specialized at one time or another in practically every form of climbing, but always I have been happiest to return to the snowy mountains to stand with one foot on ice and one on rock.

OPPOSITE: *John Cunningham and Yvon enjoying perfect rime ice conditions on Ben Nevis, Scotland.*
Paul Braithwaite

My Life on Ice:
Initiative, Boldness, Balance

First published in Planet Ice: A Climate for Change *by James Martin, Braided River, 2009*

Over my lifetime, I have been seriously involved in many outdoor sports: mountain climbing, telemark skiing, spearfishing, kayaking, surfing, and fly fishing. I have thrown myself passionately into each of these activities until I achieved 75 percent or so proficiency. Then I would move on to something else. Even with climbing, I would specialize in one form of alpinism for a time, such as big walls or jam cracks or expeditions to the highest peaks, until I reached sufficiency, but not perfect mastery. Overspecialization, the last 25 percent, did not seem worth the effort.

The closest I have come to mastery, though, is climbing snow and ice. My favorite is mixed climbing, with one foot on *verglas* (thin ice covering rock) and the other on snow. Starting in 1966 and for the next couple of decades, I climbed during summers and winters on the snowy ranges of every continent. When I began, ice equipment was primitive and provincial—in fact, it was different in each country where climbing was practiced.

Technique was primitive too and was divided roughly into two schools: those who used flat-footed (or French) cramponing techniques and those who relied on front points. Neither side was willing to admit the worth of the other.

OPPOSITE: *Yvon demonstrates* piolet ramasse *French technique. "While I was working on my book* Climbing Ice, *I taught classes in snow and ice technique for much-needed income and because I thought the best way to learn to communicate a craft was to teach it. With each class I learned to describe the techniques with fewer words." Mount Hood, Oregon.* Ray Conklin

It is possible to do all your ice climbing with only one technique, but it isn't efficient, nor does it make for a very interesting experience—like knowing only one dance: when the music changes, you are still dancing, but rather out of step.

When I returned from winter climbing in the Alps or from Ben Nevis in

---

When I returned from winter climbing … my head would spin with excitement about what I had learned—and with ideas for improving the gear.

Scotland, my head would spin with excitement about what I had learned—and with ideas for improving the gear. Tom Frost (my partner at Chouinard Equipment) and I had already redesigned and improved almost every rock-climbing tool. Now we turned to ice gear, to new crampons, ice axes and hammers, and ice screws.

I have been fortunate to have participated in several of my "passion" sports during their golden age. It's always exciting to be involved in the evolution of any sport in the early days, when new techniques and equipment are invented almost daily. And it's easy to improve equipment when what you start with is so primitive.

I first put my head underwater with a face mask in 1951 at La Jolla Cove in California, when I was thirteen. Afterward, I would practice holding my breath in high-school math class so I could freedive more deeply for lobster and abalone. To ward off the cold, I wore an army-surplus wool flight suit. For a weight belt, I used an army cartridge belt filled with lead from melted car batteries; the "safety" clasp was made from a door hinge.

When I first was learning to surf in 1954, I made my own surfboard out of balsa wood and wore a wool sweater to stay warm. When telemark skiing

OPPOSITE: *The Chouinard bamboo ax was displayed at the Museum of Modern Art in New York City. Art or function?* Patagonia archives

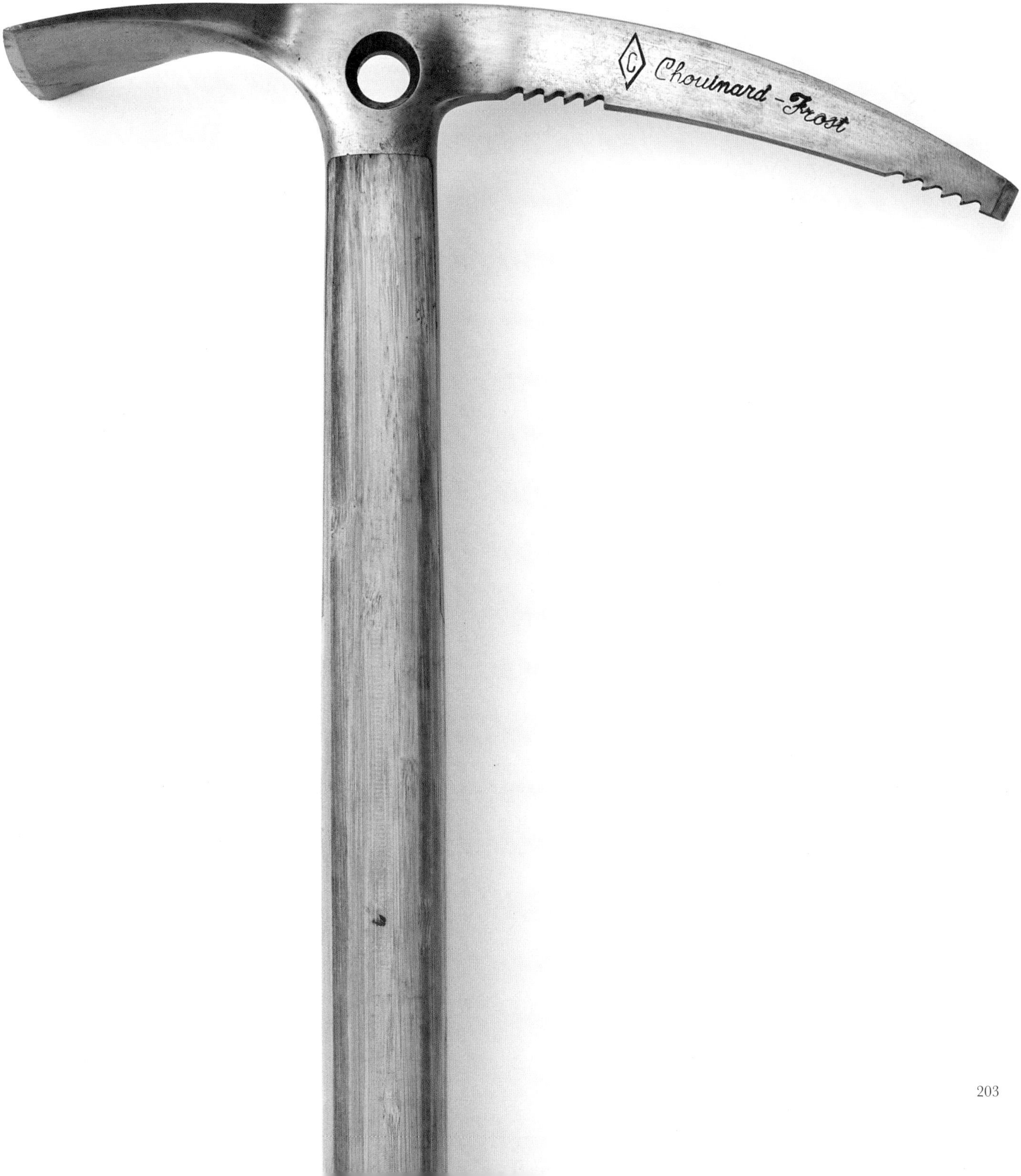
C
Chouinard-Frost

was reinvented in the early 1970s in the California Sierras and the Colorado Rockies, we started with ordinary cross-country skis with no side cut, then gradually evolved the technique and equipment to the point where, today, people can "free-heel" even in the most extreme conditions.

Inventing better equipment made climbing ice easier and less tiring; we could spend more time concentrating on the climb itself and less on cursing our gear. But technological development, even in climbing, comes not without cost.

Although a designer and innovator, I have always believed that rejecting a possible technology is the first step in allowing human values to govern the pursuit of progress—just because we can doesn't mean we *should*. Climbing itself—with its emphasis on initiative, boldness, and balance—moves against the technological solution. As I developed new ice equipment, I worked on creating new techniques that relied less on gear. I stretched myself, used only my ice ax for clawing in situations with steeper and more brittle ice. I kept my second ice tool holstered for whole pitches and climbs. The idea was technological inversion: to apply fewer tools with more sophisticated technique. I was rewarded for walking this edge by seeing more sharply what was around me, and I felt more deeply what comes boiling up from within. Henry David Thoreau put it that "simplification of means and elevation of ends is the goal." The two can't help but happen together.

Or not happen all. I believe sport follows politics, and in this age of fear-based conservative government, the kids of the wigged-out parents of the 1960s generation are living risk-averse, even virtual-reality, lifestyles. Businesspeople and their political lackeys know what needs to be done to keep the planet from warming, but they are afraid to do it, afraid that their actions might affect the bottom line and kill national and worldwide economics. No wonder rock climbing has become a sport for boulders, gyms, and bolted crags—little real-world climbing is still popular, but fewer and fewer practitioners take the time and the risk to learn what it requires to climb ice in the high mountains far from cities.

Climbing snow and ice slopes is dangerous, particularly on snow slopes, where most accidents happen. Judging the condition of a snow slope is a deep

and complicated art. A slope prone to avalanche can hide its weak layer several yards below the probing skier or climber. A slope that is safe one day can be a death trap the next, when the temperature goes up or down or the wind blows. Everyone I know who teaches avalanche safety has triggered or been

———

All of a sudden, my rectum clutched like a poodle's after it sees a bulldog. … "Hey man, this snow feels really funny. …"

———

caught in at least one avalanche. Of the three that I have been involved in, two were set off by myself or one of my partners.

The first time was in Scotland: Doug Tompkins and I were well into the day on a climb when I asked him for the rope, and he said, "You've got it." Well, I didn't, and we weren't about to go all the way back to the lodge. So we decided to drop down into the cirque and solo some Grade II routes on Hell's Lum. It was blowing a blizzard up on the plateau but not snowing lower down, and there were patches of blue sky. Frost feathers were growing on our wool clothes, and our eyelids and nose hairs were all frozen over; it was a typical day in the Cairngorms.

Doug was ahead, cramponing and traversing across what we thought was hard, wind-packed snow. All of a sudden my rectum clutched like a poodle's after it sees a bulldog. And I said to Doug, "Hey man, this snow feels really funny. Let's get. …"

Pop! And off it went. A yard-thick slab broke off right at our feet, and we were both left hanging by our ice axes, which, luckily, we had planted high.

My second close call also came in Scotland, on Ben Nevis, where we were working on an ice-climbing film for National Geographic. We were filming from near the base of Comb Buttress, and though the spring thaw was on,

OPPOSITE: *Doug Tompkins soloing Hell's Lum crag, Cairngorms, Scotland.* Yvon Chouinard

the snow didn't seem overly dangerous. I had the rope on and was standing at the base of Number Two Gully when, off to the side, I caught a glimpse of Johnny Cunningham and Hamish MacInnes running off. Almost immediately I got hit by chunks of snow. I thought it was only falling icicles, so I had just hunched down to protect my head when a wet snow avalanche hit me. They say I did a bunch of slow flips before I landed on my back. The rope was wrapped around my legs, and all I could do was try to stay on top of the sliding snow until I worked my way off to the side. Gear was strewn all over the place, and the big twenty-kilogram (forty-four-pound) tripod I had been standing next to had its legs sheared right off. It turns out that a cornice had fallen, setting off an avalanche in the gully.

The third incident occurred on Minya Konka in eastern Tibet. Rick Ridgeway, Kim Schmitz, Jonathan Wright, and I had just taken a load up to Camp II and were coming back down at a fast pace, stomping and sliding down the soft snow. I was leading and should have recognized the obvious danger signs: the several feet of fresh snow was only a couple days old, we were on the ice side of a corniced ridge, and the temperature had risen considerably since morning. At the moment when I first intuitively felt the danger, a soft slab broke just above us and carried us down 457 meters (1,500 feet) and over a 9-meter (30-foot) cliff. I had a concussion and broken ribs; Rick, various cuts and bruises; Kim, a broken back—and Jonathan died from a broken neck.

Avalanches aren't the only danger to the alpine climber. The single most difficult mixed snow and ice pitch I've climbed was on a first winter ascent of Raven's Gully Direct in the Scottish Highlands, again with Doug Tompkins.

My coldest climb was in Alaska on Denali, which is lower in elevation than Everest but far colder, the latter being at the same latitude as Miami. On our summit day, with temperatures around minus forty degrees Celsius (minus forty Fahrenheit), the plastic buckles on our packs shattered from the frost. Even the plastic lid of our thermos broke. The black ice was so old and hard that our ice screws were useless.

My most frightening experience on ice was not on a climb but in a tent in Antarctica where we endured brutal gale-force winds.

OPPOSITE: *Yvon and Rick Ridgeway in Homer, Alaska, celebrating a successful ascent of Denali in 1980. This photo has gained a certain notoriety, as Rick says, "Let's just say there's a little more than alcohol involved, and leave it at that."* Peter Hackett

Not all memorable moments in ice climbing involve the fear of death. Once I stood at the tip-top of snow-covered Mount Stanley in Uganda having a pee—and for a moment was the source of the Nile.

The most complex and enjoyable pitch of ice I've ever climbed was also in Africa, on Mount Kenya. The Diamond Glacier, high on the southern side, drains and refreezes into a narrow couloir that cascades in a series of frozen waterfalls, one of which creates a vertical curtain of melded-together icicles. My partner, Mike Covington, wrote about it in the *American Alpine Journal*: "Although the headwall seemed to loom just above, I climbed almost a full pitch past [Yvon's] belay before getting to the base of the fragile obstacle. We were in the clouds now, and the setting had changed drastically from a warm and friendly environment into a safer but more eerie one. The climbing was steep, and the visibility was usually less than a pitch. An occasional icicle fell, or running water dripped from ledge to ledge. Otherwise the silence was all-consuming. Peaceful but spooky."

The right side of the headwall was barred by multiple rows of sharp-fanged icicles. The best ice, on the left side, disappeared into the mist at an intimidating angle. We decided to climb the thin ice at the center, and I made my way up, jamming my hands between the ice and the rock, to a small cave at the top of a twelve-meter (forty-foot) outcrop. From the cave, I had to cut a hole through an ice curtain. As Covington recalled, "Two or three whacks, and some huge icicles departed the face, exploded onto the ramp near me, and then fired off down the couloir in the mist below." To get back out onto the smooth, nearly vertical sheet of ice above, I crawled through the hole and placed my ice hammer up inside the cave, then leaned out as if trying to reach over a roof. One swing of the ax, and it was buried in the ice above. Then I removed my hammer and placed it up alongside the ax. Both tools gave off a precariously dull *thunk*. "I tensed," wrote Covington, "expecting a fall as he leaned way out and engaged a crampon inches above the lip of the curtain. Slowly he moved up onto the ice and then removed a tool and swung again. This time the ax found good ice, and Yvon let out a welcome 'Wha hoo!'

OPPOSITE: *Kim Schmitz, Yvon, Rick Ridgeway, and Jonathan Wright had been attempting Minya Konka in eastern Tibet. Carrying supplies to their second camp triggered an avalanche that swept them down the peak 1,500 vertical feet. Jonathan was killed; Kim (on stretcher) suffered serious injuries and had to be evacuated. 1980.* Rick Ridgeway

There was still twenty feet [six meters] of nearly vertical ice before the angle eased, but it was in the bag now."

The Diamond Couloir no longer exists as we climbed it. On occasional heavy-snow years, it still exists as a snow couloir, but it's no longer cold enough for the ice curtain to form.

In thinking back on the snow and ice climbs I've done, I realize that many of them no longer exist. The Black Ice Couloir on Wyoming's Grand Teton is gone. Its classic alpine north face, like the north faces of the Alps' Eiger and Matterhorn, is too dangerous to climb in summer. The ice in the fissures that once helped hold these faces together is gone, and the rockfall is now much more prevalent.

When I first climbed in the Canadian Rockies in 1958, the Columbia Icefield flowed down almost to the then-dirt road between Banff and Jasper, Alberta. Now it's a forty-five-minute walk to its terminus. The classic ice climb on the north face of nearby Mount Athabasca is now all rock.

It's September in Jackson Hole, and as I work on this essay I'm looking up at the Tetons. From my view, from the southeast, they are completely bare of snow. The Otter Body Snowfield, and the patch on the east ridge of the Grand Teton, is melted out. In my fifty years of living here, I have never seen these mountains without snow. Spring has come five weeks early for the last two years. Last year, before the young red-tailed hawks had grown protective feathers, they were bitten to death by horseflies that hatched early, or they jumped out of their nests to escape them. The mountain pine bark beetles, which are killing pine and spruce forests all over the western United States, are reproducing in numbers four times greater than usual without the weeks of minus forty degrees Celsius (minus forty Fahrenheit) winter days to keep them in check. Grizzlies and black bears, starving from berry and whitebark pine nut failures, are roaming backyards looking for dog food and birdseed. So they are turning into "problem bears." Nineteen were shot this summer. We have had weeks of temperatures over thirty-two degrees Celsius (ninety Fahrenheit) this summer; we used to have maybe one or two days like that in a summer. It looks and feels like Nevada, not Wyoming. Many days this summer, it was so hot I couldn't

OPPOSITE: *Yvon on the first ascent of the Diamond Couloir (which is no longer in existence due to climate change), Mount Kenya. 1975.* Tom Frost

spend time outside doing the things I love to do. Streams in Yellowstone Park were closed to fishing because the trout were stressed by the heated waters. My neighbor grew tomatoes at more than 2,100 meters (almost 7,000 feet).

I rarely climb anymore, but I particularly like to fly fish for steelhead and

———

... we are in danger of losing one in four mammal species, one in eight birds, a third of all amphibians, and 70 percent of all the plant species that have been studied. ... we are not exempt.

———

salmon. When I fly over the Coast Mountains in British Columbia on my way to the steelhead rivers, I look down at pocket glaciers that are half or even a third the size they were when I first climbed there forty years ago. Those small icefields provide cold water all summer long to the salmon rivers that in some summers are already only a few degrees from being too hot to support the anadromous fish. Combine that with drastic clear-cutting and ham-fisted fisheries management, and the long-term outlook for salmon is grim. In two weeks of concentrated fishing this year, I caught only three steelhead.

This has been my experience of climate change, whether or not each phenomenon is a direct result of global warming. The fact remains that by our own doing, we have changed the climate of our home planet—scientists all over the world agree on this, as reports from the Intergovernmental Panel on Climate Change tell us. And we are causing another great extinction; we are in danger of losing one in four mammal species, one in eight birds, a third of all amphibians, and 70 percent of all the plant species that have been studied. Because we are also largely creatures of nature, we are not exempt.

OPPOSITE: *Pink salmon push forward through cedar-stained waters on their final journey to spawn in Canada's Great Bear Rainforest, a vast wilderness supporting over 2,000 separate runs of wild salmon. Gill Island, British Columbia.* Ian McAllister

Anthropocentric thinking got us into this mess in the first place, and the same flawed logic says that we can reverse global warming merely by changing technology. Consider the futility of trying to save the ski piste of the Pitztal Glacier in Austria by covering it with an insulated blanket. Instead, the solution to our overheating of the planet has to begin with us in the developed world consuming less and more intelligently—and using technology, but *appropriate* technology. In some cases this may mean that we "turn around and take a forward step," as the conservationist David Brower advocated.

The icefalls, snow gullies, and glaciers that have carved me into who I am today are melting, and I am perhaps bearing witness to the last of the great salmon and polar bears, the end of cold, free-flowing rivers. The Zen philosopher part of me says that the value of the climbs I've made, the business I've grown, and the fish I've caught and released was in the doing. I accept that the only sure thing is change.

At the same time, living a life close to nature has taught me to try and protect what I love by leading an examined life, bearing witness to the evils and injustices of the world, and acting with whatever resources I have to fight those evils. This is something everyone needs to do in his or her own way.

A few days after Doug Tompkins and I spooked ourselves in the hurricane winds of Antarctica, we did climb again, up to the top of a minor peak. Looking east from the Ellsworth Range to the flat expanse of ice and through the ozone-free air, we could see the curvature of Earth.

I realized that it's not only a fragile planet but a pretty small one too.

OPPOSITE: *A possible casualty of climate change, an emaciated polar bear patrols Resolution Bay for food. Northwest Territories.* Cristina Mittermeier/SeaLegacy

NEXT SPREAD: *Form follows function: spring migration of sandhill cranes on the Platte River, Nebraska.* Thomas D. Mangelsen

Zen Lessons

First published in Let My People Go Surfing: The Education of a Reluctant Businessman *by Yvon Chouinard, Penguin Books, updated edition 2016*

When I was a teenager, some fellow misfits, along with adults like Robert Klimes, a music teacher, and Tom Cade, a graduate student at UCLA, started the Southern California Falconry Club, where we trained hawks and falcons for hunting. Every weekend in the spring we went off looking for hawk nests; sometimes we banded the young for the government or we took a young hawk to train. Our club was responsible for enacting the first falconry regulations in California.

It was the most formative time of my life. When a fifteen-year-old has to trap a wild goshawk, stay up all night with her until the bird finally develops enough trust to fall asleep on his fist, and then train the proud bird using only positive reinforcement, well, the Zen master would have to ask, "Just who is getting trained here?"

Studying Zen has taught me to simplify; to simplify yields a richer result. The rock climber becomes a master when he can leave his aid climbing, big-wall gear at the base, when he so perfects his skill that he can climb the wall free, relying only on his skill and the features of the rock.

I also learned Zen as a blacksmith forging my steel pitons eight or ten hours a day. I'd grab a piton, bang on it, put it back in to reheat, and grab another, never crossing my hands or wasting energy with excess movement until the work had the fluidity and grace of Zen archery or a tea ceremony.

OPPOSITE: *At the forge, Ventura, California. 2007.* Tim Davis

At the end of a long day I could stare at an old rusty oil barrel and see it just gleam and glisten like a billion tiny rubies. You can approach Zen through contemplation or action.

Some years later I made a big breakthrough in my kayaking. I had just

———

You can approach Zen through contemplation or action.

———

learned to do a hand roll; that's where you can roll up in the kayak just by using your hands, no paddle. I got a wild hair to run the Gros Ventre River in Jackson Hole, Wyoming, without a paddle. This river is a Class 4 in high water, drops one hundred feet a mile, and if you bail out of your boat you can't pick it up until miles downstream.

Now, a paddle is a powerful piece of equipment and to not use one meant I had to sit low down in my seat with hands in the water, leaning forward on the drops; I had to look far ahead and anticipate turning the boat by banking and carving. I never went over and, in fact by acting more like a fish, I had a cleaner run than if I'd used a paddle.

Take fly fishing: If you want to only catch fish, use a worm. But fishing with artificial flies takes the same approach as Zen archery. You learn the life cycles of insects. You study rivers like a rock climber reads a rock cliff, and you practice the motion of casting the line. Finally, after 10,000 hours you begin to think like a fish.

If you're climbing a wall in Yosemite, the important thing is how you climb, how you get to the top, because there's no point in just getting to the top. There is no summit, in fact there's a trail to the top. The opposite of the Zen approach is climbing Everest if—like many a plastic surgeon or CEO— you pay $80,000 and have Sherpas put all the ladders in place and 8,000 feet of fixed rope, and you don't even have to carry a pack. There's a Sherpa in

OPPOSITE: *A hand-forged Lost Arrow piton.* Rick Ridgeway

front and he's got a three-foot rope on you, and there's a Sherpa in the back and he's carrying extra oxygen bottles. You get to a camp and you don't even have to lay out your sleeping bag. It's already laid out with a little mint on top. Your guides have computers dialed into the daily weather report. You bullshit yourself into thinking you climbed Everest, but you didn't climb Everest. You climbed a subdued mountain with all these ropes holding it down.

The whole point of climbing something is a spiritual and physical game. If you compromise the process, and you're an asshole when you start out, then you're an asshole when you get back: Nothing's changed.

The Zen lessons I learned in sports I also applied to running my business. Most public corporations operate to maximize profits for the shareholders. Decisions are made for the short-term health and growth of the company; the books are cooked to show profits every quarter.

At Patagonia, we make our important decisions based on wanting to be here one hundred years from now. We know that if all is going well with our work, the profits are bound to come.

OPPOSITE: *"Be particularly careful to keep your heels low when pulling over the top of a bulge."* *Scotland.* John Cunningham

NEXT SPREAD: *Yvon descending from the summit of an unnamed and previously unclimbed 20,000-foot peak in central Bhutan. The team had a permit for Gangkhar Puensum, the highest peak in Bhutan, but there were no maps and they ended up in the wrong valley, so they climbed peaks in an area no Westerner had ever seen. The Bhutan government would go on to give Gangkhar Puensum sacred status with no climbing allowed, and today it is the highest peak in the world that is off limits to climbers.* Rick Ridgeway

PAGES 228–229: *The Mount Everest conga line: a procession of "climbers" ascends fixed ropes up the Lhotse Face to the South Col.* Andy Bardon/NG Image Collection

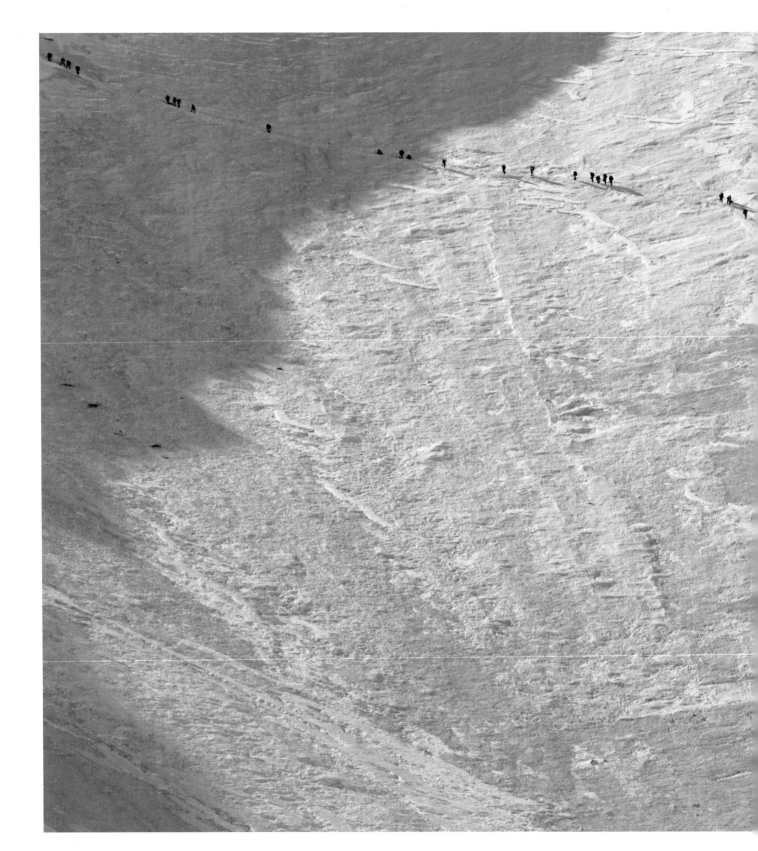

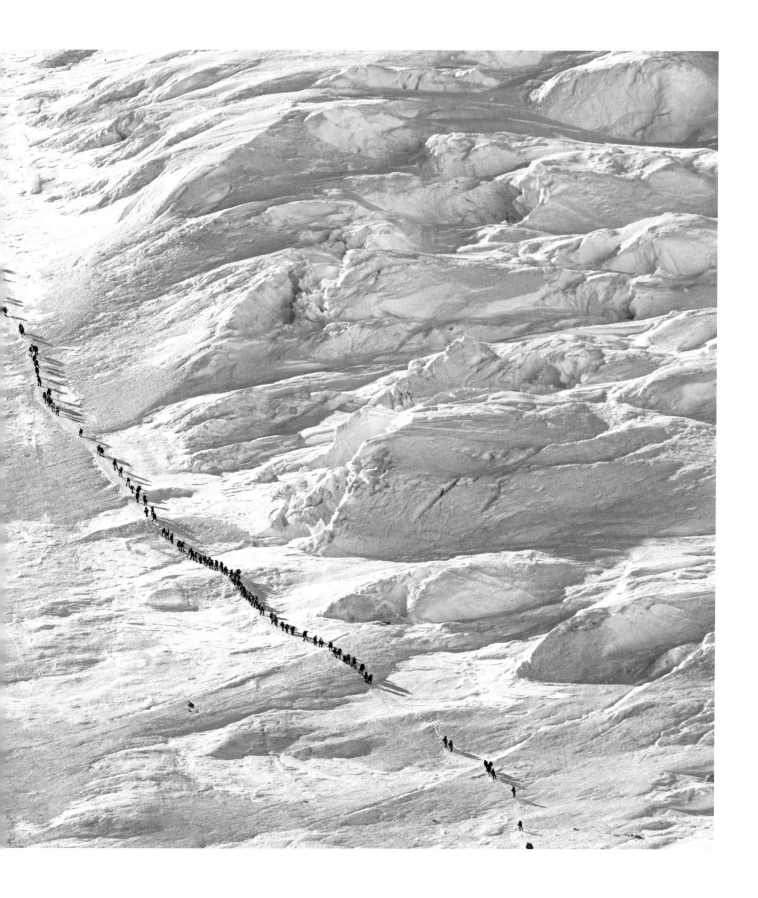

An Introduction to Glenn Exum

First published in the book Glenn Exum: Never a Bad Word or a Twisted Rope *by Charlie Craighead, Grand Teton Natural History Association, 1998*

One summer day in 1931 a young college student stood poised on some precarious footholds high up on the Grand Teton in Wyoming. Ahead lay a gap in the ramp he had climbed up. On the other side of the 1,000-foot abyss ran a wall of virgin rock that could prove to be too difficult for a first-year aspiring mountain guide. He pondered the consequences of a fall, wondered whether his football cleats would hold on the slick orange granite, and then he jumped.

The young music student, Glenn Exum, continued on that day to make the first ascent of the Exum Route and meet up with his mentor, Paul Petzoldt, on the summit. Over the next thirty years he safely led hundreds of clients to the summit of the Grand in the course of his more than 300 successful ascents. He failed to summit only once. In his modest style, Glenn claims his success came from being able to read the clouds and predict the weather. But there had to be more to it than that.

The old-school Matterhorn guide would cajole and tug and swear until the client became more afraid of the guide than of the mountain. Glenn would also be firm, but his genius lay in taking the time and effort to allow the client to build confidence in his or her own abilities. What client would not

OPPOSITE: *Glenn Exum was a meticulous climber, both in his technique and his gear. "Being a musician as well as a climber, he always climbed with gloves until the going got tough, and then he took them off no matter what. He probably took better care of his hands than any other climber I know." Grand Teton, Wyoming.* Leigh Ortenburger

trust a guide who was supremely confident himself—and was a dead ringer for Errol Flynn?

After he took over the Petzoldt-Exum School of American Mountaineering from Paul in 1956, he refined it into one of the most respected companies

---

Glenn has always known that
his role in life is to lead men.

---

of guides in the world, now employing over fifty guides in a summer. It was Glenn Exum, more than anyone in America, who transformed mountain guiding from a summer job for itinerant climbers and college students into a genuine and respected profession. Some of his guides were veterans of Denali and Mount Everest, or El Capitan in Yosemite. Others had less impressive credentials. However, when Glenn stood outside the guide shack to introduce a group of clients to their guide, it was very clear that they were to be guided by one of the best climbers in the world.

I spent many summers climbing in the Tetons, from 1956 to the present. I never worked for Glenn although, Lord knows, many times I could have used the money. The "dirtbag" climber's life existed on the fringes of society—climbing hard and sleeping in an old CCC (Civilian Conservation Corps) camp incinerator. A diet of mostly oatmeal supplemented with the occasional poached (not a cooking term) "fool's hen," marmot, or porcupine. On special days, spaghetti with a can of cat tuna from the dented can store in San Francisco. My lifestyle and demeanor were less professional than that required by the Exum Guide Service. In fact, I was on the outs with the Exums because of a little unauthorized guiding of Jackson Lake Lodge employees.

One day Glenn announced to his guides that perhaps I wasn't such a bad sort. He had seen me out in Lupine Meadows that morning enjoying the beautiful sunrise. The truth was I had been staggering about barefoot, as usual, after an all-night Vulgarian rave at the climbers' camp near Guide's Hill.

Not long after that I was walking by the guides' shack when I saw Glenn teaching his son, Eddie, to fly cast. He invited me to join in, and from that summer on I never went back to my spinning rod. Glenn was a beautiful fly caster and a dry fly fisherman. His favorite flies were the delicate light and dark Cahills and the more gaudy Bob Carmichael's Mormon Girl. These would cover most of the limited hatches on the freestone Snake River. Eddie Exum became one of the best fly fishermen I've ever fished with. One of his notable accomplishments is a thirty-three-pound steelhead taken on a dry fly.

Glenn sold the guide service to his four chief guides in 1982. It was after this date that I finally did get to work for the Exum Guide Service. I taught some special snow and ice courses and did some "overflow" guiding for a few years. That experience helped me to appreciate the skill and commitment it takes before one should accept the responsibility of putting people's lives into your own hands. I felt nothing but pride to be a part of the profession and company of guides.

There was hardly a prouder time in my life than when I was honored to be asked to share a rope with Glenn on his last ascent of the Grand at age of seventy-one. Even then he climbed as elegantly as he fly fished—graceful, effortless, never breathing hard or clutching around. He was always under control.

The idea for the Glenn Exum book came from Glenn himself. He has always been a storyteller. He has always been most alive and happy when storytelling. Relating tales of his early Jackson Hole days to rapt young guides is his best relief from the constant pain of a debilitating illness.

At his home in Moose several years ago, I read a few chapters he had written and I encouraged him to keep writing. I taped him for hours as he recounted, with amazing accuracy, the stories of his music and climbing careers.

Glenn's life is the story of a man who exemplifies Saint-Exupéry's "Freedom is acceptance of responsibility." Glenn has always known that his role in life is to lead men.

Memorial for Dick Pownall

Jackson, Wyoming, Unpublished, 2017

Dick first came to the Tetons as a teenager in 1944. He eventually guided for the Exum Mountain Guides for fifteen years. He made several important ascents in the Tetons, including the Direct Finish to the North Face of the Grand in 1949 and the first traverse from Nez Perce to the Grand Teton in fourteen hours.

On the 1963 American Everest expedition, he was considered the strongest climber on the team but missed out on being the first American to summit Everest when he and Jake Breitenbach were hit by a falling sérac that took Jake's life.

When I was a young climber in the Tetons, the mountain guides like Pownall, Glenn Exum, and Willi Unsoeld were the climbers we aspiring alpinists looked up to as our heroes.

In 1957, Howard Friedman, a climber and photographer, teamed up with Hans Kraus, Herb and Jan Conn, Glenn Exum, and Dick Pownall to do a climb on the North Face of the Grand Teton for a major article for *Life* magazine. Barry Corbet and I were each paid five dollars a day to take two horseloads of equipment that were left at Amphitheater Lake and carry them up the Teepee Glacier to the Upper Saddle. I had to help Barry stand up with his monstrous ninety-pound load and watched him stagger off while I did two trips with my loads. We set up their camp on the saddle, laid out their sleeping bags in the tents, and then found a spot nearby to bivouac.

As it turned out, the climbing party got caught in a storm and couldn't finish the route. They traversed off the face via the second ledge and got to their camp at 2 am, wet and cold. The next morning, they intended to traverse back

Dick Pownall, Herb Conn, Jan Conn, and Glenn Exum after climbing the North Face of the Grand Teton. Howard Friedman

onto the face and complete the climb. To my surprise, Dick asked me if I wanted to come along. One of the pitches was covered in ice from yesterday's storm and Dick asked me if I wanted to lead it. I couldn't believe my luck! I completed the pitch in good style and was told so by the group. Dick could have easily led that pitch but, being a teacher, he knew how important it would be for a young aspiring alpinist to lead that pitch. Since that day, mixed climbing—one foot on rock and one foot on ice—has become my favorite form of climbing.

Besides the ten dollars we each earned, Hans Kraus later sent us each a nine-millimeter Perlon rope, the first nonlayed ropes to come to America. Later on, I was tied-in to that rope when I took a 160-foot fall on the overhanging north face of the Crooked Thumb. This was before harnesses and before I knew that the nine-millimeter rope was not intended to be used as a single rope. Lucky for me, the wall was overhanging and the rope's elasticity saved my life.

Pinhead's Progress: Around the World on 210cm in Search of the Perfect Telemark Turn

First published in Powder *magazine, Volume 14, Issue 5, January 1986*

I've never been one to do well in team sports. I could hit home runs all day long in grammar school baseball practice, but in a real game I'd clutch and couldn't even hit the ball. Being more of an artistic sort, I've not been able to grasp abstract concepts through books or classes. Whatever sports I do, I've had to learn on my own or be at the mercy of my ruthless friends. For instance, my first mountain was Gannett Peak in the Winds, soloing a new route in my Sears work boots. On only my fifth day of kayaking, I found myself on the Tuolumne with thirteen stitches in my face from a Merced River rock the day before.

After escaping high school, I was fortunate to do a lot of climbing with Fred Beckey, certainly the finest mountaineer to come out of America. From him I learned how to stay alive in the high mountains. He also taught me how to do standing glissades on summer corn the correct way—with feet together and knees bent, acting like shock absorbers, and the upper body always facing the fall line. The first time I had skis strapped to my feet was in the early 1960s at Les Diablerets in Switzerland. Royal and Lis Robbins put me on a lift to the top of the mountain and said, "Just follow us." I pointed the skis down,

OPPOSITE: *A standing glissade. Tetons, Wyoming.* Tom Frost

assumed my glissade position, and carved some fairly decent parallel turns. *Piece of cake*, I thought.

The next time I had skis on my feet was on the top of Volcan Llaima, a 12,000-foot volcano at the tip of South America. Dick Dorworth, Lito Tejada-Flores, Chris Jones, Doug Tompkins, and I had driven down there from California, surfing the coasts of Mexico, Central America, Ecuador, and Peru. We were making a "Fun Hog" movie about the trip and Lito was filming Doug and Dick skiing down this smoking volcano. My job was to carry the forty pounds of gear back down to 5,000 feet. Well, even the two best ski instructors in the world couldn't get me down that mountain without a hundred crashes and head-plants.

After that, I pretty much taught myself to ski by just going out and doing it, never really spending enough time at it to become very good. I did have short, strong legs and I did enough backcountry skiing to get pretty good at survival turns. My attitude toward becoming an excellent skier has always been like that of the fat person who has always wanted to be skinny but not badly enough to actually lose any weight.

The skiers I wished I skied like had all come from alpine racing backgrounds. Well, not only was I too old for that, but I probably would have done no better at racing than I did at baseball. I was introduced to cross-country skis and the telemark turn in the mid-1970s by Doug Robinson and the "armadillos" of the east side of the Sierra. I never could understand why they insisted on messing with the pine tar and klister, and zig-zagging around instead of just slapping on some skins and going straight up the hill. And this stupid drop-knee turn. Why not just parallel or do survival stem christies?

In 1980, I found myself coming down Denali pulling a fifty-pound sled through eighteen inches of heavy, new snow. I put the load on my back thinking I could easily ski this stuff on my 180-centimeter alpine touring skis, but I soon realized that with the load, the wet snow, and floppy mountain boots I couldn't begin to initiate a turn; so I unlatched my heels and headed down with a sort of snowplow/stem/telemark/steering turn. No unweighting necessary—or possible. Modern man reinvents skiing.

This experience was a revelation for me and, soon after, I hung up my fat boards and went skinny. Corn was the new diet. A typical morning in May or early June would usually find me hiking up some slope in the Tetons or Absarokas, maybe sitting on top for an hour or so to let the corn become velvet, then cutting down in wide classic telemarks. Making it back to the house in Moose for lunch, then off for an afternoon of kayaking the upper Gros Ventre. A pine-cone eater to the core!

Later on, skiing in Aspen with Artie Burrows, Julie Niels, and Murray

———

... even the two best ski instructors in the world couldn't get me down that mountain without a hundred crashes and head-plants.

———

Cunningham opened my eyes to the potential of skinny skis. Not only were these guys out-skiing nearly everyone on the mountain regardless of the gear, but this wasn't the Peruvian-hat-double-poling-Al-Jolson-mammie-turn back-country technique I was used to. These were jaded ex-alpine racers who had blended the old with the new and created a whole new sport. On a late winter trip to the Selkirks with Eric Sanford and Don Portman, I watched these guys handle breakable crust, powder, and junk as if they were on a groomed-out piste. And then there was Mister Phun coming off jumps in a long, low tuck, not like a daffy or a yahoo, but streamlined and fast like Lopez in the tube. I was stoked, but I had some work to do!

In the summer of 1984 I went off a drop in my kayak upside down and landed on my head in a hard place, which resulted in a weird compression scoliosis thing in my back. Then, in September, after forty-five years of black-smithing, tennis, fly fishing, big-wall nailing, ice climbing, and other forms of self-abuse, my right elbow crapped out and had to be operated on. By late October I had learned to cast with my left arm but it was obvious that the only dynamic sport I would do that winter was skiing. So, this was the year I was really going to learn to ski like I'd always wanted.

DECEMBER – COLORADO
Paul Parker, who is on the PSIA demo team, is my kind of instructor. He gives you a one-sentence technique tip then leaves you alone until he sees

you've digested it before he gives you another. At Steamboat on hard pack, we parallel the steep stuff and telemark the intermediate hills. I've always had trouble with my left-hand teles, so he asks me to think about pressing the little toe of my back foot against the slope. This gets my feet closer together and my skis on edge, thus correcting my habit of going into my left turns from a stem. A foot of heavy, skied-out cement in Breckenridge stops me cold but Paul says to exaggerate the up and down the way they used to before high-top plastic boots. I also learn to lift up and place my downhill ski. The telemark turn provides great fore and aft stability because it's really one long ski.

It snows four feet in Arapahoe. As light as it ever gets and the heaviest dump of the year, but I can't handle it. My skinny skis are gophering instead of moling. Can't get any rhythm, can't pole plant, can't see my skis. My mind goes on me and I'm finished by noon.

DECEMBER/JANUARY – SKI LOS ANGELES

It's been a winter of north swells and that means cold fronts and snow in Southern California every weekend! I join the hoards of Iranians, Guatemalans, Koreans, and the occasional Yankee (saw six Sikhs ski one day). I love L.A.! I'm getting my poling down. It's no different than alpine poling. Just plant your inside pole and turn around it.

No more mammies. On the steep slopes I'm staying low and punching my fist to the opposite ski tip like I've seen the slalom racers do. It really gives you lots of angulation and edge-set on the hard stuff. Only saw two other pinheads all season. Friends of friends, of course. Just like climbing in the 1950s.

FEBRUARY – HOKKAIDO, JAPAN

The owner of my local sushi bar is from Sapporo and she keeps telling me about the great skiing and smoked squid of Hokkaido. So, Paul Parker and I are met at the Sapporo airport by Mr. Kanai and his father. The car is an old, mint-condition Mercedes, ex-Korean Embassy. The old man with the combed-back white hair is now retired from the sport shop and loves nothing more than driving around Hokkaido in a comfortable car. He is an excellent driver. We have a follow-car for the mountains of baggage. Kanai-san drops us off at a small log lodge run by a climber, and he goes off to soak in the hot springs for a few days. We meet up with 15 of the 200 members of the Japanese Telemark Association. None of them have skied outside Japan and they are anxious to watch Paul

"In 1980 I joined some friends on an early season—and very cold—ascent of Denali. Mike Jauregui, showing why they call it 'man-hauling.'" Rick Ridgeway

Parker ski to see if they are on the right track. It turns out they are excellent skiers on the pistes with solid alpine backgrounds. Generally, the Japanese ski quietly and controlled. No yelling or screaming, and no smiling. Everyone skis with perfect, Austrian feet-locked-together, ski school style. They even have one-person lifts so no one needs to embarrass themselves and yell, "single!"

It snows a meter and we head for the trees. They are all birch and giant bamboo, pretty far apart and there is no one there. Paul tells me to try and grip a pencil between my hip and waist (remember the 1960s bra test?). This gets my skis off to the side and together. Switching from side to side gets that powder rhythm going and I make five or six good turns before I blow it. Not bad, though, and the Japanese are not much better at powder. I sense they are wondering why we don't just go back to those nice packed slopes—this is all so disorganized. The next day I learn not to let my hand drop down and back. As soon as I plant my pole the other arm is coming forward. Paul yells, "Let out a big aggressive grunt every time you do a turn!" We do and suddenly it all comes together. Hooting kamikazes, grunting and screaming through the trees, finally breaking out of the woods under the lifts covered from head to toe in the white stuff, and laughing our heads off. Very un-Japanese.

He's got a unique gonzo style that's his alone. … he can run the speed trials in Les Arcs in his wool pants, Peruvian hat, and bunting jacket while chewing his Red Man."

The squid? She forgot to mention it was soaked in sugar syrup after smoking.

FEBRUARY/MARCH – EUROPE

Paul and I had to go to Munich for the ski show, so bringing along our skis seemed like a good idea. With no snow in the eastern Alps we head west. We stop off in Arosa, which is smack-dab in the middle of the most conservative and reactionary part of Switzerland. My friend Ruedi Homberger, who is a photographer and mountain guide, laughs at our skinny skis. Says his father's happiest day was when he learned the Christiana and didn't have to telemark anymore. Ruedi offers to take us on a tour the next day and something tells me he is going to try and prove that skinny skis don't belong in the high Alps.

From the top of the lifts we go down a steep, icy slope then a long traverse on steep ice. If you fall, it's 800 feet to probable death or at least total paralysis. One of us falls and goes about 200 feet before hitting some rocks and stopping at the only place on the traverse that isn't a death fall. We get to a col and I look up at our intended ridge—it's half rock, half ice, and half cornice. I whisper to the others, "Turn back, it's a sandbag." Some of us decide to take an easier way but the next five miles are on breakable crust on top of ten millimeters of depth hoar. It's so bad even the guys on their alpine touring skis are sandbagged. The others even had a worse time, coming back with purple shins.

We escape to Chamonix where there is snow, and I duck into the Bar National for a beer and old memories. There I run into Jorge Colon from Jackson. He has the town wired, so we follow him around for the next ten days. The dollar hits an all-time apogee against the franc and we dine like kings. All the years I've bummed around this town, sleeping in the rain, in the Biolay and Snell's field and living hand-to-mouth. Now I'm loaded with dollars and the franc is worthless, so I attack with a vengeance.

The clouds drop a foot of snow every night on the Grands Montets, where we meet up with Billy Barnham from Snowbird who is now working ski patrol here on his 205 Karhu XCD Comps. He and Jorge have the more progressive locals all jazzed to get some gear, but edged cross-country skis and good boots are not available anywhere in Europe except for Norway.

If you want to ski powder in Chamonix, you have to take risks and ski between, over, and around the crevasses. Billy knows the slots and we get the best skiing of the year. I concentrate on watching my hands. I tell myself, *Don't let them drop behind, keep them in sight,* over and over again, and *Don't break the rhythm even when the snow gets heavy down low.* Barnham likes air and tries to get it every chance he can. He's got a unique gonzo style that's his alone. I leave him a pair of my three-pin bindings to put on his 223-centimeter Dynastars so he can run the speed trials in Les Arcs in his wool pants, Peruvian hat, and bunting jacket while chewing his Red Man.

MARCH – THE ADAMANTS

I come back from Europe in pretty good shape so I accept an invitation to ski with climbing buddy Yuri Kristjanson, who is guiding for Mike Wiegele in Canada. The first day, I climb in the helicopter with a bunch of doctors from Colorado who come every year on a medical seminar scam. These are the hardcore skiers with one purpose in mind: to get the maximum vertical. After a few runs, their leader—a real jerk—tells me to let them go first because my telemark turns are not tight enough and I'm taking more than my share of slope. The snow varies from excellent powder to spring slush and wind crust, and after 25,000 feet my legs aren't bankrupt but definitely Chapter 11. Next day, I ski with the wives and have a lot more fun. They don't tell me to make tighter turns. I come away very impressed with Wiegele's avalanche forecasting. Having misjudged three times, I'm very sensitive about the topic and it's good to be with the professionals.

MARCH – SUN VALLEY

After the Vegas ski show, my family and I are invited to Sun Valley by Hollywood mogul Frank Wells, who I climbed Aconcagua with a few years ago. It's all hardpack skiing on wide, well-groomed slopes. No slalom cut or short skis here. Everyone is on their 210 or 215 GS's. A few hours of trying to keep up with my Idaho sales rep John Taylor, and Wayne Poulson and Rosemary Bogner has me wishing I had my old alpine skis for the first time in four years. I stick close to my ten-year-old boy, Fletcher (a perfect excuse to stop—a lot). I make parallel turns most of the time with the occasional tele to use different muscles. As I get more tired, Taylor tells me to drive my pole arm up sooner for the next turn. Old habits die hard.

My kid and I are entered in the Seventh Annual Wells Cup Race and I have one good run out of three on my three-pins. I think I beat out Clint Eastwood by a second. That made my day.

APRIL – CRESTED BUTTE

Know what the third prize is at the World Telemark Championships? A Patagonia sweatshirt. This sport is really underground. There are 120 men and 30 women competing in their purple and peacock-blue lycra suits and customized, chopped, and channeled Stein comps (homemade plastic cuffs mostly made from plastic pickle barrels). Some have old leather Molitors with a door hinge and studs in the sole. I'm there to observe because I know there's something going on, but I don't know quite what it is. Mark Lance, who lost only two races this year, qualified and was impressive to watch. The master of the early lead change, he initiates a turn in a telemark then quickly brings up the back ski to parallel, ready to initiate the next turn from a parallel. This allows him to go from edge to edge, turn to turn, without having to weight and unweight, and keeps him low with his skis on the snow so he goes even faster.

MAY – MINERAL KING

I can see why Disney wanted to put a ski area in here. There's no doubt this place has the best backcountry bowls in the Sierra. Nine of us made a camp on a patch of the last bare ground at 9,500 feet, then everyone split

OPPOSITE: *Yvon riding telemark skis when they were still narrow.* Yvon Chouinard Collection

to climb the surrounding 12,000-foot peaks via feet, skins, and klister. The sky stayed blue for the five days and the snow, a perfect velvet corn. Not a bowl, ridge, or gully was left untracked. Some of the gullies were very steep and here tele-turns failed me. I knew what needed to be done. Dive into the fall-line, drive those fists forward, crunch down low, and set the edges; lots of angulation, keep that pencil tucked into the hip and then rebound up and windshield-wiper the skis over to the next edge set. And don't let that stupid hand drop back! The theory was all there but very steep, fast corn is unforgiving. The slightest mistake and you don't recover until the deposition zone. Lots to work on next season.

On the way out, we opted to ski a twisting, narrow avalanche gully instead of trudging down the switchbacks. "Better a bad ski than a good walk. …"

OPPOSITE: *"Keep those arms in front!" Hokkaido, Japan.* Eric Sanford

The Myth of Powder

First published in the Chouinard Equipment for Alpinists Catalog, Winter 1987

I've had my share of the white stuff this past winter, but I can count on the fingers of one hand the times I've skied powder. I don't mean "packed powder" or that four inches of fresh snow that smooths out all your bad habits. I mean the real stuff, that deep, light, feathery snow that's had the moisture sucked out of it travelling over the Bonneville Salt Flats or that's been solar radiated by a cold clear night in the Tetons. That thigh-deep soft stuff is about as rare as the proverbial "six- to eight-foot hot and glassy surf."

Even if you're lucky enough to wake up to a major powder dump at a ski area, there's little chance of getting to it before the ski patrol, friends of the patrol, and the Piston Bullies pack it down by 9:30 am. The local powder Nazis and even the chili server from the warming hut will have violated all those little secret shots and slots the Bullies leave. What's left by ten o'clock is packed powder, junk, but still untouched in the too-tight trees. The yahoos will still be out there making believe and inventing stories to brag about back in Van Nuys.

I gave up fat boards five years ago for the skinny. Like a lot of pinheads I was bored with doing the same turn on packed slopes and I was too much of a realist to only live for those powder days. Turning to the backcountry, I lived some memorable days of corn and untracked Sierra cement. Being a survivor of a couple serious avalanches I really don't care to go into the backcountry in midwinter anymore. My days of powder have to come in the spring, right after

OPPOSITE: *John Wasson skiing on the north face of the Grands Montets, Argentière, France.*
Gary Bigham

a dump or occasionally on some north-facing bowl. A few times I've been lucky enough to scam a seat on the occasional chopper or snow cat. Still I'd have to say my big regrets in life—along with not having gotten enough sex as a teenager—is not getting enough of that perfect up and down, three-dimensional skiing.

Some of my more radical friends changed the rules even more and became crud freaks—only going out when conditions where shitty and actually searching out the most difficult snow they could find. I've always known that they were on to something but I've never been that good of a skier so I'm always careful to be back down before the corn turns to slush or the powder starts setting up.

That changed this past spring. I had to go out and test these new prototype Chouinard skis at Mammoth Mountain (somebody had to do it). Conditions were perfect for trying out the short, fat Magnums—over two feet of new cement so heavy that even the lift operators and locals were in their raincoats and kayak-paddling jackets. Somehow I managed to be the first in line as the different lifts opened on the upper mountain and I was able to get some nice runs on the untouched slopes. Heavy snow or not, it was dead-easy skiing those 180-centimeter floaters. As the day progressed I switched over to the trees and got several good, clean runs and had a new discovery; tight trees and short skis go together!

Back up at the cornice, I wanted one more shot at the steep slope below. It looked skied out, but by now I was pretty cocky and I attacked it as if the two-foot-deep ruts and soft death cookies weren't even there. Lo and behold I found myself at the bottom without crashing and with a grin from ear to ear. *My God*, I thought, *these skis are magic. I've never been able to ski crud like this before.* Off I went in search of the worst. By now I had left behind all the rest of my friends except for Abe San, a Samurai telemarker from Hokkaido whom I finally lost in the breakable wind crust out on the flats. I put the Magnums on their edges and came busting through the crust but immediately snapping back up before the skis had a chance to run under and catch a tip. I couldn't believe I was skiing this crud! Right then and there it all came to me, on my best day of skiing of the year. I finally understood why Dorworth, Lito, and Bridwell live for those shitty days. I was born again.

OPPOSITE: *Telemark skiing the steeps of the La Flégère ski area in Chamonix. Behind the clouds and blowing snow is the Aiguille des Charmoz. France.* Gary Bigham

One-Way Trip on the Clarks Fork

First published in First Descents: In Search of Wild Rivers *by John Lazenby, Menasha Ridge Press, 1989*

After this trip, I gave a $5,000 grant to the Greater Yellowstone Coalition, which passed it on to Lamar Empey, founder of the Clarks Fork Conservation Movement. Lamar's goal was to stop a proposed dam that was going to impound 450,000 acre-feet of water and cost $225 million. He also went to Washington, DC, and convinced Senator Alan Simpson to help pass legislation protecting the Clarks Fork as Wyoming's first Wild and Scenic River in 1990.

Back in the midseventies, while I was into surfing and ice climbing, some of my old climbing friends got into kayaking. Being adrenalin junkies, Class 5 water provided them with plenty of risk to support their habits. But, not wishing to forsake their climbing roots or their need for wilderness adventure, they adapted the sport to suit their own needs. From 1980 to 1985 two of them, Royal Robbins and Doug Tompkins, along with Reg Lake and a few others, pulled off first descents of three major western Sierra rivers: the Kings, the Kern, and the San Joaquin. What was notable was that they humped their boats over 13,000-foot passes on the east side to put in at the headwaters.

PREVIOUS SPREAD: *Doug Tompkins and Jim Donini paddling up Fiordo de las Montañas in southern Chile. With Yvon and Rick Ridgeway, the four spent a month exploring the region and Jim and Yvon climbed a rock spire that looked like a miniature Fitz Roy. 1988.* Rick Ridgeway

OPPOSITE: *Reg Lake (on the river) lowers Doug Tompkins down ... until the rope stuck. Doug had to climb out of his hanging boat. Some experiments just don't work as planned. Clarks Fork, Wyoming.* Rob Lesser

The crew sees an impossible waterfall thirty yards below. They learned the character of the Clarks Fork on the first day. Wyoming. Rob Lesser

Big-wall climbing philosophy was applied with absolute commitment to the no-turn-back rock gorges. Even the equipment of rock climbing was used to belay blind corners and rappel unrunnable waterfalls. Being a later-day boater, I missed out on this era and now I'm trying to play catch-up. So when I heard about an unrun river gorge near Yellowstone National Park, I was definitely interested.

The Clarks Fork of the Yellowstone River comes out of the Beartooth Range near Cooke City, Montana. It drops down a sheer-walled granite canyon at the rate of 2,000 feet in 25 miles. As near as we could tell, no one had ever been all the way through the inner recesses of the gorge. Chief Joseph probably followed the ledge systems on the canyon walls to escape the Feds, who thought they had him and 800 of his people trapped in the Lamar Valley in Yellowstone in 1877. I've also heard rumors of some Montana ice climbers who have gone a ways up the gorge in winter from the bottom, using crampons and ice axes. Some fellows tried to kayak it in 1976 but after thirty-three portages and three days with starvation rations and beat-up boats, they left their kayaks and climbed 1,500 feet out of the canyon.

In the summer of 1984, five friends and I were ready to try it.

The team:

Yvon Chouinard, an aging surfer/climber who's always willing to be irresponsible to further good adventure. He likes to think of himself as a badger.

Reg Lake, who owns a paddling shop near San Francisco and practices what he preaches. A veteran of the steep and deep.

Rob Lesser, a whitewater paddler/photographer who has explored the world in a kayak. Somehow each new river expedition is a piece of the "big puzzle."

Doug Tompkins, a fashion-maker. He's been around the world more times than you've been to McDonald's. Always first to take risks, but deadly practical.

John Wasson, a known sucker for terra incognita. The only one with a girlfriend who wishes she had come along.

The gear:

Personal gear: plastic kayak, fiberglass paddle, one-inch webbing runner, spray skirt, sponge, helmet, lifejacket, pile paddling sweater, farmer john wetsuit, paddling jacket, baggie shorts, reef walkers or old running shoes, midweight underwear, quarter-inch-thick foam pad, two-pound (total weight) down sleeping bag, waterproof sleeping bag cover or tarp, plastic spoon and cup, camera and film, toothbrush, aspirin, adhesive tape, waterproof stuffsacks.

Group gear: one throw rope, 120-foot 8-millimeter rope, 120-foot 5-millimeter rope, 5 carabiners, 15-foot tubular webbing, Swiss army knife, two break-down paddles, matches, one cook pot, aluminum foil, one fly rod and flies.

Food for three days: muesli, powdered milk, tea and hot chocolate, cheese and crackers, sardines and oysters, salami, dried fruit, chocolate-covered espresso coffee beans, rice and pasta, dehydrated vegetable soup.

As we leave the house in Moose, Wyoming, my wife says if we aren't back in four days she is going to chicken-wire the end of the canyon and see what comes out. Doug and Reg meet up with us in Cody, where they have been trying for two days to fly over the river for a look-see, but the weather's been awful. We want low water; that's why we're here in mid-August. Because of the rain, Rob thinks the river has come up to an "interesting" level. The shuttle, like all shuttles, is intricate. When is someone going to come up with a computer program for shuttles?

We arrive at the put-in, where the Sunlight Basin Road crosses the river,

———

... the local redneck sheriff with his CB, bill cap, and cowboy boots. He's so fat we can't understand how he crammed himself into his little Bronco.

———

and who should show up but Kay Swanson from Billings, who was on the first kayak attempt of the Clarks Fork. He and some friends just happened to be driving by after having done a lower section of the river. This unbelievable coincidence reminds me of the early days of American climbing when, if you saw a cleated footprint on the trail, it was that of a climber, and if you caught up with him, it was a friend or a friend of a friend. There are a lot of people boating these days, but still damn few willing to accept the risks of going beyond the Class 3 or 4. We ask Swanson for information, but he is a classic understater in the art of gamesmanship, so the only useful nugget we get is that they did not have climbing gear on their attempt.

Next to drive by is the local redneck sheriff with his CB, bill cap, and cowboy boots. He is so fat we can't understand how he crammed himself into his little Bronco. "You boys aren't planning on going down that river, are you? We had to pull the last guys out with ropes." Swanson jumps up and says that's bullshit, they didn't have help from anybody. This is all too much for our sixth teammate; Paul Driscoll from Jackson. He decides that the Clarks Fork on this day in these conditions is just not for him and hitchhikes back to Jackson.

OPPOSITE: *"Hauling my boat through the woods at the waterfall portage on the first day." Clarks Fork, Wyoming.* Rob Lesser

Some of the 'Do Boys' after a three-day descent of the Clarks Fork of the Yellowstone River. Doug Tompkins, Rob Lesser, John Wasson, Yvon, and Reg Lake. 1986. Rob Lesser Collection

We finally put in at three in the afternoon and head downriver. Right away the boating is unbelievably enjoyable Class 3 and easy 4. Very technical, but not hard. We run everything except one long portage before making camp at 7:30. We did pass two bait fishermen armed like Mexican bandits, bandoliers full of bullets across the chest and, of course, billed caps, camouflage clothes, and their redneck cooler. Now that no one backpacks anymore all you ever see in the wilderness are madmen and survivalists. We later joked about how these two guys looked like the two mountain men, the Nichols father and son, wanted for murder in Big Sky, Montana. (The FBI later talked to each of us wondering the same thing.)

The next day started out with four miles of flatwater through a valley reminiscent of the Merced through Yosemite. After passing a rancher's cable ford, the river enters the Box, and from here on you need better eyes than I have to count the contour lines on the map. It's difficult to remember the Clarks Fork with much sense of chronology because of the constant interplay of rapids and scouting, waterfalls and portaging. The scenery was fantastic but there really was no need to remember and register the passing rapids and canyon, for turning back was not an option. We were committed to a one-way trip.

In the three days, we experienced technical boating as enjoyable as it gets. Except for two long and arduous portages, most of the carries were short and easy. However, there were two places where we had to use the ropes. Once we had to ferry the boats horizontally across a cliff and do a little 5.7 climbing; and another time, to avoid a waterfall, we traversed a ledge and rappelled in our boats down to a pool below. Each person was lowered end-first in his boat, and the last man let himself down and pulled the double rope through. Great fun, actually! Reg compared the canyon to being in the Remarkables in New Zealand and Doug thought it was like the San Joaquin. I thought of all the great climbs you could do on this beautiful granite. The approach would be easy by foot to the canyon rim, and then you could scramble down a gully to the river. I'd guess in all we ran 200 rapids, portaged 20 times, ate plenty of rainbow/cutthroat hybrid trout, and thoroughly enjoyed our chocolate-covered coffee beans (ten dollars a pound). These should be illegal.

After Dead Indian Creek comes in, the contour lines go back to 100 feet per mile and in two hours we equaled the mileage of the previous two days. We bounced through the easy Class 3 and 4 stuff of the lower canyon and spied the truck on the dirt road that crosses the river near Wyoming Route 120. We took a "foto di grupo," drank a bottle of good red, ate the rest of the food, loaded up, and split. Recommended. Do it before they dam it.

'Opihi Man *and*
The Rest of the Story

"'Ophihi Man" *first published in* Patagonia: Notes from the Field, *Nora Gallagher (ed), Chronicle Books, 1999; "The Rest of the Story" is unpublished*

This is an essay written by my daughter, Claire, when she was in high school. We had been on a kayaking trip of seven days around the North Coast of Moloka'i Island in Hawai'i.

'OPIHI MAN *Claire Chouinard*

The tropical sky was stained with blotches of darkening thunderclouds and a plume of smoke curled up from a bamboo structure at the end of the beach. Our group had paddled to this beach earlier in the day while the sun was still hot. My dad and I paddled in a plump, hot dog–shaped kayak. It was twenty feet long and inflatable. It caught the wind like a kite. I fought the water, and the wind. Every plunge of my paddle was like a blow to an enemy. As I stared ahead, I imagined my father doing the same behind me, squinting his eyes into the sun and wind. When he squinted, the creases around his eyes and across his tanned forehead became deeper and darker. But when I glanced over my shoulder, there was no strain in those eyes. He just casually dipped his paddle into the water and pulled. The muscles in his thick arms and shoulders shifted beneath his thin sleeves; I was reminded of the burning

OPPOSITE: *"Hunting and gathering at an early age. My friends Doug Peacock and Rick Ridgeway along with my daughter, Claire, and son, Fletcher, spent a week in the Sea of Cortez on uninhabited Tiburón Island, living mostly on the fish we caught and the sea snails we gathered."* Rick Ridgeway

Waiting for the airlift out, Molokaʻi, Hawaiʻi. 1996. Rell Sunn

in my own forearms. It had been a long day and my stomach was starting to complain in a low voice.

We were now crouched like crabs on the rocks. The rocks just below the tide line were big, pink, and smooth. They were only uncovered briefly as the ocean took a deep breath and pulled the waves back into its gut. During these seconds when the ocean seemed to part, we scampered forward with our bent knives to pry off the *ʻopihi*. We had to be quick. If we were sloppy and had to try again, we'd find their glossy orange lip sucked back under the dishlike shells. When they reacted they became impossible to dislodge. By the end of the afternoon our knuckles were bleeding and stiff from scraping rocks. The mesh dive bags secured around our waists began to sag and droop and catch between our legs. Finally finished, we began the trek back to our camp at the far end of the cove.

From a distance, we could see the rest of the group huddled cooking in the shelter. Earlier, we had worked for hours digging through the rocks to clear a floor of flat, hard sand. We had then bound bamboo poles together with strips of black inner-tube rubber and tied on a blue tarp as a roof. A few of the pieces of rubber were wrapped around knobs of lava that protruded from the mountain. They held the structure up and prevented it from catching the wind and blowing away.

My three aunties and I waded through the water, letting our bags hang in the current. The smell of buttery fried *moi* filled the air, and as we arrived the sight of the glistening sashimi gave me a mouthwatering pang. I grabbed one of the slick slices of fish and let it slide down my throat. My stomach purred with relief. Keola and Jaya were slumped in the corner drinking amaretto from teacups and Dave was massaging Rell's neck. There was little talking as the four of us began placing our *'opihi* on the grill. We cooked them with soy sauce, Hawaiian salt, lemon, and hot pepper oil. They lay soft belly side to the sky with their own shells as little bowls. I had to look away when they poked their heads out.

"Claire, what is your father doing? Does he ever stop?" I looked from Rell's laughing smile to where my dad was climbing at the edge of the water. I couldn't see him from where I was sitting. He was blocked by the blue tarp. I looked back to the grill and watched the orange meat of the *'opihi* start to curl inward from the heat. I swayed slightly as I sipped my tea.

I didn't notice until I was alone in the shelter that everyone had moved. Even when Keola yelled to me that my father had fallen I didn't react. It couldn't be a big deal. Not until I saw him lying on his back curled inward in pain did I feel any fear. What was he doing? He looked like a little boy and then he looked like an ancient old man. He had been about fifteen feet up an overhang when the knob he was holding broke. The white spot where it had come loose glowed against the black lava. The bone from his elbow poked out and strained against his long white sleeve.

Rell and I used two pareus for a sling. He had lost the cap to his front tooth and hadn't shaved in six days. His face was shiny with sweat, and he cried out twice as we slowly helped him up through the rocks to the camp. I walked holding tightly to his good arm like I used to with my grandma in Chatsworth. He wouldn't let the boys carry him. While Glen radioed a friend who owned a helicopter, I watched my dad as if he were a television. He had his feet up on a cooler and a red sleeping bag up to his neck to prevent shock. It wasn't working very well.

His usually dark face looked like skim milk with a tint of blue under his eyes and on his lips. I was afraid to talk to him. He looked like I could hurt him. Something was missing from his face, or maybe something had been added. I didn't know this look. I didn't know those soft spots around his eyes. For the first time that evening I sat back on my heels and without shame, let myself feel the exhaustion and tightness in my own arms and back.

I wasn't watching at first when his orange tan briefly returned. He opened his eyes and lifted half of his mouth into a grin.

"Hey, how're the *'opihi?*"

THE REST OF THE STORY *Yvon Chouinard*

A rescue Cessna took me to the Queen's Medical Center in Honolulu, an inner-city hospital in a rough part of town. Most of the emergency cases this time of night are knife or gunshot wounds or crazed meth addicts. I can't show any identification or proof of insurance as my wallet is still on Moloka'i. All I have is a small pocketknife which they let me keep.

The emergency room doctor is only required by law to stabilize my situation. He cuts off my T-shirt, cleans the wound, wraps it up, and puts my arm in a sling. He gives me pain pills and says I'm free to go. It's 2 am, I'm barefoot and shirtless, with just a pair of shorts. I can't imagine myself wandering around the neighborhood in my shocked state. I protest that I have no place to go, but he says it would cost a thousand dollars to stay the rest of the night and reminds me that I have no proof of insurance. Under his breath he says to get out of Hawai'i as there is no doctor here he trusts to work on such a bad break.

Luckily a security guard takes pity on me and takes me over to the medical school where there is an empty apartment. I swallow some pain pills and lay down on the bare mattress.

In the morning, I'm in pain and deep shock. I force myself to focus. *OK, my wife is in Italy, my son in California, Claire and friends are still on Moloka'i probably rounding the leper colony at Kalaupapa today.*

There's a Patagonia store in Hale'iwa. They can help. I check the phone, it works. Information gives me the number but I immediately forget it. I find a

Yvon attends a conference with President Bill Clinton, Vice President Al Gore, and several business leaders as they discuss how companies can achieve the goals of improving employee training and involving them more in the corporate decision-making process. Georgetown University, Washington, DC. 1996.
William J. Clinton Library and Museum

bar of soap, call Information again, and with my trusty pocketknife carve the number on the bar.

Now all I have to do is to wait until the store opens at ten and I'm out of here. I turn the TV on to CNN and in my dazed state I see myself talking to President Clinton! The week before the trip, myself and Howard Schultz, CEO of Starbucks, had been invited to a business breakfast at the White House. There's Clinton telling me how much he enjoys shopping at our Georgetown store. I want to shout out to everyone at Queen's, "Look! That's me talking to the president of the United States. I do have insurance!"

Dear Mum

First published in the Patagonia Spring Catalog, 1986

This was a story written for the 1986 Patagonia catalog to promote a polyester tweed sport coat that you could pack in a stuffsack.

Dear Mum,

As you know, most of the coats that leave the Trinity Garment Factory in Hong Kong go to Dunhill in London, but, since I was a special order for Mr. Y. Chouinard in California, I thought that mine was to be a far greater destiny. I imagined my master being a Frenchman living perhaps in Montecito and attending dinner parties with Julia Child or even rubbing shoulders with Jane Fonda. The butler would drive me down to the cleaners in the Rolls every fortnight to clean off the odd long blond hair or spot of Sutter Home Late Harvest Zinfandel. But bloody hell, if only I had known what was in store for me!

I no sooner arrived in this oil town of Ventura than my new owner, who happens to be an aging surfer and alpinist, grabbed me, shoved my shoulders back until they touched, turned me inside out, and folded me into thirds, and crammed me into a stuff bag and then into a monstrous ruck-sack. I overheard that I was being taken on a mountain climbing expedition to Bhutan with a gang called the Do Boys. The closest I got to Montecito

OPPOSITE: *Thirty-Eight Short and his master on a layover in Calcutta, India, waiting for a flight to Bhutan, all set to meet the King. 1985.* Rick Ridgeway

was driving by on Highway 1 on the way to the Santa Barbara airport. What rotten luck.

We spent a few days in Hong Kong. It was bloody nice to be back. We had supper at the posh Swiss Restaurant of the Peninsula Hotel. Not your

———

... a city park with people sitting on benches reading newspapers, babies in strollers, but instead of feeding pigeons, they were feeding hordes of great grey rats.

———

usual garment industry or tourist crowd there. More like heavy industry from the Ruhr, arms merchants, and Swiss bankers. Leaving Hong Kong, my master bought twenty-four one-pound tins of cheese for the expedition which had to be added to his already overloaded hand-baggage rucksack. We went through security, me loaded down with tins in each pocket. It was awfully embarrassing.

In Singapore, the penalty for possession of seven ounces or more of marijuana is death. Driving a car with more than four passengers will get you a month in the pokey. But the people are wonderful, no one is starving, and they love trees. Even the water fountains all over the country are working, a sure sign of a first-world country. Take note, America.

Guess what, Mum? We had breakfast at Raffles in classic Raj style. Brown-edged fried eggs, bangers, cooked tomatoes, Heinz beans, kippers, and chips. They even cut away the crust on the toast. That made it perfect! Thank the Lord this man's taste still includes room for proper British cuisine.

A few days before we arrived in Thailand, there was an attempted coup which was put down in three hours. It would have been over sooner but the loyalist army tanks got caught up in the rush-hour traffic. There was a notice

OPPOSITE: *In a Calcutta city park, an iron fence encloses a warren of thousands of rats. Parkgoers throw tidbits of food. "Other cities, they feed pigeons," John Roskelley said as he takes a photo.*
Rick Ridgeway

still up in the hotel, "Sorry for the inconvenience. We are having a light revolution. Things should be normal soon."

In Calcutta, some of the expedition members swore they went by a city park with people sitting on benches reading newspapers, babies in strollers, but instead of feeding pigeons, they were feeding hordes of great grey rats. My master took great pleasure in reading the classifieds in the Indian newspapers. One said: "Wanted: Twenty-nine-year-old Punjabi woman, game left leg, wishes to meet man with own teeth for matrimony. Dowry seekers will be disappointed."

At the airport, we saw our first Bhutanese getting on Druk Air. They were nice young fellows all dressed in Comme des Garçons–looking clothes and loaded down with microwave ovens and Trinitrons. Turned out they were a Bhutanese basketball team coming back from a match in Kobe, Japan. How did they like Japan? "Oh man, it freaked us out."

Other than the glitterati of Thimphu, the capital, most of the people of Bhutan are farmers or yak herders. While the expedition was off climbing, I was left in my stuffsack in a cardboard box in storage along with all the expedition's extra clothes. All of the cotton, of course, got mildew but I've had my shots for that.

The Do Boys returned a week earlier than I expected them, mumbling something about getting lost and being on the wrong mountain. We went off to see the King of Bhutan, who plays basketball. Kings don't run so he waited under the basket for the game to come to him. His teammates handed him the ball and he made the score to cheering from both sides. He was sort of like a Doctor Seuss king.

Well, when we finally returned to California I was ready to "kick back." Now I hear the man talking about a trip to Antarctica in November. Well Mum, it's strange but I think it's all going to be interesting. I'm even starting to like veggies.

Love,
Your son, Thirty-Eight Short

OPPOSITE: *Gangkhar Puensum, "White Peak of the Three Spiritual Brothers," is the highest mountain in Bhutan.* John Roskelley

The Secret Weapon

First published in River Runner, *September 1986*

For over thirty years, surfing has been my number one passion. In 1975, I bought a house right on the water at a surf spot so that I would have to walk only fifty feet to enter the water. I could sit in my living room and assess the wind, swell, tide, and crowd. I soon set up an early warning surf report with my wife and neighbors so when I went to the shop, I wouldn't get caught unaware of a new swell. It's no exaggeration to say that I had the best setup for surfing in California except for perhaps Richard M. Nixon at Cotton's Point in San Clemente—but that's mostly a left break anyway.

Even with all the odds stacked in my favor, I still wasn't getting enough waves. There were too many days when the tide was too high, the wind was too strong, the crowd was too big, or there was just no swell. There's nothing you can do with a flat ocean, but I discovered that during high tides or blown-out surf I could take out my slalom kayak and still feel like I was surfing. The shitty conditions usually took care of the crowds.

It wasn't long before I felt like I needed something with higher performance. On big waves, I was exceeding the hull speed of my river kayak and on small hollow waves, I was spinning out and broaching. I tried an old surf shoe that turned easier and, with the shorter stern, allowed me to get out of a broach by cutting back. I bought one of those short surf kayaks made for the average two-foot Virginia Beach wave. It was too stiff with fins in place,

OPPOSITE: *Yvon at Ventura Overhead, a classic reef break just north of Patagonia's headquarters, in the late 1980s. California.* Rick Ridgeway

275

and with its hard rails and flat bottom, all I could do was pivot turns back and forth across the soup. I tried a wave ski, but I didn't like not being able to use my knees to bank, and paddling with my knees together hurt my back. Besides, I had no interest in doing 360s; I wanted a craft that acted more like

———

Basically, I was a surfer wanting to kayak rather than a kayaker wanting to surf. These are vastly different approaches to design. …

———

a surfboard—one with a skeg that lets you take a more vertical line without spinning out. I also wanted a boat in which I could sit down low to be better poised for punching through waves on my way out. And being inside a boat eliminated the need for a wetsuit.

Basically, I was a surfer wanting to kayak rather than a kayaker wanting to surf. These are vastly different approaches to design and produce wildly different performing boats. Rather than approaching a kayak builder, I worked with my surfboard builder friend Greg Liddle to produce the boat to fit what I wanted.

We began with an 8'4" surfboard hull hollowed out with a kayak deck on top. The deck didn't extend over the rails but left four inches of them sticking out all around. This is important if you want to carve turns rather than do the jerk with pivot turns. Also, soft round rails at midlength hold you better on the face of a steep wave.

Our fin solution was to use a windsurfing one with a very narrow base. It kept the boat loose yet prevented it from spinning out in hollow waves.

This first boat had a parallel rail outline and not much bottom rocker. It was very fast, good for down-the-line point surf and unbelievable for getting tubed. I started going out on those junky wind-swell days that Ventura has so many of in the spring. I'd catch and ride ten to fifteen waves to every surfer's one. I was also going out a lot on crowded days to the seldom-surfed outer reefs, like the Overhead, where with my ease of paddling, I could drop in sooner and be gone before the wave hit the reef and pitched forward. I was able to even occasionally backdoor the peak. This boat did have a drawback in that it was difficult to break all that speed with a radical cutback. It was stiff, particularly on big waves.

Boat number two was a turning boat. It had more curve in the outline, with a pulled-in nose and tail, more rocker fore and aft and double chines on the bottom made it easier to bank and carve. I could take off going left in the curl and turn before hitting the bottom and go right, climbing up and peeling off the lip to go back into the pocket again just like a surfboard. I was able to make sections that surfriders couldn't by getting maximum speed and climbing and peeling off. By going way out ahead of the whitewater, banking my boat back into the soup, and taking a few strokes, I was back up onto the green shoulder ready to ace out the next pocket of surfers getting ready to drop in. The only problem with this boat was that, by adding curve and rocker to the design, I compromised on speed. In boat design, everything is a compromise. You can't have ultimate speed and total maneuverability at the same time.

The third boat kept the rounded outline but had a flatter bottom for better water release and was four inches shorter for easier turning. I compromised on floatability. Yes, it was faster, but it was hard to put on its edge because of increased water suction from the flat bottom.

Boat number four is a work in progress. If a surfboard is 100 percent efficient for surfing ocean waves, and a kayak is 30 percent, then I'm at about 60 percent there.

Still, there are drawbacks with these boats. With the skegs, it's tough getting out on rocky beaches; I can see working on a movable skeg for getting in and out of difficult beaches. The other problem is that wiping out on big waves puts a lot of torque on your body; you can't just bail out and dive under the big sets like you can on a wave ski. But I'm having fun with my surf-yak, and I'm getting a lot more waves with no one else out, and that's what I was after.

Attack of the Killer Limpets

First published in The Surfers Journal, *Volume Three, Number One, Spring 1994*

"Sounds like thunder. Gotta head for the high ground. White water's comin', no fooling around." – "'Opihi Man," Ka'au Crater Boys

What would you say is the biggest cause of drowning in Hawai'i? Caught inside at Pipeline? Bodyboarding the Waimea shorebreak? Olive drab cutoffs and the Sunset rip? Although steely-eyed veterans of the North Shore would like to think that surfing big waves is a death-defying experience, to date no one has been turned down for life insurance because they surf. No, by far the biggest cause of drownings in Hawai'i is a large, coin-sized limpet known in the islands as '*opihi*.

'*Opihi* are little nuggets of sweet, briny protein that are considered *ono grinds* (good eating) by Hawaiians. The '*opihi* is part of the gastropoda or 'stomach-foot' family that include snails, abalone, slugs, and other such creatures that people wouldn't normally put themselves in dire peril to plop in their mouths. Because, like surfers and the craving for the ever-elusive Big Wave, '*opihi* hunters want the "bombucha" limpet, which puts them in the firing line between the world's wildest surf and the rough-hewn lava coastline.

"Gotta fill up your bag, with the yellow and black.
Keep your eyes on the wave, don't ever turn your back."

OPPOSITE: *Wild* '*opihi* *on the shores of Maui, Hawai'i.* Hank Gaskell

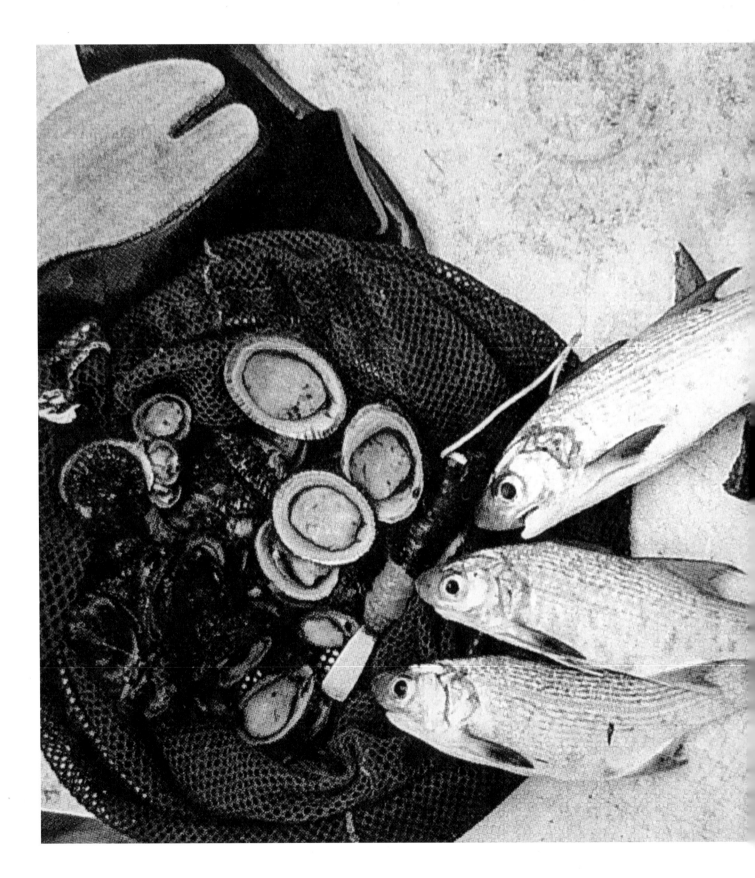

'*Opihi* attach to rocks by means of a suction-foot which also provides its locomotion. They browse for food at night, grazing algae and seaweed like a lawn mower cuts grass, and then somehow return to the exact location on their home rock. The cone-shaped shell of the '*opihi* has evolved perfectly to offer the least resistance to breakers and currents on their rocky perches— much like a pyramid-shaped tent efficiently spills an arctic wind.

The most prized Hawaiian '*opihi* is the ribbed-sided Chinaman's hat. Those above the low-tide line that are easy to get have a black foot and are called "night ones." The same type that live and feed directly in the surf zone are called "day ones" and have a yellow-orange foot, and like most forbidden fruit, taste sweeter.

To be legally harvested in Hawai'i, '*opihi* must be at least the size of a half-dollar. Some limpets, like the yellow ones, are so rare at any size that the serious '*opihi* 'pounders' (pickers) have been forced toward rougher and more remote terrain. Some even rappel down the sheer coastal *pali* using flimsy clothesline. Between sneaker sets and bad knots, the pounders are often at a disadvantage.

A Hawaiian '*opihi* can grow relatively fast, about an inch in diameter per year. It is rumored that in between the bomb craters of the isolated Kaho'olawe you can still find saucer-sized beauties. These disparities in sizes lead one to the opinion that the commercial harvest in Hawai'i of '*opihi* should be outlawed to protect this resource.

In California, I've found that limpets prefer the smooth rocks of jetties and breakwaters. That's where I get mine, without the guilt of denuding the tide pools. Of the California limpets, the taste of the sweet yellow-footed owl limpet (Lottia gigantea) prevails over the blander keyhole limpet and hinged shell chitons.

How can you tell if the limpet at hand is edible? Just like the seaweeds (or limu in Hawai'i), you just try a bit. None of them will kill you, but some are definitely better than others. It once took all day to get the bitter taste of a Chilean limpet out of my mouth. The flavor is very much affected by what the limpets have been feeding upon. Sometimes I won't eat the '*ōkole*, or stomach, if it's bitter.

OPPOSITE: *Tools of the* 'opihi *pickers: reef walkers, a small net bag, and dakine table knife. "You hold the net bag open with your teeth, freeing the hands for hanging on and manipulating the pry knife." Moloka'i, Hawai'i.* Yvon Chouinard

281

In Hawai'i, any good *lū'au* must include *'opihi*. Thus, the good host is confronted with a dilemma: face the risk of "getting deeper," or suffer open-wallet surgery at a fish market like Tamashiro's on O'ahu. Hardly anyone I know eats limpets in California other than myself. When I look at the photograph of Jeff Clark spread-eagled on the rocks at Maverick's, I salivate thinking about all those sweet mussels, limpets, and gooseneck barnacles that he is clutching for dear life. …

"'Opihi man in the sun,
'Opihi man grab your bag and run.
'Opihi man another swell's comin' your way,
'Opihi man another swell's comin' your way."

RECIPES:

1. Pry out the foot, rinse off any sand, and pop into your mouth, *'ōkole* and all. A drop of "salsa brava," a squirt of lemon, and a bottle of Bohemia is a Baja classic.

2. Place the rinsed-off meat into a dish and sprinkle on Hawaiian salt, adding half of a tomato, some olive oil, lemon juice, garlic, fresh ginger, *limu*, and a squirt of Tabasco. The best *limu* would be *manauea*, *'aki 'aki*, or *huluhulu waena*. Eat with poi. "Ho, broke da mouth!"

3. Place the limpet, shell down, on a barbeque grill and dab on a mixture of butter, minced garlic, chopped parsley, and shoyu (soy sauce). Or use the same ingredients and sauté in a pan for a few minutes.

Lyrics from "'Opihi Man," Ka'au Crater Boys, Roy Sakuna Productions.

OPPOSITE: The 'Opihi Pickers. Illustration by Dietrich Varez

Sucker Cakes

First published in The Drake, *Winter 2016*

I'm slunk down in the car seat at the Kmart parking lot, trying to avoid being seen. Jackson is a small town and it would not be good for me to be recognized. My wife, Malinda, comes out of the store with a brown paper bag with five flavors of PowerBait: crawfish, sherbet, marshmallow, Captain America, and cheese.

Have you looked at the price of fish lately? Twenty-three dollars for halibut, king salmon at thirty-five. Even toxic farmed salmon is more than twelve dollars a pound. Whack and eat that gorgeous cutthroat? No way. The options for fish eaters are getting fewer these days and the prices—like with rhino horn—are reflecting their scarcity.

What if I said there's a fish, free for the taking, that tastes as good as any freshwater fish—including walleye? And certainly a hell of a lot better than tilapia and largemouth bass.

I've been eating whitefish for years, but always drew the line at suckers, thinking like most rednecks that they are ugly, dirty, garbage eaters—and they eat trout eggs as well. But one day, with a bunch of whitefish, I caught a Utah sucker. Malinda convinced me to try eating it. After smoking the fish, I hung them all out to dry on the wood pile. A pine marten snuck in and stole the sucker, leaving the whitefish. "I told you those suckers have got to be tasty," she said.

Looking up suckers on the internet, there are all kinds of scientific papers describing every aspect of the eighty species of suckers in North America. Not one mentioned if they are edible or not.

One early summer day at Jackson Reservoir while fishing for lake trout, I caught a couple of suckers on streamers. I cooked them up in the broiler with

A suckerfish. Linda Schwerzler/Alamy

butter and garlic and they were delicious albeit boney. I remembered how they deal with that in the Bahamas, Hawai'i, and Tahiti, and I was ready for another go.

Problem is, when you actively target them, they aren't so easy to catch. If they are actively feeding it's no problem: drift any nymph by and you've got 'em. When you see a bunch of them sitting on the bottom not moving, it is a different matter—they won't take anything. Ergo the PowerBait. I went to my favorite spot on the Snake and smeared some on a nymph—I didn't have any bait-holder hooks. Cast after cast. Change flavors. No luck. *What the hell?* Do I have to sneak over to Stone Drugs for night crawlers? Basically, when they are sleeping it's hopeless.

Like with the elusive California corbina and the finicky permit, I'm sure someone has dialed in catching suckers. If so, let me know, I'll try anything.

SUCKER CAKES

You need to debone the fish. First fillet the fish then scrape the meat away from the bones with a small teaspoon. In the Bahamas, they let the bonefish soften a bit in the sun, which makes scraping easier. The bones along the lateral line are particularly fine but try to get them all.

1 to 1½ cups of grated sucker, whitefish, or *o'io* (bonefish)
2–3 eggs
3 cloves garlic
1 large stalk celery
1 small bok choy or other green leafy vegetable
½ red pepper
4 green scallions
½ cup panko
1 small handful parsley
2 Tbsp. Thai fish sauce
Creole seasoning to taste
Oil for frying

1. Mince all the vegetables.
2. Mix all the veggies, panko, and fish together.
3. Check the seasoning, then add the eggs and mix together.
4. Form into 3- to 4-inch diameter patties about ½ to ¾ inches thick.
5. Heat oil in frying pan and fry as you would a hamburger. Turn over when first side is brown.

Serves 4 to 5.

Serve as you would crab cakes, adding your favorite sauce or lemon juice on top. I like a classic Italian green sauce.

OPPOSITE: *Sucker cakes on a hot griddle.* Amy Kumler

Seaweed Salad

First published in The Surfers Journal, *Volume Three, Number One, Spring 1994*

People have asked me what have I gotten out of a lifetime of surfing, climbing, fly fishing, and running rivers. I tell them I've gained a sense of place. After experiencing a hundred bivouacs on mountainsides all over the world and trying to experience a river's flow the way a fish would, I feel a certain sense of comfort in these environments. So does the waterman feel at home at the littoral edge who works with the ebb and flow of the tides, swell directions, interval and seasonal changes in fish habitat, and … pollution.

The California coastline is my home because I can survive there. I feel no small sense of confidence knowing in an hour's time I can gather enough periwinkles, limpets, mussels, and seaweed to feed my family. To a lesser extent, I can also keep from starving in a mountain environment, but I've yet to come to grips with the desert.

There are hundreds of edible seaweeds on the west coast of North America, but you wouldn't know it by reading the 752-page *Marine Algae of the Monterey Peninsula*. It doesn't bother to state the edibility. For that, it is better to have a Japanese or Korean friend who will assure you that they are all edible, but some are definitely better than others.

I particularly enjoy the *Gelidium* and *Cystoseira*, or *matsu-mo* in Japanese, which translates to "pine needle seaweed." They occur in shallow waters from Oregon to Baja. You can think of seaweed as lettuce; the younger it is the better. My favorite gathering place for the *matsu-mo* is in Ventura and Santa Barbara Counties around the reef and point breaks. I only pick it during the months of April, May, and June when it is young and succulent. How do you know if you have the right seaweed? Go ahead and experiment; this isn't like mushroom hunting.

A seaweed salad prepared by Patagonia chef Tracy On. Tim Davis

THE RECIPE

Strip off the younger, tan-colored branches from the main stem. The darker, older blackish/brown parts are not so tender and have a strong flavor. Rinse well in fresh seawater. Put in a pot of boiling water for five minutes. Take out and cool in refrigerator.

You can now use the seaweed in any number of ways, but I like it best as a salad. I usually dice up some tomatoes, sliced green onions and make a ponzu dressing using rice wine vinegar, soy sauce, lemon juice, and Cavender's Greek seasoning.

One plea: please don't all of you go out and strip the tide pools bare. The Earth can't accommodate all five-and-a-half billion of us going back to hunting and gathering (or eating beef). Gather only enough to show your kids where food really comes from. Make it a ritual—the goal is not to fill the stomach, but the soul.

Eat da Bait!

First published in The Surfers Journal, *Volume Nineteen, Number Six, December/January 2010–2011*

Captain Jacques Cousteau once predicted that not too long from now we'll still be eating fish "products" but no longer sitting down to a meal of whole fish, or of fish filets or steaks. The oceanographer Silvia Earle told me she no longer eats fish at all because they are all endangered. The Blue Ocean Institute, backing her up, reports that 90 percent of the world's commercially caught fish species will be wiped out by 2048.

And if you can still find big hunks of fish that fill up your dinner plate you may not be able to afford it. When I was a kid, fish was the cheapest item on a restaurant menu. Now it's often listed at "market price." The last time I checked at the seafood counter in Santa Barbara, local halibut was twenty-four dollars per pound and wild Chinook salmon, thirty-three dollars. That's ten gallons of gas or ten Big Macs—or twenty if there's a two-fer sale.

The cost of eating high on the seafood chain also includes ingesting all the accumulated toxins that we dump into the ocean—mercury, dioxins, hormones, and all the other chemicals and pharmaceuticals that pass through us. The larger the fish, the more concentrated the contaminants. You shouldn't eat meals of longer-lived fish like Alaskan halibut or swordfish more than twice a month. And eating two meals of bluefin tuna in less than twenty-four hours

OPPOSITE: *Fletcher Chouinard about a half mile out on the far side of the kelp beds going for baitfish. Central Coast, California.* Tim Davis

can more than double the amount of mercury in an adult's bloodstream. I have a friend who decided to go on a healthy diet and only eat fish and vegetables three meals a day. After a month, his eyebrows fell out and he lost hunks of hair from his head. The level of mercury in his body was nineteen points

---

Bottom line: You don't have to stop eating
fish, just switch to the little guys.

---

per million. The normal concentration of mercury in human blood is less than .01 points per million.

If you buy cheap, farmed Atlantic salmon from Costco you'll also ingest antibiotics, fungicides, and high levels of carcinogens, including dioxins, polychlorinated biphenyls (PCBs), and chlorinated pesticides. The Pew Foundation recommends eating farmed salmon no more than once a month; pregnant women should abstain. Costco scallops as well as shrimp are often soaked in sodium tripolyphosphate, a suspected neurotoxin, to keep them from drying out. Sushi-grade tuna is often treated with carbon monoxide to prevent it from turning brown.

So much for the fish we do eat. What about the fish we don't? Thousands of sardines and anchovies caught each year are ground up into fishmeal to feed farmed fish, pets, chickens, pigs, and cows. It takes three to six pounds of edible fish to grow a pound of farmed salmon and seven pounds to grow a pound of farmed bluefin tuna. Yet we could double or triple the available protein in the oceans by eating anchovies, mullet, smelt, herring, sardines, squid, and other small species. Not only would we save money, feed more people, support local small-scale fisherman, and delay the extirpation of the large noble fish, but we would be healthier for it. Baitfish eat plankton and algae that are fed by the endless energy from the sun. The algae eaters, especially, have the highest levels of omega-3 fatty acids, the good stuff that cleans your arteries and provides antioxidants to keep your heart healthy and prevent cancer.

If you haven't tried fresh grilled sardines or anchovies, you are missing out on a great treat that's prized all along the coasts of France, Spain, Portugal, and Italy. Sardines can be simply coated with salt and grilled. Fresh grilled anchovies with lemon and salt are my favorite. No scaling, no boning required.

In 1968, I spent a month surfing in San Blas, Mexico, living on fifty cents a day. The high point was always breakfast, which consisted of tropical fruit, hot rolls from the bakery, and a hot smoked mullet from a local Indian who lived near the bridge this side of Matanchén Bay.

The bad news is you are not going to find these types of fish at your local Safeway. The good news is you can go down to the local bait house or live bait barge and get two scoops of sardines or anchovies for about ten bucks. Or as a surfer/kayaker, you can catch them yourself. What? You call yourself a waterman and you don't fish? Grab your longboard or SUP (finally a valid use for your super tanker) and paddle out to the kelp beds where the birds are working. Use a small spinning rod with a train of tiny Sabiki hooks, which come five or six to a rig. Attach a sinker and pitch it out. Jig up and down until all five hooks are loaded.

Mullet can be caught in estuaries by chumming with balls of Wonder bread, followed by casting a simple fly—a bare hook impaled with a bit of cotton fluff. In the mid-Pacific, I once caught the ultimate algae-eating milkfish with a floating fly that looks like frisée lettuce.

Bottom line: You don't have to stop eating fish, just switch to the little guys.

Bad Day at Flat Rock

First published in Patagonia: Notes from the Field, *Nora Gallagher (ed), Chronicle Books, 1999*

Surfers still talk about the winter of 1969 as having the best surf of the century in California. I was renting a beach cabin in the cove at Mondos and creating and forging climbers' equipment out of the old boiler room of the Hobson/Smith Packing Company.

Bob McTavish, the Australian surfer, was wintering in a cabin up the point, and he and I spent a lot of time surfing together at the cobblestone point breaks of Ventura and Santa Barbara. Conditions there were ideal for perfecting his revolutionary wide, deep-V shortboards.

He mentioned one day that he wouldn't mind trying a bit of climbing, even though he admitted to not liking heights very much. In those days, there were so few climbers that few climbs in Southern California had seen first ascents: Whenever we went climbing, we did new routes. For his introduction to rock climbing, we knocked off a fine first ascent at Sespe, which is now called McTavish. The climb turned out to be more difficult than I had expected— especially the part going over the overhang and the vertical wall above. Bob remembers the day as a horrifying adventure, and he's never climbed again. I've always felt a bit guilty about the whole affair.

Twenty-four years later I'm at Bob's shop in Byron Bay in Queensland, and we two gray hairs are talking about having a surf together for old times' sake, even though we both know that the conditions are Victory at Sea, with

OPPOSITE: *The surf industry traditionally slowed down during the winter months on the north coast of New South Wales, so Bob McTavish made a few George Greenough–inspired kneeboard spoons to help supplement his income. Lennox Head, Australia. 1976.* Peter Green

howling onshore wind and big wind waves. Bob knows a spot next to Flat Rock that might be more protected. On the way there, he casually mentions that he has surfed this place fifty or eighty times and about 50 percent of the time he's seen a huge tiger shark that lives there, but "Don't worry mate, he's never bothered anyone yet."

Flat Rock is a reef that extends from shore and drops off suddenly in deeper water. With the waves so close together, the only way to get out is to go off the end of the reef, but with the medium high tide, the rock is awash with white water from the waves crashing over the end. Bob waits for a lull, then runs and wades and jumps off the end and just barely paddles over the next set, leaving me on the rock, gripping my surfboard with both arms to keep it from blowing away. Did I mention I'd forgotten my wetsuit, so all I had for protection was a rash guard?

I couldn't just chicken out, so off I go and near the end of the reef, my right leg drops into a hole up to my crotch and gets stuck. Right away I remember the warnings I've heard about the blue-ringed octopi that live in these holes. One bite and you have mere seconds to live. I manage to get unstuck and I run back before the next wave crashes over. Now I'm really pumped, but I finally get outside and it's horrible. Just massive wind waves with no form sucking out over huge rock boils. As the adrenaline wears off I become aware that blood is pouring out of my leg and then my mind flashes on the shark. *Thanks, Bob,* I think. *We're even.*

OPPOSITE: *Bob McTavish on his V-bottom board at Honolua Bay in 1967. Maui, Hawai'i.*
John Witzig

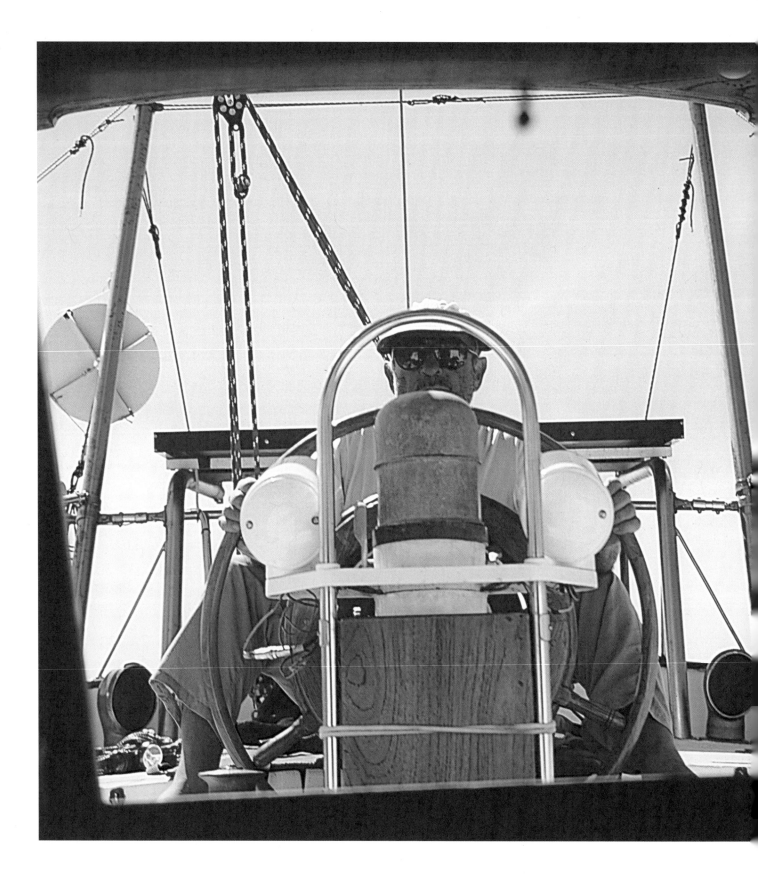

Further Adventures with the Atoll Man: A Month at Sea and on Land

First published in The Surfers Journal, *Volume 10, Number 2, Spring 2001*

When I was a young man I was a student of the South Pacific. I read every book written on the subject. I had Gauguin prints on the walls of my blacksmith shop in my parents' backyard in Burbank. Later, I imagined myself selling my company and disappearing into the Pacific on a sailboat with my fly rod and surfboard looking for the perfect surf break and bonefish flat. I even had a name picked out for the boat: *Close to the Bone*.

Thirty years ago, I was flying back from a climbing trip in New Zealand and I had planned to stop over in Tahiti. As we circled the Papeete airport I could already smell the Tiaré flowers from a thousand feet up. It was two in the morning when we landed and the airport was quiet except for a few women sweeping and cleaning. They were of Asian, French, and Polynesian mixed blood with exotic eyes and smooth brown skin. They were fat and they were beautiful. The soft air, the perfume smells, the wide friendly smiles; I knew I wasn't ready for this. I had recently married and was anxious to get home. If I stayed, I knew I'd go "troppo." It would be the end of my productive years, and I had plenty more dragons to slay. I got right back on a plane to Los Angeles.

OPPOSITE: *The ancient mariner, somewhere in the Pacific Ocean.* Yvon Chouinard Collection

Since then, I've been on lots of surfing and fishing trips to tropical areas including one to the Society Islands where, at age fifty-one, I rode the best wave of my life: a deep stand-up tube at Temae on Moorea. But on all these trips, there were jet flights and deadlines and no opportunities to cut loose and seize opportunities as they came.

Last July I received a phone call from Trevor Mullen, manager of the Patagonia store in Santa Monica, asking if I knew anything about Fanning Island. "Are you kidding?" I said, "I've been trying to get there ever since I was on Christmas Island with Rell in 1993." Chuck Corbett had told us about this perfect left at the lagoon entrance on Fanning. Then in 1994, I received a map from my friend Terry Baird, who had sailed there and said it was a bonefish paradise. The trouble is there's no way to get there except by private boat. Corbett's been living there for seven years, going out of his mind because he has no one to share the waves with. "Why are you asking?" I said.

"My friend and I are sailing there on his boat. He's going to drop me off at Christmas Island and I'll fly home. He's going on to Tahiti."

"No way," I said. "Ask him if I can come. I'll pay for the food. I'll cook." I suggested we stop off at Palmyra on the way. The Nature Conservancy was buying the island and I could get permission to stop over for some great bone-fishing and maybe some surf.

Ten days before our sail date, I got another call from my friend Marilyn Links on O'ahu, who was working for the Conservancy's Palmyra project. She said there was a plane going down on Monday with lots of space available. Did I want to go down early and hang out, fishing and diving for a couple of weeks, and wait for the boys to pick me up?

"I'd love to," I said, "but this time I want to grind it out all the way. I'm not going to approach paradise from the window of a Gulfstream. I want to see these atolls from low down on the horizon."

July 19: Ala Wai Yacht Harbor. Trevor and I go on the *Tahitian Moon*, a thirty-eight-foot northeast ketch. Twenty-six-year-old Luke Tansil, owner and captain, and Dan Doolan, twenty-two, welcome us aboard. The boat looks

OPPOSITE: *The* Tahitian Moon *at anchor at Fanning Island, Line Islands.* Yvon Chouinard Collection

good, but what do I know? I've only had a Red Cross dinghy sailing course about twenty years ago. I go downstairs and check out their library: Melville, Slocum, Moitessier, T.E. Lawrence, Theroux, Henry Miller. This is good. I look into the cupboards and see cases and cases of Budweiser. Not so good.

———

How far can the boat tilt over before it fills completely?

———

There are 300 CDs, 40 videos. That's good. But there is no sextant, the compass has never been swung, and everything on the boat is electronic. That's not good at all. I hate electricity; never trusted it. A technician is installing even more electronics—a depth gauge and electronic self-steering to go with the digital compass.

Trevor and I go off and shop at Safeway. We buy a thousand dollars worth of wine, wasabi, canned chili, four kinds of hot sauce, brown rice, and fruit. We drive back slowly over several speed bumps, or is it the car's flat springs?

I find an old hippie masseuse in Waikiki and get a "fifty/fifty": a fifty-dollar massage for my fifty-year-old shoulder (actually sixty-one).

July 20: We fill up the boat with diesel, more beer, and head out of the harbor. Surf at Ala Moana Bowls is one to two feet. After only an hour, a mahi mahi takes the lure and provides us with enough fish to get to Palmyra. Dinner is potatoes, onions, tomatoes, and mahi roe scramble. Doing five-and-a-half knots with sails and motor. There's a tropical storm reported at Palmyra, but it's moving west at fifteen knots. She's a slow boat, but seems solid.

July 21: Bad sleep. Everyone except Luke is seasick. Mahi, wine, and veggies for dinner, but after cooking my appetite is gone. Two light meals a day from now on. The seas are building.

July 22: Twenty-five to thirty-knot winds with ten-foot seas out of the east. We are on one tack from 160 to 185 degrees. It takes Luke and Dan (who has never sailed before) twenty minutes to reef the mainsail. This is really not good.

July 23: Scary night. Twelve-foot seas. I just don't know the limits of sailing. How far can the boat tilt over before it fills completely? How do you know when there's too much sail? We double-reef the stay sail. Also use the engine to keep the boat stable in the confused seas. Alternating cold and warm squalls pass by, luckily to the north and south of us. Halfway to Palmyra at 6 pm.

July 24: Cloudy and humid. We are now out of the Hawaiian subtropics and into full-on tropics. Trevor and I do the 12-to-4 am watch. At seven knots, we're really moving. Perfect sailing. The moon comes up at 1 am. Good thing we don't have to fool with the sails much. There's not much experience on this boat. Luke has a background in trading stocks, like his father, but hated it and cashed out. He bought this old boat, and has been refurbishing it for the last year. Dan, the first mate, is taking a year off from school. Their goal for this trip is to discover adventure, women, and themselves, not necessarily in that order.

July 26: Fair weather, good winds, no squalls. Lots more birds in sight. Petrels and shearwaters preying on small flying fish. I wonder, *What do those birds do at night? Fly about aimlessly? Sleep in flight? Sit on the water like shark bait?*

We haven't seen a ship or plane go by. I realize this is the real wilderness. The most remote spot in the United States outside of Alaska is only twenty-five miles from a road or civilization. Here, we have nothing for at least 400 miles. Our radios have a range of only twenty miles. Even our Grundig (made in China) shortwave radio gets only Chinese stations.

July 27: Starting to see boobies; we must be close. The farthest away you can see an atoll with coconut palms is ten to twelve miles. Finally, we sight Palmyra. A school of dolphins greets us. I wish we could ask them how to get into the lagoon. The charts say the entrance is a narrow, dredged channel with coral heads and breaking waves all around it. We go too far to the northeast until I see boils around us. Just in time, we turn and someone on the island comes on the radio and says he better come out and show us in. We aren't too good at reading charts yet.

Palmyra is a privately owned atoll with 700 acres of land encircling a 16,000-acre lagoon. It supports three times as many coral species as Hawai'i does and, because the equatorial currents here add nutrients from a large seabird population and heavy rainfall, Palmyra has an incredibly high level of natural productivity in its reef and lagoon ecosystems.

The Conservancy staff gives us a tour of the Palmyra Yacht Club, a funky tin building with names and messages from all the visiting boats since 1970 inscribed on the walls. I noticed a lot of inscriptions from *Cous Cous*, the boat of Roger, the eccentric French caretaker who lived here for twenty years. He

is gone now but left his two dogs, who have learned to work the flats for reef sharks. They herd the sharks up onto the beach to kill and eat them.

We are anchored next to a small double-ender ketch owned by a middle-aged, felon-looking character from Maui. He has a crew of two sassy-looking girls. They say they are on their way to American Samoa, the pit of the South Pacific. Later I hear he has no passport, so that is the only place he can go. It took them fourteen days to sail from Hawai'i because of bad winds and not enough diesel. When the *Tahitian Moon* boys tell the girls they are on their way to Tahiti, I can see their pupils widen. No doubt in my mind that they would jump ship in a minute. The boys are beside themselves at the thought. "Listen," I say, "if you want them to come along just go over there and whisper softly in their ears, 'We've got plenty of diesel.'"

The boys go over with a couple of cold six-packs and end up drinking most of it themselves and never get up the nerve to close the deal.

July 28: Nick and John from the Conservancy take us around in their new flats boat. The sea life is amazing with huge turtles, manta rays, spotted bat rays, and black tip and white tip sharks everywhere. Three kinds of trevally—bluefin (pāpio), striped, and giant ulua—are busting bait everywhere. There are big milkfish in the back of the flats where the water is hot. The Conservancy guys are just learning to fly fish and I see them casting in frustration to the milkfish not knowing they are algae eaters and won't take flies.

Albula vulpes is, to those who know it, perhaps the most beautiful fish in the ocean. Fishing for bonefish is done on the sandy flats of lagoons in one to two feet of water. You walk around searching and don't cast until you see a fish. It doesn't take patience; it requires intense concentration to see these "ghosts of the flats." It's more like hunting than fishing. A four-pound bonefish will pounce on a tiny fly that looks like a shrimp and rip 400 feet of line in just a few seconds.

We follow the bonefish from the incoming tide at the lagoon entrance in the morning to the far east flats in the afternoon. The best fishing is where the bottom is somewhat softer, perfect for wading. These fish don't spook; I've never seen such naïve fish. Some cruise right by my feet, too close to cast to. Luke, on his first time bonefishing, lands fourteen fish.

OPPOSITE: *Atoll Man with prey. Fanning Island.* Yvon Chouinard Collection

We motor out of the lagoon at 6 pm, anxious to get to Fanning. A small, clean wave breaks outside the entrance. They say it breaks perfectly on a strong south swell. It even closes out the channel, which is twenty feet deep. We set our course at 120 degrees, next stop Fanning. There's no wind, only sea and yellowfin tuna busting bait just outside the reef. We use up some of our diesel.

July 28: The trades change to southeast this time of year and our course is right into the wind. We motor. Rain, but no squalls, all over the black skies. Horrible sleep, the boat rocks and pitches.

July 30: In the morning, we do three-plus knots with a slight headwind. We put out the trolling line hoping to get some ahi. I purposely put on a small lure hoping to catch a small one as our fridge has stopped working.

We spot Fanning at 4:30 pm and head for the pass. We sail by the wave. It's two to three feet and perfect! We anchor and go look for Chuck Corbett.

Chuck grew up in Orange County where he learned to surf at 56th Street and the Santa Ana River mouth in Newport. At sixteen, he left home with his surfboard under his arm. He headed for Hawai'i where he worked construction for five years, then went to Guam to work as a diver, traveling to all eighteen islands of the Gilbert group, and then ended up in Tarawa, the capital of Kiribati. There he saw a young girl being beaten up by some man. He fought the guy off, rescued the girl, and took her back to her parents.

They thanked him and said, "Well, what are you going to do with her? You've saved her; now she's yours."

He looked over at the pretty seventeen-year-old girl and said, "I guess I'll marry her."

Over the years, he organized the Line Islanders to dive for sea cucumbers. He would dry and smoke them and the island freighters would come by and pack them up and sell them to the Chinese. At the peak of his business, he was traveling to Shanghai and grossing half a million a year. He had over twenty boards stashed away on islands like Christmas and Canton, but the downside was that he would sometimes get stuck for three to five months waiting for the freighters, with no one to share the waves, living in utter social isolation. He finally found his perfect left point at Fanning, but his wife and now two young daughters wanted to stay on Tarawa. So, they broke up and Chuck gave up the cucumber business. He was burned out on the travel anyway.

In1994 I received a letter from him. "Last week I got my first ever hundred-yard dry tube ride on Dave's Stub Vector 7'2". It's amazing after

These children will be married in three to five years. Fanning Island. Yvon Chouinard Collection

twenty-seven years of barrels to go out and get a best ever."

We anchor in the lagoon and ask around for Chuck. People point here and there and I realize no one speaks English. We take a dinghy over to his "home," a homemade ugly plywood catamaran moored against a partially sunken barge. Chuck finally shows up in a decrepit skiff with three local divers. The bottom of the skiff is loaded with five or six large octopi, assorted reef fish, and a five-foot moray.

He greets me like George Greenough used to, which is to act like it hasn't been years since we've seen each other, but as if we were just chatting a few minutes ago.

Tabata shows up in his canoe with two eight-foot-long sailfish that took at the same time. He landed both by himself on handlines. He cuts off a big piece of fatty belly and tosses it to us. I think I'm going to like this place.

July 31: We clear customs and immigration. No problem here. The official is one of Chuck's diving friends.

The surf is three to four feet with occasional five-foot faces. Because of its proximity to the lagoon entrance, you have to surf the incoming or high tide, otherwise the current is too strong. We paddle out 150 feet. The ride parallels the shore like Rifle Range on Kaua'i. You kick out twenty feet from the shore and walk back up.

Some waves are easily makeable, especially the larger ones; others pull down-the-line and are freight trains. I'm forced to go into my backside survival mode: paddle straight down the face and, before standing, turn the board down-the-line and take an extra stroke, then go right into a pig dog stance, pulling my nose into the curl so I'm tight in the wave and don't get hit by the lip. If I make the initial section, then I can stand for the rest of the wave. Chuck has it wired but he's broken all his shortboards, so I let him use my 7'2" five-fin rocket sled. He surfs off his back foot and at first tries to ride it like a thruster, but after a day or so he adjusts and starts flying. With his long hair flying back, he looks like he is right out of *Free Ride*.

Dan and Luke are the struggling beginners, and this is not a beginner's wave. Trevor, who surfs Santa Monica Bay, is wave hogging until I call him on it and introduce him to the concept of taking turns. Here in the tropics, we all have to slow down except on the waves.

This wave, Chuck's Corner, works best on south swells from March to mid-July when the trade winds are out of the east. Later, the winds shift to southeast, and you can get a slight side bump, but we never saw anything except perfection. It also works during El Niño's west swell years. After seven years of surfing alone, Chuck admits he doesn't go out until it's at least over-head. He's totally excited about being able to share his wave.

We go fishing midday and surf the incoming tide again in the afternoon.

August 3: I have Terry Baird's 1994 map showing all the good fishing flats. At that time, there were only seventy families living on Fanning. Now there are nearly 2,000 souls, most of them dumped here from the overpopulated and polluted island of Tarawa. They came over with fishing nets and not much else. It's the continuing history of the Pacific.

Fanning has five villages made up primarily of family groups. They have fished out the waters near their villages so they go farther out. We watched one canoe carrying two locals handlining, with sandworms for bait. They caught forty fat bonefish. The fish are dried and sold on Tarawa for two cents each. It's nearly the only cash economy on the island.

To find bonefish, Chuck and I have to go out in his skiff to the far west of the lagoon, which is a taboo area for collecting bird eggs or killing fish. We

———

No doctor on the island; there's a nurse "who will hold your hand while you die."

———

found bonefish, but also three illegal fishing camps using gill nets.

We are invited to a party in the communal house (*maneaba*) of Chuck's new wife's village. The whole village is out and everyone brings potluck. They serve us heaps of rice, breadfruit, squash, bonefish, and manta shrimp. They do a semitraditional half-hula, half-Tahitian dance to the blare of a big boom box. Each of us gives a short speech and some important village people welcome us, wish us a good time on the island, and ask, "By the way, do you have any videos?"

August 4: The swell died and Chuck and I go off fishing in the mornings. The boys sleep in. Dishes go undone. No maintenance on the boat. The living area must be a giant Petri dish of organisms. About as much discipline as you'd expect from young guys on their first time in the tropics.

We dive in the pass and can't believe the variety of big fish, giant wrasses that are not fished here because of ciguatera poisoning: ulua, pāpio everywhere, but very wary of the speargun. We have octopus and rice for dinner. There's no soil on the island, so no farming. The store only sells palm oil, rice, and corned beef. Coconut in every meal. I remember to take my cholesterol pills. No doctor on the island; there's a nurse "who will hold your hand while you die." Break a leg and you wait three to five months for the supply boat to take you out.

We meet Bruno, a fiftyish Frenchman who has been living on Fanning for ten years. He is a dead ringer for the solo sailor Bernard Moitessier. In fact, they were friends. Bruno's skin is like cracked leather, what my dermatologist would call "a colossal amount of sun damage."

Sailing alone eleven years ago, Bruno ended up at Washington Island fifty miles north of here. There he contracted ciguatera from eating reef fish and got so sick he thought he was going to die unless he got medical help. He sailed off in his thirty-foot boat for Tahiti 1,200 miles away. In his delirium, he sailed around in circles and shipwrecked back on Washington Island three days later. He survived and eventually found a fourteen-year-old girl to marry, and ended up on Fanning where they are raising a beautiful nine-year-old daughter. He occasionally sails back to Tahiti and works a while to make enough money to live a few more years on Fanning.

Every morning I see Bruno row out to an old wreck and shoot enough fish for *poisson cru* for lunch and fried fish for supper. He works on building a house of coral and cement, tends a small garden, has a glass of "toddy" and a midday smoke. His wife is lively and strong. His child speaks four languages, Bruno's shit is tight.

Chuck, on the other hand, has paid dearly for having surf breaks all to himself. He's dead broke. His bank records on Christmas Island show him being overdrawn by $11,000. That's because someone cleaned out his account. He gave up a US passport to become a Kiribati citizen, but the official on Christmas Island won't approve his application because she is the best friend of his first wife who he thinks has divorced him. He was doing shark fins for income but fished them out. His surfboards are all broken and he can't afford fuel for his skiff. He lives on his boat, but I noticed that his dog and his wife, Temoaiti, are mostly living in the village. In a Micronesian society, you're never really accepted into a village unless directly related to a villager and if you're not part of the village, you're less than tolerated. As Chuck says, "Village life is playing cards, smoking, sleeping, and gossiping."

August 5: A new swell arrives with four- to eight-foot faces. The larger waves are perfection. We surf until the low tide boils freak us out and don't go out again until evening.

We motor across the lagoon to the north side, and Chuck shows us where there is a perfect right, "just like Sunset," and two more lefts during the winter season. It looked like a perfect setup: a reef-cut made while laying the old trans-Pacific cable, a sand bottom, and offshore winds.

OPPOSITE: *Yvon "pig dogging" the left at Fanning Island.* Yvon Chouinard Collection

August 6: We have to leave Fanning in order to make the once-weekly plane from Christmas Island to Hawai'i. We plan on three days to do the 150 miles. The direction is straight into the trades, and we have a two-knot westerly current to contend with. Bruno tells us stories of boats trying for two weeks to get to Christmas at this time of year, then turning back to Fanning when they run out of food and water. Luke says we have lots of fuel, so no worries.

August 9: A tough evening. Squalls blasting us. Headwinds. We use the motor and, surprisingly, run out of fuel in the morning. Turns out the captain thought the tanks held a hundred gallons—they hold only sixty.

It's looking grim for getting to that Wednesday flight in time. In fact, I'm worried about making it at all. There is no option but back to Fanning. We're having to endlessly tack. We are making only one knot toward Christmas. Then, sure enough, we lose electricity. God knows why. With no electricity, we lose our digital compass, the self-steering, the freshwater pump. The one-burner stove runs out of propane. The compass was never swung, so it is off between three and twenty degrees depending on our heading. Trevor's reef cuts on his foot are infected. He is feverish, glands are swollen, and one wound looks a lot like the staph volcanoes one sees on the feral Aussies of Desert Island in Indo. We break open capsules of dicloxacillin and put the powder directly on the wound. Even my new water-resistant Timex packs it in. It's a worried boat.

I've been reading one modern sailing book after another, all with the same themes. Wife or girlfriend leaves, guy with little sailing experience takes to the sea to discover himself. I wonder what I am doing here. I have a loving wife and family. I didn't sign up for an adventure. I was just following my curiosity because that's what makes me happy.

At some point, Trevor and I admit we are not catching that plane and suddenly we relax and the mood changes on the boat. Screw it all. What's the hurry? A school of tuna slides under the boat with two pelagic white tip sharks trailing. One bumps the boat hard, another does a 720 in the air. We are sailing so slowly we can't even troll.

August 10: The wind picks up and turns more to our port beam. The genoa fills in. I even enjoy my 2-to-6 am watch steering by the stars. The Southern Cross is low on the horizon and the only other stars and constellations I know—Orion's Belt, Pleiades, the Big Dipper, and the North Star—are not much help. I just pick any old star that's in the general direction we want to go and head for it until a cloud comes by, then I pick another.

Having trimmed surfboards for forty-five years is of great help. Sails, keels, and rudders are just like rails and skegs. When the sails are properly trimmed, the boat steers itself. You can feel the sideways thrust of the keel and rudder translating into forward motion, like projecting out of a good bottom turn. I'm even starting to understand the synergistic relationship between the jib and mainsail and how it is like a Bonzer five-fin setup.

At 11 pm we make one last tack, and a school of 200 spinner porpoises guides us into the anchorage just off the Catholic church in London. In the morning, we row onto the beach because the outboard has crapped out.

August 21: I spend the days bonefishing while the boys repair the boat. The day before we are to catch the plane to Hawai'i, I get a call from Marilyn who asks if I want a ride back to Palmyra. There's a plane coming from Hawai'i and they could pick me up. I could spend five or six days on Palmyra fishing and surfing and then fly back to Hawai'i.

I wish the boys good luck and leave them with a little Zen message: "Forget about getting yourselves to Tahiti: focus on getting the boat there."

Epilogue

When I returned to Palmyra, I surfed the reef pass on a decent south swell. The Conservancy guys said the two sassy girls were kicking themselves for not getting up the nerve to ask for a ride from the boys.

The boys made it to Tahiti, but only after barely surviving a sixty-knot gale and running out of fuel. They sent a photo of themselves lounging on the deck with some brown-skinned local girls. Chuck left Fanning for Tarawa on the freighter two days after us—to "get his life in order." The last message I got said, "I am still stuck on Tarawa, but doing OK, and looking to get back to Fanning. I promise My Wizard I will never leave Fanning again. What a dream place."

NEXT SPREAD: *Why people dream of escaping to the South Seas. Kiribati.* Yvon Chouinard Collection

Foreword to *No Bad Waves*

First published in No Bad Waves *by Mickey Muñoz, Patagonia Books, 2011*

In 1957, six young men made surfing history by being the first to ride the giant waves at Waimea on the North Shore of Oʻahu. One of them, Pat Curren, went on to father the World Champion, Tom Curren. Another of them was Greg 'Da Bull' Noll. People who were there can't remember whether Harry Church or Greg Noll caught the first wave, but without doubt, a young kid from California by the name of Mickey Muñoz caught the second wave.

Mickey does not look like he's a big-wave rider. He's my size—only five feet four inches tall and about 130 pounds. Since then, Mickey has become one of the greatest all-around water sportsmen in history. He is an excellent skin diver, fisherman, and multihull boat sailor. He also skis and snowboards. Mickey surfs every day there is swell and makes his living shaping some of the best surfboards in the world.

Like me, Mickey believes in never putting more than 75 percent into any endeavor. He would rather become proficient at a multitude of sports than become an expert at one.

For a while in my climbing career, I specialized at climbing only cracks; then I climbed only big walls; then I specialized in ice climbing and, eventually, Himalayan peaks. When I felt satisfied with my abilities, I would move on to another aspect of the sport or maybe even into another sport altogether. Mickey takes the same approach, but he has been involved in surfing since

OPPOSITE: *"The Quasimodo," a stance that Mickey Muñoz made famous. Arroyo Sequit, California. 1959.* John Severson

before the shortboard revolution, pioneered multihull design and sailing, and dabbled in everything from stunt doubling, to underwater demolition work, to designing soapbox racers, to wrestling bears in the circus.

I took a surfing trip to Indonesia with Mickey where we surfed some of the most exciting and dangerous waves either of us had ever experienced. On the last day of the trip, at Desert Point on the island of Lombok, I took off on the first wave of what turned out to be the largest set of the day. It was one of my best waves of the trip. I slid in and out of the tube twice before I finally punched out just before the curl crashed onto the reef. Bad mistake!

I tried to paddle outside before the next, and larger, waves caught me. No luck! That three-meter wave broke on my head and snapped my board into three pieces. The next wave was even bigger, and Mickey was on it! He was completely locked into the tube, racing for his life. He passed between the reef and me, and went for another seventy-five meters before kicking out.

Here are Mickey's words about that ride: "The sound of the water sucking off the reef, roaring as it sweeps down hundreds of yards of coral shelf, draws you into the eye. Time becomes meaningless, as if it was faster than light. You emerge younger, mindless, uncluttered—like a child laughing with stoke! Hooting! Hooting! Hooting! *Awhoo*!"

Today, Mickey is just as stoked as ever to surf, shape, boat, dive, or just hang out on the water.

OPPOSITE: *"The Aquatic Ape" was a contest proposed by Mickey Muñoz that would be judged for the longest wave ridden. Other rules included that the surfer build his own board out of natural materials and that the surfer couldn't wear a wetsuit. Jeffreys Bay, South Africa.* Robert Weaver

Dear Claire

A letter to my daughter as she is going off to school. Upper Dean River Camp. Unpublished, September 1994

D^{ear Claire,}

It's been raining the last two days and this morning the river is in spate and muddy. The sun is out now and if the river drops a few inches we may be able to fish this afternoon.

Tom McGuane and I have had great steelhead fishing so far, and we've landed about twenty fish between the two of us. The longest ones were males of thirty-six and thirty-seven inches—about nineteen or twenty pounds. The males come earlier into the river so they have already begun to regain their rainbow trout colors. The gill plates and their lateral lines are rosy red. These males rarely jump but are dogged in their fight.

The greatest fish though are the fresh-from-the-sea females of ten to twelve pounds. They are as bright as new dimes, with small heads and fat bodies. Some are so fresh they still have sea lice on their skin. As soon as they feel the hook, they jump and roll all over the place. They know they are carrying the eggs of their prodigy and they don't want to give up.

I'm using the flies that I tied in Moose, the best one is a Green Butt Skunk with a mohawk on top. The hooks are barbless to make it easier to release these beautiful creatures. Remember those rainbows we caught last year on the Blackwater? Well, if they went out to sea for three or four years and fed

OPPOSITE: *Yvon "spots" his daughter. San Sebatián, Spain. 1990.* Susie Graetz

A wild California steelhead. Eel River, California. Andrew Burr

on prawns and fat sardines and herring, then they would look like these big silver bullets. They would have gotten tough from swimming all over the North Pacific dodging other fish and seals and drift nets. The Dean River fish are especially strong because to enter the river they have to jump over a twenty-foot waterfall. Only the strongest steelhead and the Chinook salmon can make it over.

Fishing for these steelhead is my favorite kind of fishing. These fish are not difficult to catch but there's so few of them, it takes countless repetitive casts until you get into a hypnotic rhythm. Then you start seeing the bright fall colors and snow-capped peaks. Catching one or two of these fish a day is going to be heaven for me.

The anglers who are fanatic steelhead fishermen are different from other anglers. They are tough, eccentric, more interesting, and seem to have a far-away look in their eyes. You could write a book about any of these codgers. Just like Doug Peacock has become a subadult grizzly, so have these guys become like their totem steelhead. I really believe the fish makes the person. Just like the mountains one chooses to climb influences your personality.

A person is born with certain genetic traits and early childhood experiences will influence you, but the greatest changes come after you become deeply involved in a passionate activity. The falcon, the steelhead, the waves, your art will all be great influences. We are who we are because of what we do.

I wanted to say this to you now, Claire, because going away to school is like those steelhead smolts going out to sea. What an adventure! You've shown many times that you are capable of doing anything you want to. You learned to surf and tandem surf in just a couple of hours. You could easily become an artist or great designer. Your strong body and mind have no limitations. Ventura High School would not have been enough of a challenge.

Now is the time in your life when you should be exposed to the most opportunities and challenges you will ever have. Some, like having to take care of a horse, may not be your first choices I'm sure, but what the heck, "What doesn't kill you makes you stronger."

I miss you terribly; it will be a sad and empty house without you. That's why your mother and I plan to do some traveling and will spend a lot of busy time building the rock house at the ranch.

I thought that by writing this letter I could feel a bit closer, and I knew you would understand. I hope we can still go off on more trips together. You let me know when and where.

I love you,
Your Pop

A Miracle in Calcutta

Unpublished, 2005

Some years ago, I went on a surf trip to the remote Andaman Islands in the Indian Ocean. We surfed a few days off of North Sentinel Island. This small island of twenty-three square miles is inhabited by between 50 and 400 indigenous people who may be the most primitive people on Earth. They don't seem to be closely related to anyone else and there is no one in the world who can speak their language. They probably can't even make fire from scratch but have to keep hot embers alight in their huts between cooking fires.

There have been several shipwrecks around the island of which there were no survivors. Anytime anyone has tried to make contact, they were given an extremely hostile reception. Sometime in the 1990s some Indian special forces soldiers parachuted onto the island to try and take a census. They made no formal contact except to come away with Stone Age arrows embedded in their bulletproof vests. These people want to be left alone.

The Indian government requires you to stay at least five miles from their island, but one day we broke the rules to surf a reef close to shore. We observed a group of natives who seemed to be gathering shellfish on the beach.

Whenever I've been in close contact with very primitive people, it's been a very disturbing experience for me. I can't explain why, but it's left me questioning my very being as a human. With fewer than 400 of these Sentinelese people left, it's just a matter of time before they go extinct, taking along with them all their accumulated knowledge of how to live and survive on their little piece of our planet—without fossil fuels.

Back in Calcutta, we take a room in a cheap hotel to wait for a flight out the next day. In the morning, I look through my luggage for my passport …

Locals on the beach of North Sentinel Island, Andaman Islands. Christian Caron/Creative Commons

look all over the room … look again. Nothing. My friends leave for the airport without me.

On the way to the American Consulate, I pass child beggars with horrible wounds, open and oozing; entire families living in cardboard boxes; lepers and HIV victims laying here and there on the sidewalks waiting to die. Waiting to cross a busy street, suddenly the traffic stops to let an armless and legless man undulate his way across. An elegant woman hires a severely handicapped person to carry her small grocery bag. I watch another woman leave a carefully wrapped box of leftovers from dinner on a bench for any hungry person to take. This city of the most wretched people I've ever seen also has the most compassion of any place I've ever been.

The consulate people are nice but can't issue passports. The best they can do is give me a letter that will perhaps convince the immigration and airline people to let me go. Bribes have always worked for me in India and Pakistan but not this time. It's holiday season and all the chiefs are on vacation and the small bureaucrats are afraid to risk a bribe.

I spend the next three days pounding the pavement in 100-degree heat and 95 percent humidity going from one office to another of the Indian bureaucracy. No one will take a bribe and no one can get me out.

At one ministry office, I wait in a long line behind some Sisters of Charity nuns. They have on pure white robes and are joking and laughing among themselves. I can't believe that they would be so cheerful when their job is to administer to the most wretched of the dying lepers.

In a futile effort, I walk one more time to the American Consulate. Sweating like a roasting pig, in the same clothes I've been wearing for days, I step in a hole in the sidewalk into the open sewer. I am covered from head to toe in human shit. I just stand there, afraid to move. *That's it, I'm done in.*

I looked up at the sky and said to who or whatever, "OK, you've got me. Let's make a deal. If you get me out of here, I'll send five grand to Mother Teresa and the sisters." One more attempt at bribing.

Seeing the state I'm in, the consulate desperately wants me out of there and gives me another letter. A Ministry of Immigration guy takes twenty bucks from me and gives me a piece of paper to take to another office, and another twenty gets me another form. I rush to the airport to find there are no seats available for a month! Another twenty bucks gets someone bumped and I have a ticket for a flight in the morning! I go back to the hotel and walk into the shower, clothes and all.

The next day I don't take any chances and get there six hours early. I sit down at the gate, open my pack and all I have left to read is an *Earth First! Journal*. I open it and between an article on how to spike a tree and the "Dear Shit for Brains" column is my passport. It falls into my lap.

I get on the plane without even having to show my passport.

The moral of the story: Someone is trying to tell me that maybe I've been too focused on saving the natural world and not doing enough to alleviate the suffering of humankind.

During the terrible earthquake and tidal wave of 2004 I heard nobody was killed on North Sentinel Island because old knowledge told them you head for high ground in an earthquake.

OPPOSITE: *Vendors, pedestrians, and iconic ambassador taxis jam the street near the Sealdah railway station, Calcutta, India.* Steve Raymer/NG Image Collection

Eulogy for Bruce Hill

Terrace, British Columbia, Unpublished, 2017

Bruce was a close friend and one of the most effective conservationists in western Canada.

Many of you here have probably heard Bruce say that I was influential in how he conducted his life's work. I can tell you it was mutual—we learned from each other.

We had many good times sitting at the Hills' dinner table, eating good food and drinking great wine. We tried to eat locally, but I confess we drank globally. We were partial to the old-world wines. Particularly the old Bordeaux and Rioja with the funky, barnyard finishes. I remember one particularly stinky red that Bruce was really excited about; it "smelled like Sophia Loren's bicycle seat."

Typically, Bruce was going off about the injustice of the political system and about how the large foundations and the mainstream NGOs were noncreative, wasteful, and noneffective. And the best way to win our environmental battles is through small grassroots activism. No large environmental organization would have thought of having First Nation grandmothers blocking the bulldozers, getting handcuffed by the Mounties, and then having it all appear on national television. That's great marketing, and that's how the battles are won.

He liked to say the bigger the behemoth, the better chance you are going to hit solid meat when you swing a punch. You can hear him now, railing on

OPPOSITE: *Bruce Hill would always plan multiday brainstorming rendezvous set somewhere stunningly beautiful, knowing that the surroundings would emphasize just how important it was to fight for these places. Kowesas River Estuary, British Columbia.* Steve Perih

with lots of swear words and with Anne, his wife, in her strong, quiet way, supporting the whole clan. I can tell you I was listening—so were his kids, Aaron and Julia, and everyone else in the room.

I could go on and name persons who were similarly affected by Bruce, but I would leave out too many important people. I would guess it's every one of us here.

Bruce told me he was not afraid of death—like most people who have lived full and righteous lives. But he was sad to be leaving his family and friends—and he was frustrated that there was a lot of work still to do to protect our Mother Earth.

He has taught us well, and now it's up to us to carry on his work. I think this credo describes Bruce Hill's approach to life perfectly:

Respect the elders,
Teach the young,
Cooperate with the pack.
Play when you can,
Hunt when you must,
Rest in between.
Share your affections,
Voice your feelings,
Leave your mark.
– Wolf Credo

OPPOSITE: *A Tahltan elder being arrested while protecting the Sacred Headwaters, British Columbia.* Taylor Fox

NEXT SPREAD: *Iskut River in the Sacred Headwaters, a subalpine basin in northern British Columbia that is the source of three wild salmon rivers: the Skeena, the Nass, and the Stikine.* Paul Colangelo

We Lost a Chief – Doug Tompkins

Unpublished, 2015

Doug was my friend for almost sixty years. We first met climbing in the Shawangunks of New York. He was only fifteen and had either dropped out or been kicked out of school. In any case, he probably thought the teachers had nothing important to teach him. If you want to understand the entrepreneur, study the juvenile delinquent. That was Doug.

Over the years, I taught him to surf. He taught me to kayak. We learned to climb mountains together. We boldly broke the rules of business—and made it work.

Doug was good at many "do" sports: skiing, fencing, tennis, squash, and, of course, climbing. Together we did an early ascent of the Salathé Wall of El Capitan in Yosemite, which, at the time, was considered one of the most difficult rock climbs in the world. We climbed in Canada, Scotland (in the winter), the Karakoram Range, Bhutan, Antarctica, and, of course, Patagonia—where we climbed Fitz Roy. We fell in love with the area and later, I built a company around that mysterious name and Doug spent a fortune in protecting its natural beauty.

From so many days living among the mountains and rivers, we expanded our love of nature to include the whole of this lovely planet. Doug was especially influenced by the Norwegian climber Arne Næss and his philosophy of Deep Ecology. Early on, we recognized that we humans were destroying our home planet, and that each of us, in our own way, was responsible to protect and restore the wild nature that we loved.

OPPOSITE: *Yvon and Doug Tompkins survey the route up Cerro Kristine, Chile.* Jeff Johnson

We were always looking for an adventure, but there is no possibility of adventure without risk. Sometimes you have to purposely leave the door open a crack, for the opportunity of a good fight or possible serendipity. We loved life and were not afraid of death—but did not wish to die.

Doug had little respect for authority. He didn't like anyone telling him what to do—but he didn't hesitate in lecturing others.

On a Do Boys kayaking trip to the Russian Far East, our only maps went flying out the window of the helicopter. We all exchanged high-fives. We were on our way to an adventure!

Another time, we made the first descent of the Maipo River outside of Santiago. We eddied out before a blind turn and Doug got out to scout. Two soldiers came up from behind, with guns pointed, and demanded to see his papers. Basically, he told them to "get stuffed," ran down the hill, jumped into his boat, and took off around the bend. Hearing a roar of whitewater around the corner, I was freaked out not knowing how bad it was—and by the thought of getting shot. Sure enough, I hit a big keeper and went over. I questioned whether to roll up or not. Later we found out that the river flowed through the dictator Pinochet's summer grounds.

On that fateful trip last December, I was a little shocked to see how frail the old fig looked. But then, he probably thought the same of me. Doug was dressed in his signature pressed chinos, his Brooks Brothers shirt, a light wool sweater, and a light rain jacket. This was the same outfit he wore to climb the last mountain we did together: Cerro Kristine.

On the lake, we ran into a perfect trap: a forty-knot wind at our back and an equally strong wind from the side, making for large and confused waves. We could not even miss one paddle stroke for fear of going over. The boys made a valiant effort—but we lost Doug. We lost a Chief.

By his actions, Doug became the teacher we all needed—and he still is.

OPPOSITE: *Doug and Kris Tompkins with Lake Cochrane behind and also his favorite peak in the world: Cerro San Lorenzo, Chile.* Rick Ridgeway

NEXT SPREAD: *The headwaters of Lago Inexplorado in Hornopirén National Park, Chile.* Chantal Henderson

Measuring Time

First published in Bonefishing! *by Randall Kaufmann, Western Fisherman's Press, 2000*

When a man reaches a certain age, he begins to measure his wealth not in terms of how much he has accumulated, but in how much time he has left. Often, panic sets in. Forget about the *process*, or Zen, of activities like fly fishing or mountain climbing; the process takes too much time. He doesn't want to learn how to climb well; he wants to bag summits. He doesn't want to merely *fish*; he wants to *catch* fish.

Mountain guides, bonefish guides, hunting guides, river guides—all these exist to help the client hit the bull's-eye without having to spend a lifetime learning a chosen craft.

My father was a tough French Canadian from Quebec. Papa completed only three years of schooling before he had to begin working on the family farm at the age of nine. In his lifetime, he learned to become a journeyman plasterer, carpenter, electrician, and plumber. In Lisbon, Maine, where I was born, he repaired all of the machinery in the Worumbo Woolen Mill. One of the profound memories of my early childhood was seeing him sitting in the kitchen next to the wood-burning stove, drinking a bottle of whiskey, and proceeding to pull out his teeth, both good ones and bad, with his electrician's pliers. He needed dentures but felt that the local dentist was asking too much money to do a job he could just as easily do himself.

Because I inherited some of those genes, I have a preference for learning and doing things on my own and a visceral dislike of authority—like the

OPPOSITE: *Yvon on the wave at the lagoon entrance, Christmas Island, Kiribati.* Bernie Baker

No guide, no problem. Christmas Island, Kiribati. Bernie Baker

old-school Florida bonefish guide who barks orders like a Marine drill sergeant: "I said one o'clock, not eleven! Strip! Strip! Not too fast! Strip again!"

The classic example of excessive guiding can be seen on Oregon's Rogue River. The guide asks you to let sixty feet of line out from the stern of the dory and tells you to hold the rod with both hands. "Keep the tip up, and don't move it," he orders. He then ferry-glides your fly right into the mouth of the fish. There is no doubt that the guide is doing the fishing and, with luck, the client may be doing the catching. What should be a deeply personal and fun experience can turn into "Surviving a blizzard of micromanagement," as Tom McGuane described an encounter with a particularly zealous guide in South America.

I prefer to walk and wade my home river, the Snake, in Wyoming, but I may go through the whole summer never seeing another angler on his own—just one drift boat after another with the "sport" throwing Pepperoni Yuk Bugs

"Andy Carlson, Rell Sunn, and myself pounding down lobster on Christmas Island." 1993.
Bernie Baker

at the bank. One shot at each fish, and the floating shooting gallery drifts by. Anyone with that view of the sport can't possibly have an experience like the time I worked on a big feeding cutthroat for over an hour. I finally put it all together with a combination of 7X tippet, a difficult reach cast to the precise location, and a stripped-down size 20 PMD dry that I converted into a "physically challenged" emerger. The final solution was to put spittle on the tail end so it floated at just the right angle in the surface film.

My most memorable fishing experiences have not been the days when most of the fish were spotted for me by my guide but, rather, those singular experiences when I worked out a tough problem on my own. Don't get me wrong, I fish with guides. I've fished with great guides. The best see their role as teachers, not manservants.

These are just a few flashes of pleasant experiences and fond memories.

They are enhanced by a sense of satisfaction and confidence gained in each case by exercising a degree of self-reliance.

The best bonefish guide I've ever fished with is Moana from Christmas Island. One time I did "Moana's Walk" with him. It's a six-mile, all-day affair. You can only do this walk during the right tide cycle when the water isn't too deep to cross the cuts and when you can hit the different flats when there are fish on them. Moana has only one eye, but there is no way you can spot a fish before he does. You have to listen as he says quietly, "Over there, thirty feet." He won't tell you how to fish or rush over to take the hook out of your fish—unless that's what you want. If you ask, he will teach you the identity of every bird in the air or tell you the life history of the *Edward Scissorhands* manta shrimp and how his grandfather taught him how to catch them. He will show you what bonefish eat at Christmas Island and explain why the biggest ones come on the flats during the August full moon. We caught a lot of fish on "Moana's Walk," but that's not what I remember. I remember watching a master fisherman work those flats perfectly, so in tune with the environment and so adept at his craft that he has no need to actually catch a fish. I'll probably never do that walk with Moana again, but I've got two halfway decent eyes and two strong legs. There's nothing to keep me from trying to become as good a bonefisherman as Moana.

On my last few trips to Christmas Island, I've taken along my surfboard and fly rod and stayed in a shack in London Village—near the dock. My daily routine consists of getting up early, grabbing my surfboard, and walking barefoot along the coconut palm–lined path to the surf break at the lagoon entrance. I often hear someone singing in the distance or see a young girl brushing her sister's long black hair. They smile when I walk past and, since they don't see many surfers here, a few kids and dogs follow me out to the point to watch. There's a lot of fish action at the lagoon entrance. Once, a friend had a giant black trevally busting at his surfboard leash as he rode down a twelve-foot wave at twenty-five miles per hour.

The inhabitants of Christmas Island, the Kiribati, are not necessarily seafaring people. Most of them are uprooted farmers from Tarawa who were dumped on this barren atoll. I witnessed a near disaster during the occurrence of the largest surf of the year with the waves closing out the mouth of the lagoon. An unseaworthy old barge laden with eighty souls, dogs, pigs, and

OPPOSITE: *Fishing guide extraordinare Moana Kofe with bonefish on Christmas Island.* Val Atkinson

baggage attempted to navigate out of the lagoon powered only by a straining twenty-five-horsepower outboard. Of the three of us surfing, one was concerned about the babies, one was concerned about the puppies, and one saw the opportunity to catch the best waves of the day.

When the trades come up too strong to surf or the outgoing tidal rip messes with the incoming waves, it's time to fish the flats around London. They may not be the best flats on the island, but they're within walking distance. I've gotten to understand their tides and the movements of the fish. Even when the flats are nearly dry, there are always deeper channels where the bones are hanging out waiting for the tides to flood the flats. It's satisfying to learn on your own as simple a fact as the bonefish will be tailing on a certain flat at four o'clock.

Once, within sight of the docks, I hooked and landed a giant bra. A friend nearby yelled a challenge, "Can you still unhook it with one hand?"

From years of trying to hook a milkfish with a fly, I've found that they will, indeed, take a fly—a dry fly dressed to look like bright green frisée lettuce. If you think bonefish are good fighters, check out those fifteen-pound gulpers on a glassy day just outside the lagoon.

After surfing one of the other reef passes near Cook Island, I spent a couple of hours fishing for trevally. They were riding in with the tide through a pass. Under the watchful eye of a beautiful Polynesian friend, I was catching one after another. Though she could not understand the concept of catch and release, she took great joy in wading out and unhooking them for me. I did save a couple of fish for *poisson cru* for lunch. Dinner that evening consisted of a huge pile of lobster bodies. We cooked them ourselves, blissful in the knowledge that we had bought the whole pile for ten cents Australian per pound from the divers, who export only the tails.

The purpose of doing passionate sports like fly fishing or mountain climbing should be to learn and grow, and ultimately, to effect some higher personal change. It won't happen on Everest if, before you ever step onto the mountain, there are 28 ladders in place and 6,000 feet of rope, and you have a Sherpa in the front pulling, and one in the back pushing.

Learn all you can from the guide or teacher, but at some point, you need to cut loose from the catered experience and, for better or for worse, muddle through on your own.

OPPOSITE: *The bra. Christmas Island, Kiribati.* Bernie Baker

The Minestrone Hatch

First published in The FlyFish Journal, *Volume Four, Issue Two, Winter 2012*

During the 1960s, I spent summers climbing in the high Alps of France and Switzerland. When the weather turned foul, which it often did, we headed east to the sunnier Dolomites of Italy. If the weather followed us, we escaped south to the topless beaches and limestone cliffs between Marseille and Cannes.

Driving through Italy, I never dreamed there could be fish in the rivers that tumble from the Alps. How could there be? These rivers were all dammed, diverted, channelized, polluted, and mined for gravel. I thought trout fishing in Italy must have suffered the same fate as hunting. Nearly every Italian male owns a shotgun but is reduced to shooting songbirds on their migration to and from Africa. They are plucked, impaled on a stick, drizzled with olive oil, and end up as *uccelli carbon*.

Five years ago, I discovered I was wrong about the fishing. The streams of northern Italy flow through limestone, creating an alkaline environment (think San Pellegrino mineral water) that supports abundant insect life. I've found the fishing so good in Piemonte and Lombardia that several times I've had grand slams of rainbows, browns, grayling, marble trout, and marble brown hybrids. Now when I pass through Europe, I include a trip to the pre-Alps of Italy with my friend and rabid fisher Mauro Mazzo. The search is for trout, old Barolos, and the fabulous foods of northern Italy.

Driving through the Valtellina, the villages have sprawled so much that it's tough to tell where one ends and the next begins. One time, stopping to

OPPOSITE: *The Hotel Giardini pool on the Sesia River, Italy.* Mauro Mazzo

fish the Adda River downstream of the village of Chiuro, I was filled with doubt. Traffic careened along several major highways bordering the river, and houses, hotels, and restaurants lined the banks. Crowds of tourists filled the streets. But we were catching fish—fat, red-finned grayling up to two and a half pounds. I thought the fishing was great, but Mauro promised that at about 2 pm the fishing would get even better. We moved up to a long pool with a sewer pipe coming in from the village. Promptly at two, gray water poured from the pipe, dishwater from lunches of bresaola, pizzoccheri, cheese dumplings, and polenta. A veritable soup of leftovers.

Tiny red worms crawled out of the bottom muck to feed on the minestrone, and the grayling went nuts feeding on the worms. Mauro gave me a small fly tied with only thick red thread wrapped around the shank. The world's simplest fly?

My tenkara rod stayed bent for the next two hours, until all the dishes were washed and it was time to recharge with an espresso.

OPPOSITE: *A nice fat grayling. Italy.* Mauro Mazzo

Bhutan Brown Trout:
Here Be Caddis

First published in The Drake, *Winter 2012*

In 1985, I was in Bhutan to climb Gangkhar Puensum, then the highest unclimbed mountain on the planet. Our worthless Chinese and Indian military maps put us on the wrong side of the mountain, so we gave up and settled for making first ascents on some unauthorized 20,000-footers. We corrected the flawed maps and planned to tell our sponsors (National Geographic and Rolex) about our corrections. But standing around the campfire one day, we decided to burn our notes instead. There need to be a few places left on this crowded planet where "here be dragons" still defines the unknown regions of maps. Then I went fishing.

I knew that King Jigme Wangchuck was a fly fisher who had some spring creeks to himself, where he avoided wading by casting from atop an elephant. He was also married to two beautiful sisters and loved playing basketball. We watched a game in the capital city of Thimphu one day. The king waited under the basket (kings don't run) until the game came to him. When he scored, both sides cheered. It's good to be king in Bhutan.

Many of the rivers in Bhutan run clear and cold, and brown trout, introduced by the British, thrive there. Being at the same latitude as Miami, the insect life is prodigious. Some of the caddis cases I saw looked like small cigars.

OPPOSITE: *Yvon and a young monk near Jakar, Bhutan. 1985.* John Roskelley

Fishing near a small village one day, I was ignored by the women washing clothes along the bank next to me. Until I landed a pretty big brown. When I released the fish, the women began screaming, pounding me on the back, and indicating with fingers pointed at their mouths and bellies that they wanted to eat that fish. Their religion wouldn't allow them to kill the fish themselves, but if I killed it. ...

On another river, just outside Thimphu, the air reverberated with a deep *Ohmmmmm* coming from hundreds of chanting monks in the monastery near-by. I wasn't having much luck, so I sat on the bank, taking in the chants and searching my fly box for answers. I looked up to see a tall monk walking toward me. My gut cramped with fear. You are not allowed to fish within a mile of a temple, or monastery, in this strict Buddhist country, so I recognized trouble.

As the monk drew closer, I imagined myself being strung up in a dark dungeon of some sixteenth-century building. When he reached down and grabbed my fly box, I thought maybe I'd get by with just having my gear confiscated. Then he reached into the box, picked out a large gray nymph, and handed it to me. On the first cast, I hooked a fat twelve-inch brown and released it. The monk clapped and laughed from deep in his belly, just like the Dalai Lama.

OPPOSITE: *Yvon and Doug Tompkins on the summit of an unnamed, previously unclimbed, and un-mapped 20,000-foot peak in central Bhutan. 1985.* Rick Ridgeway

The Pack

First published in The FlyFish Journal, *Volume Eight, Issue Two, Winter 2016*

I've never had the pleasure of owning a dog, but I have hunted behind some great bird-dogs and I've known some equally great fishing dogs. I don't mean the ubiquitous Labrador standing proud on the bow of the guide boat. I am talking about dogs who actually fish for sustenance and sport.

There was Tom Brokaw's yellow lab, Sage. She was a Manhattan apartment dog for nine months of the year, but the other three she turned into the best South Dakota pheasant hunter I've ever known. One day in her retirement years in Montana, I was walking by her on my way to fish the farm pond and, though she was old and arthritic, she forced herself up off the cool lawn and hobbled down the trail with me. She stood quietly by my side while I cast big dry flies over the still waters. She stared intensely at the fly and just before a big rainbow would take the fly, she brought one leg up in a perfect point. What's with that? Polaroid eyeballs? Or a sixth sense that I've been trying to develop for seventy years?

Cruiser was Doug Moore's yellow retriever at Turneffe Flats Lodge. The dog knew to be in the shallows near the pier on an incoming tide. Cruiser hunted with two other mutts that the dog had trained to herd box fish toward him. He would jump on the fish and pin it down. Best of all, he knew that box fish were right up there with fugu and lionfish in delicacy. Cruiser himself was finally eaten by a saltwater croc.

PREVIOUS SPREAD: *Bonefishing in the Bahamas.* Marcos Furer

OPPOSITE: *The pack finds something interesting in the Palmyra shallows, Line Islands.* Yvon Chouinard

The best job I've ever had was on Palmyra Island when I was deputized by The Nature Conservancy to catch and tag as many bonefish as I could. This was in the early days when the bones were country bumpkins—I actually had one swim between my legs.

Palmyra was a private island that was sold to The Nature Conservancy in 2000. When the owners departed before the sale, three dogs—Floppy, Tut, and Dadu—were left to fend for themselves until the Conservancy and US Fish and Wildlife Service moved in. When I sailed there in July of the same year, Dadu and one other dog were still there. Even though the Conservancy provided them with all the dog food they could eat, they still had that fishing gene that has nothing to do with survival.

At camp one day I saw the two dogs get up and do a big downward-facing dog. "Oh, they're going fishing," one of the scientists remarked. I grabbed my rod and followed, busting through bushes and mangroves, and swimming across cuts all the way to the southeast flats.

All abreast, we walked the shoreline looking for fish. I stopped for a moment to look at some far-off bonefish. Dadu stopped, looked back at me and I swear he was saying, "Come on, man, keep up. We're here for sharks, not bonefish." Sure enough, we cornered a small black tip and drove it on to the beach where they commenced to eat it. Feeling pretty proud of myself and grateful to be part of the pack, I wandered off searching for my bonefish.

OPPOSITE: *Coming back from a successful fishing trip, Palmyra Atoll.* Yvon Chouinard

A Good Skunking

First published in the Atlantic Salmon Journal, *Spring 2013*

When the fishing is always better the week before you arrive, or after you leave, there is only one thing to do. Go Zen.

Huzzah! I'm invited on a trip to the Lakselva River in arctic Norway. They tell me the average salmon this time of year is twenty-five pounds! This is my big chance to catch a fish of a lifetime without having to pay $25K to share a rod for a week on the Alta, a few miles to the south.

After months of anticipation, I am standing on the banks of the Lakselva, stringing up my rod with shaking hands. The river is running high and cold. The few fish coming in are not stopping on the lower beats. I have the lower beats.

We hear that the commercial netters in the sea are regularly catching thirty- to fifty-pound fish. I finally hook a fish. When it rolls to the surface, a friend standing on the bank above estimates it at more than thirty pounds. After ten minutes, he throws my size 10 Blue Charm. My spirits plummet. I blame myself for using single hooks instead of doubles. I should have sharpened the hook. Or loosened the drag. Or set the hook harder. Or pulled from a different angle. …

While casting my 575-grain Skagit line, it breaks and goes flying across the river. I borrow an intermediate line, but it neither floats nor sinks enough. After beating the river to a froth for six days, my total catch is one eight-pound Atlantic salmon.

OPPOSITE: *On the way to getting skunked. Kola Peninsula, Russia.* Håkan Stenlund

ABOVE: *Atlantic salmon on the move. Dartmouth River, Quebec.* Gilbert Van Ryckevorsel

I fly down south, where I have four days on the Gaula with two good friends, a cabin, no guides, and five beats to ourselves. Heaven. But the river is too high—a familiar tune—and very few fish can ascend the Gaulafoss, a waterfall that is, of course, below where we are fishing. The worm and harling "anglers" below the falls have caught twenty-three tons of corralled salmon. The five-year moratorium on commercial fishing in the estuary has ended, and netters are out fishing with a vengeance to prove they should be paid to stop netting again.

A "hundred-year" flood last year changed the course of the river and there is no holding water. I've bought a Snowbee Scandi line with no instructions in the box, so for four days I struggle to cast with the floating tip on backward. Beautiful. My running line snaps on a cast. I save the head, but have to use the back end of an old fly line, resulting in even worse casts. A few fish are showing on the other side of the river, but I can't reach them.

After repeatedly attempting thousands of single and double Speys, circle, overhead, and poke casts, all the while expecting vastly different results, my total catch is zero. I hate myself.

Back home in Wyoming I call my friend, writer Dylan Tomine, and recount my failures. He provides a rousing pep talk, saying he hopes I continue my streak when I go to Canada because "it would make a better story."

I decide I'm not obsessive enough to be a good salmon fisherman. I don't sharpen my hooks, check for wind knots, and lay the line out perfectly straight every time. I keep stepping on my line. But now, with my Canadian trip approaching, I'm going to prepare like never before. I make sure my lines are matched to my rods; the tips are on the right way. I whip finish some mono to back up the factory-fused loops. I tie new leaders, glue the knots, check the running line for nicks. I also realize that maybe I'm trying too hard. We all know the best fish are caught by the worst fishermen. I work on a Zen mind. I tell myself I no longer care about the fifty-pound salmon. I'm just going to lose myself in the casting and if a fish happens to intercept my fly as it swims past its nose. …

At Lorne Cottage on the Grand Cascapédia, I casually gaze at the wood cutouts of all the forty- and fifty-pound salmon caught over the years in this greatest of all Gaspé rivers. I remind myself I'm just here to enjoy casting my now perfectly rigged Spey gear. My mind is calm.

It's early August and the river is very low. The guides say the fish all came in the first week of June, and went right up to the cooler waters of the upper river. The fish knew.

I cast over a few dark, dour fish but they won't take. All I get is one boil under a waking muddler. Then days of nothing.

We move on to the Petit Cascapédia, where the water is also extremely low. All we can find are a few old fish concentrated in only three pools. I entice a couple of fish to rise, but no takes. My Italian friend Mauro Mazzo, who has a history of creative juvenile delinquency, follows behind me throwing a huge Snaelda on a fast sink tip and nails a fifteen-pounder nearly at my boots.

It's hot and humid on the Bonaventure—perfect weather for being eaten alive by blackflies. The water is again, guess what? Historically low. One guide says the salmon won't take when it's this hot. Another says they won't take when it's this humid. My Zen façade crumbles.

I'm beginning to loathe Atlantic salmon. They are just big brown trout with all their neuroses, the moodiness, the undirected viciousness. Like vampires, salmon hate the sun and are active only at night. They are the Dick Cheneys of the fish world.

It occurs to me that in order to be a successful salmon angler, you need to stay at the most expensive lodges before, during, and after the best weeks. You have to take the constant abuse of guides telling you what to do and where to cast. If salmon were the size of trout and still required all this money and effort to catch, no one would even fish for them. They are merely big.

Yet I continue to fish. I see a pod of good fish in a pool and just as I start to cast, a flotilla of a hundred canoes goes right over them. And so it goes for two more days on the Bonaventure.

One of Lee Wulff's favorite rivers is the beautiful Serpentine in Newfoundland. Gorgeous country, but it hasn't rained in a month. No one can remember such a dry spell. They say salmon won't take in water temperatures above sixty degrees Fahrenheit, their metabolism slowed by lack of oxygen. When we arrive, the Serpentine is sixty-eight degrees in the morning, and seventy-three by late afternoon.

We coax and drag our canoe for two hours to the falls, where there are several good pools. When we arrive, a family of five is camped there. They give us the news that they have already fished the runs and killed two grilse.

The only possibility for success is to fish very small hitched flies in the surface film. All my small wet flies are tied on heavy hooks and won't wake on the low, slow water. Unless we get rain, it's hopeless. We hear rivers are closing all over eastern Canada.

Where a tiny spring of cold water flows into the river, I discover twenty large salmon nosed into the rivulet, gasping for oxygen. I sit down and watch for a while.

OK, I get it. The lesson here is bigger than simply trying to catch a fish. Maybe it's about global warming—and we are the Cheneys and Stephen Harpers of the world. I now feel compassion for these poor salmon.

With the recent extreme swings of weather, added to all the old problems of water diversion, dams, pollution, commercial fisheries, fish farms, disease, and sea lice, these great creatures need help. God help us as well.

OPPOSITE: *"I had a Pancho Villa mustache in the mid-1960s and Sheridan Anderson drew this caricature of me and the White Whale."* Illustration by Sheridan Anderson

367

Lessons from a Simple Fly

First published in Trout and Salmon, *May 2013*

In the various outdoor pursuits and crafts in which I've been involved—from mountaineering and whitewater kayaking to spearfishing and tool-making—the progression from novice to master has always been a journey from the complex to the simple. An illustrator becomes an artist when he can convey his message with fewer brushstrokes.

Fishing with a fly seems to have gone in the opposite direction: it has become a needlessly complex and expensive pastime where anglers choose from hundreds of fly lines, high-tech rods, and trout reels with drags that can stop a truck. We all know that palming the rim of a reel with a simple click-drag can stop any trout or salmon, but the industry has become dependent on building insecurity in the minds of the customers. "If we aren't outfitted with the latest gear and *au courant* signature fly, can we really be enjoying ourselves?" (I must admit that I, too, have multiple rods and reels and I've caught myself cursing the fact that I don't have the exact fly for that specific stage of that particular mayfly.)

More than thirty years ago, I was introduced to the original method of fishing with a fly first described in the second century AD by Claudius Aelianus. This form of fishing is still practiced in parts of Spain, Italy, and Japan, in addition to places where people cannot afford modern gear. I've adapted this simple tenkara style to the large rivers of the Americas with great success. The combination of the long tenkara rod (no reel) and soft-hackle wet flies has proven for me to be the most effective way to catch trout on a fly.

OPPOSITE: *Where are those damn glasses? Río Nirehuao, Chile. 1991.* Rick Ridgeway

I used to fish the soft hackles with a brace of different flies. Then I started noticing that most times, regardless of the hatch, the fish took the Pheasant Tail and Partridge. If that was so, why bother with the other patterns? Why not see how far I could go fishing an entire season with only one style of fly?

Like most new ideas in fishing, this one had been thought of before: Arthur Wood—the great English salmon fisherman who used only the March Brown for a whole season and a Blue Charm for another. He caught as many salmon as before and, in fact, found his success with either fly was hardly different. Art Flick, the Catskill angler and flytyer who wrote *The Streamside Guide to Naturals and Their Imitations*, ended up using mostly one fly, the Grey Fox variant. Jim Teeny has used only the Teeny Nymph since 1971. Some of the most successful salmon fishermen in Canada use only the Muddler Minnow.

My scheme was to use only one style of fly for all trout, salmon, and saltwater fish.

Years ago, the American angler George LaBranche considered the myriad aspects of using dry flies to catch trout and ranked their importance. The position of the fly on the water he ranked first. Second, the action of the fly. Third, the fly's size. Fourth and fifth, the form and color of the fly. For the way I typically fish with wet flies, I rank the fly's action as most important, followed by size and presentation. I believe most anglers place too much importance on form and color.

The Pheasant Tail and Partridge (PT) is a neutral fly that fairly imitates most mayfly and caddis. It probably has its roots in the time of Dame Juliana Berners in 1496 when she wrote a treatise describing the wet-fly patterns used in England at that time. Frank Sawyer, the river keeper on the Avon, has been attributed as the developer of the modern Pheasant Tail nymph. Some years before, George Skues was already tying a version of the soft-hackle PT.

My one-fly season began in the winter and spring of 2015 when I used the PT on the flats of the Bahamas and Cuba. Bonefish that have been fished heavily can get spooky. If they "blow up" when you strip the fly, it's probably because they have seen too many shiny hooks, bright eyes, and flashabou. I tied saltwater PTs on size 6 and 8 weighted bronze-colored hooks. I used long hackles from the backs of grouse necks and tied on two at a time to give a bushier

OPPOSITE: *The Pheasant Tail and Partridge soft hackle.*

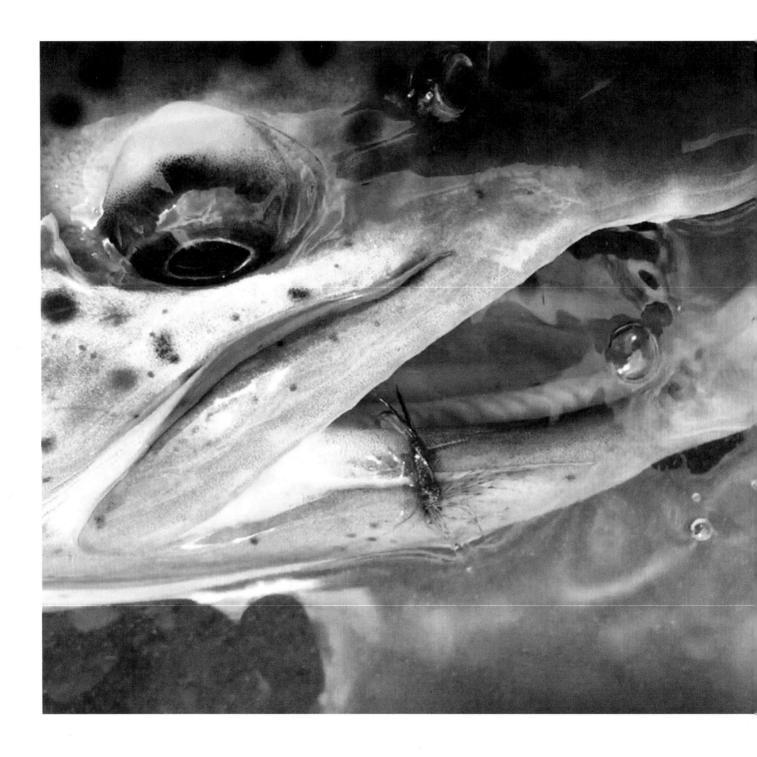

look. With a small strip, the hackles pulsate like a jellyfish or shrimp. This plain brown fly even worked on light sand bottoms where you would normally use a lighter-colored fly. I've since used the PT for many other saltwater fish.

Fishing for trout in the spring and summer in Wyoming, Montana, and Idaho, I fished a size 10 as an attractor. When a hatch came on, I would switch to the appropriate size. Regardless of the color of the naturals or whether they were mayflies, caddis, or stoneflies, the PT, in the proper size, outfished the more exact imitations.

My wet-fly technique is simple. I cast forty-five-degrees downstream and mend the line to slow the swing. When the line starts to straighten, I slowly lift the rod to straighten it even more. Once the line is straight, I give an occasional twitch with the tip of the rod. I'm trying to imitate an emerging caddis or mayfly swimming to the surface or struggling from its shuck. Nine out of ten times the take is right after the twitch. The flexible tip of the tenkara rod is perfect for imparting this subtle action. I've found that a proper twitch is the most difficult thing to master in swinging wet flies. Almost everyone overdoes it. A big twitch will send a wave of slack down the line giving time for the fish to eject the fly. Remember, you are trying to entice a take, not scare the fish. If you're getting bites but few hooked trout, it's either a small fish or there's slack in the line.

Modern fast- and medium-action rods are not designed to impart movement to the fly; they're built to cast heavy flies a long distance—usually beyond the fish. Add the typical 5- or 6-weight line and the line droop at the end of the rod prevents any sort of twitch transferring to the fly. The best you can do is lower the tip to the water and try to give the smallest hand-strip. When I want to use a rod and reel, I use a cane rod or a ten-foot 2-weight rod with a 1-weight line to avoid the line droop. I also tie knotted leaders because the increased water friction helps to straighten the line.

When fishing a brace of flies, I tie the larger fly on the point and the smaller on the dropper, keeping them about thirty inches apart. The two-fly system increases the friction further and gives a different action to each fly. I can't emphasize enough the importance of giving action to the fly. Like your

OPPOSITE: *A nice brown trout fooled with a simple olive fly on the Snake River, Wyoming.*
Katsumi Fujikura

house cat, fish are predators. Slowly pull a toy mouse across the floor and the cat will go into its predator stance. Stop pulling and give it a twitch—the cat pounces. It makes no difference if the mouse is gray or yellow. Grizzly bears and tigers love it when you run.

———

We humans think of ourselves as perpetual teenagers; maybe salmon and steelhead do, too?

———

In early July, I applied my one-fly approach to the salmon of the Hawke River in Labrador. The flies were tied on size 10 and 12 low-water salmon hooks. Later, on the Haffjardara in Iceland, I had similar luck. Most of the fish were grilse and I used the sensitivity of a ten-foot, 5-weight rod to give action to the fly. The occasional twitch with the hitched fly was especially effective at inducing a take in slower water. I wasn't trying to prove a point anymore; it was simply the most effective way to catch these salmon. I've since taken to hitching the PT for trout, which often leads to explosive takes.

In September, I had an opportunity to fish for steelhead for five days on the Babine River in British Columbia. On the first day, there was only six inches of visibility. It cleared to a foot on the second day, but I had no confidence that a fish would be able to see my small flies. I put on a sink-tip line with a big dark Intruder and caught one small steelhead.

On the third day, I still couldn't see my boots but the water was clearer and the parr were active in the shallow riffles, feeding on caddis and green drakes in the afternoon. I thought if the parr could see the tiny naturals, then surely the adults could see my size 10 PT. Sure enough, I started catching some large steelhead. I even caught two sockeye salmon, which is unusual so late in the season and so far from the sea.

Conditions continued to improve and I switched to a floating line and a hitched PT. Even fishing behind other anglers who were throwing traditional gaudy steelhead flies, the PT was producing fish up to thirty-seven inches. Many times, when using large rubber waking flies for steelhead, you get boils but no takes. I believe this is because the flies are too large. Rarely do I get only a boil with the small flies. In this situation, I'm convinced it was the most effective fly and technique I could have used.

We think anadromous fish take flies even though they are not feeding because it's a memory from when they were parr and eating insects. If that's so, it would explain why a small fly works so well especially when there's a hatch. We humans think of ourselves as perpetual teenagers; maybe salmon and steelhead do, too?

In the late autumn and through the winter, when the only hatches happening are tiny midges and blue-winged olives, most American anglers stoop to throwing streamers and gross rubber-legged and plastic concoctions—outfits for a Barbie doll, as the writer Tom McGuane calls them. But midges and BWOs are active swimmers and a size 20 or 22 sparsely tied PT fished on the surface with a tiny twitch can be as effective as any fly.

Am I going to continue using only one fly for the rest of my life? My tying table looks pretty brown and boring … also, I feel the lessons have been learned. Action and size are more important than style and color.

Limiting options forces creativity. Fishing for a year with only the PT has given me deep knowledge about what to do with that simple brown fly and a deeper understanding of fish. It has taught me that choosing a simpler life doesn't mean choosing an impoverished life. Rather, simplicity can lead to a more satisfying way of fishing and a more responsible way of living.

Threats to Coldwater Fisheries

Unpublished 2018

In 2007, I was salmon fishing on the Rynda River in Russia. It was late June in the Arctic and already the air temperatures had hit the nineties for several days in a row. The rivers there are short and come out of shallow lakes with dark, tannin-colored water. After a few days, the river heated up to the low seventies in the afternoons. Fishing was slow but I finally hooked and released a twelve-pound salmon, but it stayed alongside my legs gasping for oxygen for half an hour before it slowly swam away.

IN HOT WATER

I'm not a scientist, but I have been a fisherman for more than seventy years, and I've seen firsthand that of all the threats facing coldwater fish, climate change is the most dire. Water all over the planet is heating up, putting salmon, steelhead, and trout in danger almost everywhere.

The temperature of the Earth fifty feet down hovers around fifty-six degrees Fahrenheit. (That's also the temperature of freshwater springs and the perfect temperature for your wine cellar, by the way.) Coldwater fish need cold

PREVIOUS SPREAD: *More than 90 percent of "wild caught" salmon on the West Coast are not actually wild, instead they begin life in fish hatcheries due to the damming and destruction of rivers and spawning habitat—salmon without rivers. Here, a portion of one million hatchery salmon are trucked and released into San Francisco Bay.* Ben Moon

OPPOSITE: *Dead salmon float a few miles upriver from Klamath Glen, California, in 2002. The Yurok Tribe, which depends on Klamath River salmon for food, and environmental groups blame the Bureau of Reclamation for the fish kill, saying their management plan of full irrigation to farmers cut flows for fish.* Shaun Walker/AP Images

water. Trout and salmon thrive in water somewhere around that magical fifty-six-degree mark. In water warmer than sixty-eight degrees, all salmonids experience signs of stress, and water warmer than seventy-five degrees is lethal.

In 2007, Yellowstone National Park experienced a huge fish kill when the water temperatures in the Yellowstone River and many of its tributaries reached into the eighties. That same year, rivers were closed to fishing all over eastern Canada because of warm water.

A few years later, in 2015, the mortality rate for sockeye salmon in the warmed-up lower Columbia River was between 80 and 90 percent: 250,000 salmon died before they could spawn. In August of 2016, 350 miles of the Yellowstone River and its tributaries were closed to boating, fishing, and swimming because of a parasite that caused kidney disease in whitefish and trout. Montana's government website issued a report stating the "magnitude of the kills is unlike anything our fish health specialists have seen." The parasite, combined with historically low streamflows and seventy-degree waters, created a devastating scenario for fish populations, not to mention local businesses that rely on the fishing economy.

In my home state, no Southern California steelhead were able to spawn from 2014 to 2017 because drought made creeks so low they never broke through the sandbars to the ocean. Hot conditions in Northern California resulted in lethal blue-green algae blooms that closed many lakes to all users. By lethal, I mean, if your dog drank the lake water, it could die.

The freshwater algae known as didymo, or "rock snot," can take over rivers when the water warms. We used to think it was spread by anglers inadvertently transporting it from one body of water to another. Now scientists believe that it's naturally always there and hotter temperatures trigger its growth and spread. I've experienced it on the normally crystal-clear Bonaventure River in Quebec—it was so thick in places you could hardly wade through it. Didymo also encourages the spread of a worm that's a host for whirling disease, which causes skeletal deformation and neurological damage in salmon and trout.

Beginning in 2013 and extending through 2015, there was a large area of warm water off the northwest coast of the United States and Canada. This warm water, known as the "Blob," created a double-whammy—increased fish metabolism and very little food available—with devastating effects on juvenile and adult salmon. As a result, the returns of salmon and steelhead in 2016

Hetch Hetchy, a dam that never should have been built and needs to be taken down. Sierra Nevada, California. David Cross

and 2017 were the lowest in recorded history. The hangover effect of the Blob is expected to continue through 2019.

Winters start later and end sooner. The pocket glaciers and permanent snowfields in the Coast Ranges of British Columbia serve as an essential source of cold water all summer long, but in my lifetime, I've seen those glaciers shrink by 30 percent. In these shortened winters, precipitation often comes as rain rather than snow, resulting in catastrophic flood events that can alter the course of rivers and destroy redds.

The warming environment impacts our freshwater food chain as well. Mayflies, a critical food source for fish, now emerge earlier, are smaller in size, and produce fewer eggs. Last year on the Henrys Fork in Idaho, the famous hatches happened in April and May, way before the season opened on June 15.

Climate change may hover over all of our coldwater fisheries, but it's hardly the only problem. The others issues—loss of habitat, competition from

invasive species, increased exposure to toxins and disease, irresponsible harvesting, and loss of genetic diversity—would be bad enough on their own. But because they reduce the resilience and health of fish populations, they compound the problems of climate change, making the fish less able to adapt to our warming planet.

The bottom line is that we stand to lose close to half of the trout habitat in the inland West by 2080 (Wenger et al., 2011). Another study by UC Davis (2017) on climate change states that of the thirty-two distinct salmonoid species in California, twenty-three (74 percent) are likely to be extinct in the next 100 years.

DAMN DAMS

Wild fish evolved to overcome natural obstacles to migration—landslides, earthquakes, volcanoes, flooding, drought—but as far as I know, there aren't many fish that can scale concrete walls. The United States has built one dam a day since Thomas Jefferson's time. There are 40,000 useless dams in America. Useless, because they no longer serve a purpose or, even worse, dangerous, because they have not been maintained. Some of them, like the four dams on the Lower Snake River, prevent salmon and steelhead from utilizing 1,500 miles of streams above.

All dams lose water by evaporation, but new studies have also shown that high methane emissions are produced by dams as woody debris and organic matter trapped in the reservoirs decompose and release the potent greenhouse gas. The findings suggest that many dams around the world can contribute more greenhouse gas emissions than coal-fired power plants producing an equivalent amount of energy. So much for "green hydropower."

There's a small dam on the Madison River in Ennis, Montana, which creates a limited amount of power—only about nine megawatts—but it slows down the Madison, warms up the water, and kills the fishing below the dam for forty miles of otherwise perfect trout habitat.

My own local river, the Ventura, used to have runs of coho and Chinook salmon, and a run of 4,500 steelhead. Because of a dam (which filled up with

OPPOSITE: *Travis Rummel stands on a beautifully preserved old-growth cedar stump that was revealed after being submerged for nearly a century under Washington's "Lake" Aldwell. The Elwha River has now re-carved its course through the drained reservoir.* Ben Knight

sediment in only fifteen years), pollution, and dewatering, we now have only two dozen steelhead struggling to survive.

Admittedly, some dams have produced great coldwater fisheries downstream where none existed before. But let's not kid ourselves: many of these dams are operated by power or agricultural interests and, in winter or in drought years, the fish have the lowest priority.

A couple of decades ago, my friends and I were pheasant hunting along the banks of the Big Horn River in Montana when we noticed the river suddenly receding, leaving thousands of fish stranded in mud or shallow pools. It turns out the afterbay of the Yellowtail Dam (named for Chief Yellowtail, who vehemently opposed the dam) was being worked on, and they just shut off the flow.

California is considering building more dams even though the land in the Central Valley has subsided in some places by fifteen feet from overdrawn wells. One logical solution of course is to store water underground, but at this time, there do not appear to be any viable plans to do so. California is also proposing to build two four-story-high tunnels to take 70 percent of the water from the tributaries of the Sacramento River and send it south. It would be the end of anadromous fish runs in those rivers.

In Europe, the Balkan states are proposing to build more than 2,000 dams on some of the world's healthiest chalk streams. A recent study by Oxford University found that building large dams never makes economic sense, yet all over the world we keep building more.

INVASIVE SPECIES

With increasing globalism, invasive species of animals, plants, insects, fish, and shellfish are naturalizing all over the Earth. Many of these species create problems when the host country has no natural predators to keep them in check.

Here's just a partial list of aquatic invaders that have naturalized in the United States: purple loosestrife, Eurasian watermilfoil, hydrilla, flowering rush, Asian carp, Asian clams, quagga and zebra mussels. The mussels, which are now spreading across the West, have already sucked up 90 percent of the phytoplankton in Lake Michigan. The phytoplankton utilize carbon produced by the algae, the zooplankton eat the phytoplankton, and small fish eat the zooplankton. Remove one link in the chain, in this case, phytoplankton, and the whole interconnected web of life falls apart. There is no solution for this problem except to drain the waterways and let everything dry up and die, and then start again.

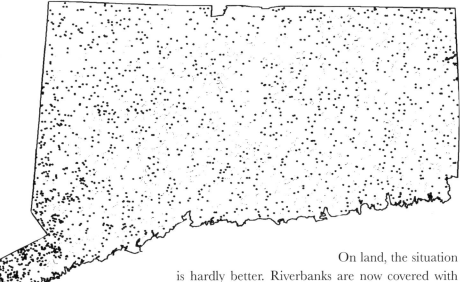

On land, the situation is hardly better. Riverbanks are now covered with Himalaya blackberries, Japanese knotweed, English ivy, Scotch broom, arundo, and other invaders, changing watershed ecosystems across the country. The aggressive growth of these plants chokes out native species, dewaters the streams, and alters runoff patterns. And once established, they're almost impossible to remove—knotweed, for example, sprout entirely new plants from even the smallest fragment of leaf or stem.

Over a twenty-five-year period, Jim Vashro, a fisheries biologist in Montana, recorded 600 illegal fish introductions in more than 300 waters in the state, these include putting warmwater fish like pike, perch, crappie, and walleye into cold waters. In the Columbia River reservoirs, these spiny-ray, nonnatives feed heavily on juvenile salmon as the juveniles attempt to migrate through the artificially warm, slack water to the sea.

Offshore net-pen salmon farms accidentally release millions of domesticated, genetically inferior salmon all over the world. In 2017, a net pen in Puget Sound collapsed, allowing more than 200,000 invasive Atlantic salmon into Pacific waters. In Scandinavia and Canada, researchers have found that

ABOVE: *A map of the many dams in Connecticut.* Graphic courtesy of Stephen Gephard

NEXT SPREAD: *There are plans to put up 10,000 dams in the Balkan states. This is a screening of the film* Blue Heart of Europe *shown against a deadbeat dam. Bosnia and Herzegovina.* Fly Fishing Nation

escaped farm fish can breed with wild salmon, polluting the gene pool with domestic traits. These farms all have problems with various viral, fungal, and bacterial disease. Escaped farm salmon can act as a vector to spread these diseases to wild populations. Under the pens themselves, there are gelatinous masses of excrement and sea lice. Many of the fish are deformed and have gill plates missing from sea lice infection. Wild salmon catch these diseases and parasites when they migrate past the farms. Because of toxic chemicals and pharmaceuticals used to treat these problems, the Pew Foundation recommends you limit your intake of farmed salmon to once a month. Pregnant women, never. Personally, I can't see why anyone would eat these fish—ever.

The Canadian government acts like it has given up on wild salmon and steelhead when it actively promotes these offshore net-pen farms. In the eastern provinces, it is releasing striped bass near scores of Atlantic salmon rivers. At the mouth of the greatest of the rivers, the Cascapédia, there is already a robust bass fishery, especially when the salmon smolts migrate to the sea.

Our own FDA has now approved a GMO "Frankenfish" salmon, a Chinook salmon with DNA from another species, the ocean pout, spliced into its genes, that grows three times faster than a wild salmon. Ninety-nine-point eight percent will be sterilized so they can't breed with wild fish—but what about the .02 percent? This could be the beginning of an entirely new kind of invasive species—one that's never existed anywhere on our planet before.

INDUSTRIAL-STRENGTH FISHING

We are treating the oceans the same way we have treated the land. We went from being hunters and gatherers until we killed off the game and then we became farmers. We have killed off 90 percent of the large fish in the oceans worldwide and now are making the same mistakes with our sea farms that we made with our industrial land farms.

We harvest unsustainable quantities of low-value fish like sardines, anchovies, mackerel, and herring in developing nations to make feed for higher-value fish like farmed salmon and tuna—not to mention pigs, chickens, and cows.

Overharvesting and nonselective fishing methods are two of the problems with industrial fishing. "Nonselective" means if you catch a Chinook salmon in the open ocean off Alaska, there's a good chance it came from a river in British Columbia or Washington state. And that river's Chinook population could be endangered. The main point, though, is that the open-ocean fisherman has no way of knowing where his fish came from. A sockeye caught at the mouth of the Columbia could be one of just a dozen or so that are meant to go a thousand miles to Redfish Lake in Idaho to spawn. The summer-run Chinook salmon returning to Puget Sound, which are harvested heavily in nonselective ocean

———

Because of toxic chemicals and pharmaceuticals used … the Pew Foundation recommends you limit your intake of farmed salmon to once a month. Pregnant women, never.

———

fisheries off British Columbia and Alaska, used to average twenty-four pounds. Now, after decades of intensive harvest, the fish that survive to reproduce are the ones that spend the least amount of time in the ocean—making the modern average just nine to eleven pounds. I've caught larger trout than that!

The summer steelhead on the Fraser and Skeena Rivers in British Columbia migrate at the same time as sockeye, chum, and pink salmon. Commercial fishermen at the mouths of these rivers target the salmon, but also catch large numbers of steelhead in their lethal gill nets. That's why one of the greatest steelhead rivers, the Thompson, a tributary of the Fraser, was down to only 430 steelhead in 2015, 380 in 2016, and I've heard there were only 180 in 2017. There used to be 10,000 in the mid-1980s.

The solution is to either fish with nonlethal selective methods using reef nets, tangle tooth nets, and fish traps, or to fish near rivers where there is little or no accidental catch of nontarget species. The Bristol Bay sockeye fishery is a great example of sustainable practices based on science and a deep connection between the salmon, the land, and the people who have relied on these fish for thousands of years.

DOWN THE DRAIN

We're all aware of the obvious sources of pollution: industrial chemicals, mining waste, toxic spills in waterways, ruptured pipelines, sewage from septic

tanks and primitive sewer plants—or in the case of Victoria, British Columbia, no sewer plant (although construction of a tertiary treatment plant finally began in April 2017 to be completed in 2020)—and the 80,000-plus chemicals and pharmaceuticals that we humans and our animals ingest. But the largest polluter, and one of the biggest causes of global warming, is industrial agriculture. Agricultural runoff carrying toxic chemicals, fertilizers, and animal waste is our fisheries' biggest pollution threat.

In 1956, I'd just escaped from high school and driven from Burbank, California, to the Wind River Range in Wyoming in my 1940 Ford, which I'd overhauled in auto-shop class. Jackrabbits were everywhere racing the cars along the roads. When was the last time you saw a jack rabbit? Whenever I passed near water on the warm June evenings, a blizzard of moths, mayflies, caddis, crane flies, stoneflies, and lightning bugs so battered my windshield and headlights that I had to constantly stop and clean them off. Have you noticed that this hardly happens anymore?

A scientist at Stanford University, Rodolfo Dirzo, estimates that we have lost 45 percent of our land invertebrates in the last forty years. The biologist Frank Craighead told me he blames the loss of giant stoneflies in Wyoming's Snake River on the fact that in the 1960s they sprayed for pine bark beetles and mosquitos. Monoculture crops such as corn and soybeans create biological deserts devoid of hedges and ponds where insects can live and reproduce. Where are the bugs? Ask Dow Chemical, DuPont, Bayer, Monsanto, and the chemical farmers who use their products.

On the Idaho side of the Teton Range lies some of the most beautiful farm landscape in the West. It's also some of the most toxic. Seed potatoes grown there are sprayed with some of the most toxic pesticides that we're allowed to use. Because the ground there is porous, eight feet of water is put on a single crop, carrying the toxic chemicals with it. Residents in the Teton Valley are warned not to drink their own well water. The chemical-laden underground runoff flows to the spring-fed Teton River where downstream, in

OPPOSITE: *One of hundreds of toxic salmon farms in Chile.* Marcelodlt/Shutterstock

NEXT SPREAD: *A farmed Atlantic salmon processing plant releases blood effluent into British Columbia's largest wild salmon migration route—Discovery Passage. This blood was found to be infected with Piscine Reovirus and the exposé prompted a government review, which found that 70 percent of processing facilities are violating their permits.* Tavish Campbell

the Teton Canyon, native cutthroats are afflicted with ugly skin lesions. I can no longer even bring myself to fish for them.

Of course, it's not just western agriculture. Pollution ends up in our waters everywhere. In fact, the government has warned us not to eat any freshwater fish from east of the Mississippi. That says something, doesn't it? Toxic copper dust from car brakes accumulates on roads and washes into streams whenever it rains. Copper is lethal to almost all aquatic life, and the results are predictable. In Seattle, adult coho salmon, which return to their natal streams to spawn after autumn rains, routinely die upon entering their freshwater streams, the victims of brake dust.

Acid rain (sulphur dioxide) from coal-fired power plants in New York and Ohio has acidified the salmon rivers of Nova Scotia, where seventeen of the nineteen salmon rivers may never have salmon again. Burning coal also sends vast quantities of mercury into the atmosphere, and eventually into the ocean, where it accumulates in the flesh of predators. Ignore the warnings not to eat any of the larger ocean fish at your own risk. I have a friend who decided to get healthy by eating only fish and vegetables. He was eating tuna, halibut, and swordfish, and in a month his eyebrows and hair were coming off in big patches. He tested positive for mercury poisoning.

The oceans are capturing so much human-produced carbon dioxide that they're acidifying, and many of the micro-organisms that form the basis of the food chain struggle to survive because they can no longer make shells and skeletons in the low-pH water. A major oyster producer in Washington state now hatches its shellfish in Hawai'i—where the effects of ocean acidification are lower—so that the baby oysters' shells aren't dissolved by increasingly acidic coastal waters.

ARTIFISHAL

Despite robust hatchery programs in the Pacific Northwest, the wild salmon and steelhead population is down to such low numbers that they are listed as threatened. In Puget Sound rivers, the wild steelhead numbers are now between 1 and 4 percent of the historical population. The only healthy streams

OPPOSITE: *The removal of the Elwha dams in Washington's Olympic National Park was part of a $320 million river restoration, the largest in history. Instead of allowing the river to naturally repopulate with wild salmon, $16 million was spent building a second fish hatchery on a river that was primarily restored for wild fish.* Ben Moon

Deformities, viruses, and toxic algae blooms—these are some of the results of fish farming in open-net ocean pens. This salmon—legally labeled "organic"—will end up in the fish section of Costco or Walmart, or on a plate at an all-you-can-eat sushi restaurant. British Columbia. SeaLegacy

where wild steelhead or trout populations are stable or increasing are those with no dams and no hatchery fish. It's very simple. When a hatchery is put in, wild fish numbers go down. Take them out and wild fish rebound.

Over millions of years, magnificent fish developed as a result of natural selection. Scientists tell us that it takes only one generation for a fish bred in a hatchery to have dumbed-down genes. After five generations, fish bred in hatcheries no longer know how to reproduce. The recreational value of hatchery fish, often touted as reason for producing them, is highly suspect as well. Hatchery fish are programmed to race back to their hatcheries without spending time in the downriver pools where fishermen can access them. Instead, hoards of anglers cram into the hole nearest to the hatchery and spend their day in shoulder-to-shoulder combat fishing. Years ago, Tom McGuane and I were fishing the North Fork Nehalem River in Oregon. We landed seventy-three hatchery steelhead in three days by nymphing with egg patterns. The fish that slipped by us and reached the gates of the hatchery were put into tanker trucks and taken downriver to run the gauntlet again for more "sport." Neither of us has sunk that low since.

The greatest of the Atlantic salmon rivers in the United States, the Connecticut, used to have twenty-five strains of salmon, each uniquely adapted to its home tributary. They were all wiped out by dams and pollution. Over the years, millions of hatchery smolts from other rivers were introduced to the river with a near-zero result. You can't fool them; it's not their home river. And even if it were their home river, hatchery-produced fish have become so domesticated that they lack the instincts to survive for more than a few generations anyway. In fact, their genetics are so poorly adapted to life in the wild, if a hatchery steelhead spawns naturally with a wild steelhead, the number of surviving offspring is reduced by 50 percent compared to two wild fish spawning. And if two hatchery fish somehow survive to meet up and spawn together naturally, their progeny have only 37 percent of the reproductive fitness found in fish born to two wild parents.

And yet, despite the mountain of peer-reviewed scientific evidence demonstrating that hatcheries don't work, our addiction continues to grow. Pacific nations such as Japan, Korea, Russia, and the United States, when combined, pour 52 billion hatchery salmon into the ocean each year. All these fish now compete with each other, and with the remaining wild salmon, for food in warmer, less nutrient-rich waters. In years with peak Asian hatchery releases, the average size of Bristol Bay sockeye and Yukon River Chinook shrinks dramatically. It's clear now that we're exceeding the current carrying capacity of the mighty North Pacific.

Hatchery steelhead return as adults at a rate of .003 percent. Despite a massive hatchery program created to save them, in 2015 only fifty-four endangered Red Fish Lake sockeye salmon made the 1,000-mile journey to the lake. In 2017 not one hatchery fish made it back. Think of all these dumb smolts getting to an estuary, or the ocean, and cruising around the surface looking for pellets to fall from the sky. Well, it makes the pelicans and cormorants happy.

In eastern Canada, the Atlantic salmon smolts migrate to the waters off Greenland to feed. The smolts from hatcheries are so slow that by the time they reach the feeding grounds, the food they are supposed to eat has grown too large to fit into their mouths.

Some anglers are rabid proponents of hatchery fish because they can kill them, show them off, and eat them. Colleges like the University of Washington, which has the largest School of Fisheries in the world, like hatcheries because they provide employment for graduates. And the hatchery industry just wants to protect itself and stay in business. With Trout in the Classroom programs, the hatchery system teaches young people that humans can do better than nature. We don't need wild fish, or wild free-flowing rivers, we can just ship salmon around dams, truck them across states, and shoot them through the air with "salmon cannons." We can create Frankenfish that are three times larger, and farmed salmon that cost half as much as wild fish.

But here's the reality: Hatcheries not only don't work, they also damage wild fish populations and cost the public enormous amounts of money in the process. A single, harvested spring Chinook salmon from the Entiat Hatchery in Washington state costs citizens—you and me—$68,031 to produce in one sample year. While that may be an outlier, none of our hatchery programs come cheap: A harvested hatchery steelhead from the North Fork Nooksack River cost as much as $2,700. On the Skagit, it's down to $1,000 per fish. On the Elk River in Oregon, the hatchery Chinook salmon are a relative bargain, coming in at about $48 per fish. If the negative biological impacts of hatcheries on wild fish aren't enough to convince you, the economics should.

Imagine if, instead of spending billions on hatcheries, we put that money into river restoration. We all agree, as does the best available science, that wild fish, because of genetic- and life-history diversity, survive adverse conditions much better than hatchery fish. If we could allow wild fish to live without the negative impact of hatcheries, in an improved habitat, it's entirely possible that on some rivers we'd end up with more fish than anyone alive today has ever seen. Think about that.

The wild salmon, steelhead, and trout we cherish are more than objects of desire for anglers, or food for hungry people, or income for commercial fishermen. They are also the proverbial canary in the coal mine for every living creature on the planet, including us humans. We all need clean, healthy water, and if the species that live in it are going extinct, what does that mean for us? Now more than ever, as we face the effects of a warming planet, it's time we pay attention.

OPPOSITE: *A diverse group of environmentalists, commercial fishers, tribal members, anglers, and concerned citizens protest Atlantic salmon fish farms; finally in 2018, Washington became the last West Coast state to ban non-native salmon farms. Bainbridge Island.* Ben Moon

I bet this isn't the most uplifting story you have read. If you're a fisherman, you're probably already tying bass and carp flies. But I hope it makes you angry, too. Angry enough to take some action. Global climate change is happening, and it amplifies all the other problems facing coldwater fish. Whether you believe the warming of our planet is human-caused or a natural occurrence makes a big difference. If it's a natural cycle, then sit back and relax because there's nothing we can do about it. But if we are the cause of any of it, we're also the solution. I've found that the cure for depression is action. What can we do? Here is a menu to choose from.

• Get involved with local organizations and help clean up and take care of your local stream. If you can't be on the front lines fighting for wild fish and wild rivers, then support those organizations and individuals who are. I don't mean $25 donations. If you're paying $500 a day plus tips for a guide and $1,000 for the rod, then dig deep into those pockets. How much is it worth to you to fish for and catch wild trout and salmon?

• Be sure the fishery-education programs in our schools are giving the right message to young people.

• Fight for clean water, fight to leave more water in our rivers, and fight for clean energy.

• Clean your gear when moving from one river to another.

• Don't eat farmed salmon from ocean net pens. Insist on sustainably caught fish. How you eat can be a revolutionary act.

• Work to take out deadbeat dams that hamper fish migrations.

• Don't vote for dumbass, climate change–denying politicians.

• Go fishing, and take a kid with you. Our kids and grandkids are the key to any long-range solution. All the factors that threaten our trout and salmon threaten our kids as well.

When we love something, we protect it. We anglers are the ones who love our trout and salmon the most. It's time to start doing the hard work of protecting them.

OPPOSITE: *All kids want to fish. Three generations of fly fishermen.* Chouinard Family Archives

NEXT SPREAD: *Genetically distinct coastal wolves feed on herring eggs on the north coast of British Columbia, Canada.* Ian McAllister

Your vote could finish the job.

The environment is in crisis.

This November 2nd, how we vote could determine whether American children will, by the time they reach middle age, face life on a dying planet. We can do better. But we don't have much time. Register. Get informed. Vote the environment November 2nd.

Vote the environment

Why Voting Is
Not a Waste of Time

First published on Patagonia's blog, The Cleanest Line, *September 12, 2016*

In the United States only 58 percent of eligible citizens bothered to vote in the 2012 presidential election. Of those, many voted only for president and left the rest of the ballot blank.

They say all politics is local. Why wouldn't all of us care about who we elect to teach our kids, or whether we clean up the local creek or canal? Should we care about preventing a developer from filling in the local swamp where you hunt and fish? Or fighting a city council to keep a vacant lot available for gardening in your town?

Ask the people of Flint, Michigan, about fresh water. Ask the children with asthma in West Virginia about clean air. Ask the people of Vernon, California, about contaminated soil.

Put very simply, without a healthy environment, we are toast.

It's mostly old, retired white men (I'm an old—active—white man myself) who vote consistently, and they tend to vote against issues like education (their kids are grown up), progressive taxes, the environment, and any change or project that won't be completed until after they are dead.

Only 25 percent of young people (eighteen to thirty) voted in the 2010 midterm elections. Most young voters feel disenfranchised and disillusioned by politics, but if they voted in full force, the politicians would have to take their issues seriously, like student debt, fair pay, and housing. It's a self-perpetuating cycle of apathy and inaction.

OPPOSITE: *A Patagonia get-out-the-vote ad for the 2004 election.* Photo: Joel Rogers

Then there's the single-issue voter who disregards what's going on in the world and only cares about a single issue be it abortion, taxes, the gender or race of a candidate—or they just hate all government. These people also tend to vote for seriously uneducated politicians.

This great country of ours is rated seventeenth in the world in quality of life, fourteenth in education, and thirty-seventh in healthcare. Most of the countries in the top ratings are socialist democracies.

Many Americans have a very negative view of socialism, equating it with communism and welfare. Yet they don't realize that we actually are a social welfare society. It's just that we are subsidizing giant agro-businesses, too-big-to-fail banks, fossil-fuel companies, and monopolistic corporations—many of which, through "legal" machinations, pay no taxes. In the United States, more than $37 billion in subsidies goes to fossil-fuel companies. The question is not government subsidies per se, but who and what is being subsidized. With our tax dollars, we are supporting the wrong entities.

Government doesn't move unless it's pushed. This can be done by you and me, or by the Koch brothers, or Wall Street. The Koch brothers have poured tens of millions of dollars into fighting climate reform. Bill McKibben of 350.org said the Kochs "hide their contributions through outfits like DonorsTrust, closely linked to the Kochs and focused not on conducting research to disprove climate change (a difficult task in a warming world), but on raising doubts about it wherever and however possible, a tactic borrowed from the tobacco industry."

We used to be called citizens. We can still act like citizens by exercising our right and responsibility to vote. It is a very serious time in the story of this planet where we have the potential to destroy our natural world or to save this lovely blue planet—our home. The politicians who deny climate change and think they are smarter than 99 percent of the world's climate scientists are either crooks or dumbasses. So why would you vote for them?

If we don't act, especially by intelligently voting for the people and issues that matter, then someone else will—someone who doesn't care about a future for our children and other wild things.

All of us working together can elect the government we need rather than be forced to live with the one we deserve.

OPPOSITE: *A Patagonia ad featuring musician Jack Johnson and the Vote for Life on Earth campaign* Photo: Thomas Campbell

NEXT SPREAD: *Feel the Verm. Go vote. A 2018 catalog spread.* Photo: John Sherman Collection

Cast a positive vote for life on earth.

"When you vote to improve water and air quality you are voting to improve human health. When you vote to provide incentives to use renewable energy you are helping create jobs and energy independence, and in turn making an investment in peace. When you Vote The Environment you are not voting for one isolated issue, you are voting for all the issues." – *Jack Johnson*

To learn more about the candidates' records on environmental issues, visit votetheenvironment.org.

Feel the Verm. Go vote. **John Sherman**

What Midterms?

You have been misled and lied to. Your communities are at risk: Our lands and waters are being sold off to the highest bidder; pesticides are replacing topsoil; and toxic factories are poisoning our rivers, streams and the air we breathe. We don't have two (more) years to lose.

It's worse than we feared.

Since the current administration took office, they've taken a rusted chainsaw to decades of hard-won environmental regulations that, if imperfect, helped millions of Americans lead healthier lives, protected millions of acres of public land and represented crucial first steps for addressing the climate crisis.

Sucking up to failing industries, they've made it OK to dump toxic waste into local streams, for obsolete power plants to spew poisons, and they're even considering letting uranium mines contaminate drinking water. They've rescinded bans on offshore oil and gas drilling in the Atlantic and Arctic, and proposed opening nearly all U.S. waters—and several national parks—to drilling, too. They've rolled back efforts to reduce methane leaks—methane being a shorter-lived, but far more potent greenhouse gas than carbon dioxide. And let's not forget the president's unilateral withdrawal from the Paris climate agreement. We're getting cooked.

However, there is a glimmer of hope in all of this—it's you.

Everywhere we look, we've been inspired by people like you who understand that if we don't change course, we'll be the next endangered species.

You've turned out in record numbers at protests. From the 200,000 of you that jammed the streets of Washington, D.C., for the April 2017 People's Climate March, to the 50,000 more who marched in sister city demonstrations, to the 6,000 of you who turned out to protest the president's proposed reduction of Bears Ears and Grand Staircase-Escalante National Monuments.

You've been in touch with government officials like they're family: 228,518 of you contacted your legislators, submitting 152,175 comments and making 5,802 phone calls in less than a week.

You've volunteered more than $1 million worth of hours to environmental nonprofits (see page 105).

But you can't let up now.

You've got to vote in this November's midterms elections.

Midterms typically lag behind the presidential years, and in 2014, the turnout was more pathetic than it's been since 1942 when many eligible voters were deployed overseas. Only 36 percent of eligible American voters cast a ballot. A little more than a third.

For those who do give a damn, there's an opportunity in this apathy—it means you can have an even bigger impact if you do show up.

Between now and November 6, we'll track several key Senate, congressional and gubernatorial races online, so you can get educated on the issues and public lands fights, and learn which candidates are committed to addressing global warming.

"It is a very serious time in the story of this planet where we have the potential to destroy our natural world or to save this lovely blue planet—our home," says Patagonia founder Yvon Chouinard. "We used to be called citizens, not consumers. We can still act like citizens by exercising our right and responsibility to vote."

Dear Mister President

Sent 1996

When Bill Clinton was first elected president, the environmental community was warned that he needed to be aggressively pushed to do the right thing for the planet. It turns out I could have sent this letter to every president since Clinton!

July 11, 1996

President William Clinton
The White House
Washington, DC

Dear Mr. President,

Thank you for inviting me to the gathering of CEOs in May and for inviting our new CEO, Dave Olsen, to the work and family discussion in Tennessee. We're flattered and humbled by your interest in our company.

I'll get to the point. I have been asked by several long-time friends and colleagues in the environmental movement, to endorse Ralph Nader for President. I have decided not to do so; I don't want Bob Dole as my President. Because I'm not writing the public letter my friends hoped I would, I want to send you a private one.

OPPOSITE: *Love Canal activist Lois Gibbs' son, Michael, protesting outside the Niagara Falls City Hall in 1980. New York.* Penelope Ploughman, courtesy of the University Archives, University at Buffalo

On February 19, 2016, Reverend Jesse Jackson led more than 500 people past the abandoned General Motors plants and to the Flint water tower to protest the water crisis in Flint, Michigan.
Zackary Canepari

Before doing so, please let me make an important point. I understand that the approaches you and I take are often quite different for an important reason. I own my own company. If I want to do something, I can. You must answer to nearly 250 million shareholders. You must share power with Congress. And you must constantly battle, and accommodate, well-funded special interest groups. There are many things, I assume, that you want to do but are prevented from doing because the shareholders (the public) or Congress may not agree. So, I acknowledge that there are pressures on you that are far beyond the pressures I know, and that what works for me will not always work for you.

In business (and elsewhere), a key element of great leadership is being willing and decisive enough to do the very things others say you should not do. We've been at our strongest when we've gone against the grain and changed to better and, ultimately, more successful practices.

You've talked supportively about values-driven companies, ones whose employees have an obvious passion. You've pointed to companies that are innovative, that are ahead of the curve. You praised our company for holding these attributes, so you clearly recognize and appreciate them in business. And I like it when I see those values in you. But there seems to be a disconnect—because I don't believe you're applying to politics the practices you respect in business.

You have fought more visibly and with more vigor on ideological ground since the 1994 election; in doing so, you helped stop the onslaught of attacks from the Republicans, and I am particularly grateful for that. But there is a large difference between stopping the Republicans (and retaining the status quo) and fighting for the genuine changes we need, given the fragile state of the world's environment and cultures.

People today are genuinely afraid—and not just for their jobs. They see their governments, their religions, their cultures collapsing around them. They hear nothing but doomsday scenarios for our planet Earth. They are doubting that their children will have clean water to drink and strong enough immune systems to fight off cancers or new exotic diseases. Giving them a greater sense of confidence in this area would help them begin to develop confidence elsewhere. They believe that jobs can follow a commitment to protect the environment, and they believe, rightfully, that we can have both a good environment and a healthy economy. They know that a focus only on jobs does nothing to address their greatest insecurity. They see that the fate of the Earth is not a separate issue: it is a unifying one.

The free trade accords have done nothing to help bring more security. Rather, they lead people to feel like we have less control over our own destinies because some faceless organization has say over our own laws and regulations. Equally important, these accords support the growing trend toward globalization. Security lies in small, healthy local economies and communities, not massive big business. The days of gigantism in warfare, in business, and in government are coming to an end, as they should. As Darwin said, diversity is strength.

We need you to take stronger stands in defense of the environment. What do I mean by a stronger stand? Tell the American people that, after twenty-five years, we will finally live up to the promise of the Clean Water Act. Two-thirds of America's rivers and streams were once unsafe for swimming

413

and fishing, that number is down to one-third. We've made great progress, but not enough for a nation that says it's the greatest one on Earth. A strong President can tell the American people that within fifteen years, every river in America will be safe for swimming and fishing. It's as bold as saying we'll go to the moon—but it's much more relevant to the everyday lives of Americans. To do this, we would need to abandon all pesticides within the next twelve years. In phasing out all pesticides, you would tell the American people that we will restore balance and beauty to the American landscape. You can tell them that their children will have fewer cancers. You will redefine patriotism. You will take on the pesticide industry (an enemy is important in politics and I can't think of a better one aside from the tobacco industry). And, if you use the right language, you can make the farmer—still an American icon—the genuine hero.

Such an approach would be fraught with danger. But it would make us a stronger and healthier nation. It would be presidential. It would be a graceful transition from a century of pillage and squandering the environment to a century of restoration. And it would help you get re-elected with a strong mandate. You could champion a tax on all of our nonrenewable resources that properly reflects their true costs. With education, the consumers would welcome such a system of taxation, but only if it replaced the unpopular and inefficient current system.

As I said, I believe the characteristics of leadership are the same in business and politics. (When I say I don't want to bankrupt my company for a cause, I assume it's very similar to you saying you don't want to risk re-election for an outlandish stand.) And the rewards of leadership are the same as well. Every single time I've taken a very strong stand—whether it's publicly supporting Planned Parenthood or committing our company to only using organically grown cotton in our clothes—I've made more money. Every time. The same can be true in politics. The stronger your stands in defense of the environment, the more votes you'll get.

I believe political capital is one of the few resources that increases with its use. The more you are willing to spend, the more you will acquire. The fact of a strong stand matters almost as much as its content, because people today want leaders who will stand up and fight. They want role models who can teach them about defending principles and ideas. The environment is the one issue where you and the Republicans are furthest apart. They won't be

Conventional, chemically intensive farming techniques. Oxnard, California. Michael Ableman

stupid enough to give you a chance to veto a major bill—they've learned their lesson. So, you are on your own on this one; if it is to be a big issue, you need to make it a big issue. But if you take the bold steps—genuinely bold steps—in the area of environmental protection, you will be a stronger President and a great leader.

I hope this letter does not sound arrogant. I don't want to pretend for a moment that my very serious consideration of a Nader endorsement will have an impact on your decisions or your presidency. But I appreciate the dialog between you and my company. Out of respect for that relationship, and for your office, I figured I owed you a direct challenge.

Respectfully,
Yvon Chouinard

Why a Tools Conference?

First published as the Introduction to Tools for Grassroots Activists, *Nora Gallagher and Lisa Meyers (eds), Patagonia Books, 2016*

Over the years, I've been influenced by many nature writers like Henry David Thoreau, Rachel Carson, and Edward Abbey. I pretty much got to know what the problems were but it was lost on me what I, as one person, could do to fix them.

The first time I came to realize the power of an individual to effect major change was in the early seventies. A group of us went to our local theater to watch a surf movie. At the end, a young surfer asked the audience to attend a city council meeting to speak out against the city's plan to channel and develop the mouth of the Ventura River, one of the best surf points in the area and only five hundred yards from Patagonia's office.

Several of us went to the meeting to protest the possible disruption of our surf break. We knew vaguely that the Ventura River had once been a major spawning creek for steelhead and Chinook salmon. In fact, in the 1940s, the river had an annual run of 4,000 to 5,000 sea-run rainbows. Then two dams were built and the water was diverted, killing the fish run and causing the bars at the mouth of the river to be starved of sand. Except for winter rains, the only water left in the river flowed from the one-stage sewage treatment plant. At the city council meeting, several city-paid experts testified that the river was

OPPOSITE: *Protect what you love! New York City climate march, 2014.* Photo: Tim Davis

NEXT SPREAD: *The sun sets over Bears Ears National Monument, north of Mexican Hat, Utah. In 2018, President Trump announced that he is scaling back Bears Ears by 1.1 million acres.* Photo: Katherine Frey/Getty

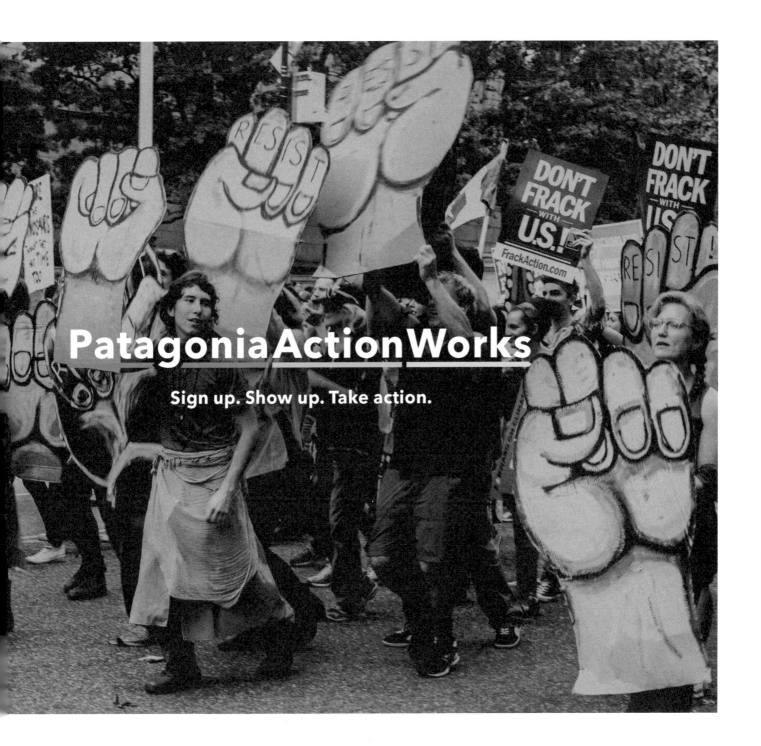

PatagoniaActionWorks

Sign up. Show up. Take action.

The President
Stole Your Land

"If you want public lands, you're going to
have to fight for them." *Yvon Chouinard*

dead and that channeling would have no effect on the birds and other wildlife at the estuary or on the surf break.

Then Mark Capelli, a young graduate student, gave a slide show of photos he had taken along the river, of the birds that lived in the willows, the muskrats, water snakes, and eels that spawned in the estuary. When he showed the slides of steelhead smolt, everyone stood up and cheered. Yes, several dozen steelhead still came to spawn in our "dead" river.

The development plan was defeated. We gave Mark office space, a mailbox, and small contributions to help fight the battle for the river. As more development plans cropped up, the Friends of the Ventura River worked to defeat them and to clean up the water and increase its flow. A second stage was added to the sewage plant and then a third. Wildlife increased and a few more steelhead began to spawn. Mark taught us two important lessons: grassroots efforts could make a difference, and degraded habitat could, with effort, be restored. Inspired by his work, we began to make regular donations to small groups working to save or restore natural habitat, rather than give money to large, nongovernmental organizations with a big staff and overhead, and corporate connections.

There are many scientists and smart people who work tirelessly to bring us knowledge and facts, but they are too introverted or afraid of losing their jobs to champion their beliefs. Science without action is dead science. I also don't have the courage to be on the front lines, but at least I've learned the power of activism and I want to support it.

We held our first Tools Conference in 1994 at Chico Hot Springs, Montana. We knew we'd hit pay dirt when the local newspaper ran a front-page story about how we "greenies" asked the hotel we were staying in not to change the sheets every day to save water, a revolutionary idea at the time.

While I am often embarrassed to admit to being a businessman—I've been known to call them sleazeballs—I realize that many activists could learn some of the skills that businesspeople possess. When I told that first group of activists that they were businesspeople, there was some snickering in the group. They all thought business was the enemy. I told them that their little NGOs had expenses, did marketing, and had to follow budgets: They had all the problems of business.

OPPOSITE: *Free the Snake Flotilla at the Wawawai Landing above the Lower Granite Dam, Washington. 2015.* Ben Moon

At that time, many universities had schools of business that had no classes in environmental responsibility, and the schools of environmental studies had no classes in business. I thought I would bring some activists together with people who knew about strategic planning, community organizing, technology, and money.

Now, twenty-one years later, the Tools Conference has really come into its own. Every two years, we bring together a hundred activists at Stanford Sierra Camp on Fallen Leaf Lake near South Lake Tahoe and let them feast on what the best trainers available in their fields can give them: grassroots organizing, lobbying, planning strategy and communications, getting the most out of social media, fundraising, using Google tools, and how to work with business. And we don't just bring in good trainers—we bring in the best.

It's easy to be depressed these days, as so much of the wild world has been denigrated or destroyed. But I like to remind myself that things change. You see nothing happening, and then all of a sudden, it changes. It was like that with tobacco. Remember when people smoked on airplanes? The tobacco industry held sway, the way the oil industry does now. They had teams of PR people and lawyers; even though the medical world knew that smoking caused lung cancer and so did they, they continued to thrive. For fifty years, people worked to connect cigarettes to lung cancer and to ban smoking. The tobacco companies appeared invincible. But the antismoking groups kept at it, year after year, slowly and steadily until smoking was banned on airplanes, and then in restaurants and bars, and, finally, CVS stopped selling cigarettes. It was like that with gay marriage, too. Unthinkable, and then … done.

The people who won these battles were like those Patagonia supports. Some examples:

Royal Dutch Shell wanted to drill 1,500–10,000 coal-bed methane gas wells in the Sacred Headwaters, where three of Canada's greatest wild salmon and steelhead rivers, the Skeena, Stikine, and Nass, are born. The Skeena Watershed Conservation Coalition—which describes itself as a mix of redneck bravado, First Nations culture, and logger work ethic with a dash of hippie passion—defeated them.

A young woman we supported in her efforts to protect mountains in Appalachia from coal mining went on to organize for the Sierra Club. When they began this phase of the campaign in 2010, the nation was getting 50 percent of its electricity from coal. Today, it's less than 40 percent.

Participants at the 2015 Patagonia Tools for Grassroots Activists conference at Fallen Leaf Lake, California. Amy Kumler

Twenty years ago, dam removal was barely even discussed, but in 2013, communities in eighteen states, working in partnership with nonprofit organizations and state and federal agencies, removed fifty-one dams. And in 2014, the people of Chile united to stop what would have been the biggest energy project in the country's history—five huge dams built on two of the wildest rivers in Patagonia.

You'll find the best practices and tricks of the trade from those who teach and lead at Patagonia's Tools Conference. We hope to reach well beyond those one hundred activists who come to Fallen Leaf Lake each year, to everyone who needs the tools to carry the work forward. Thank you and good luck.

Since 1994, we have had 1,500 activists come to our conferences.

NEXT SPREAD: *On March 2, 2009, some 12,000 young people gathered to show their elected officials that young voters demand real action on climate change. Washington, DC.* Robert Van Waarden/Survival Media

The Responsible Economy

First published in The Responsible Company: What We've Learned from Patagonia's First Forty Years *by Yvon Chouinard and Vincent Stanley, Patagonia Books, 2013*

In my three-quarters of a century of stupid stunts, I've had enough near-death experiences that I've accepted the fact that I'm going to die someday. I'm not too bothered by it. There's a beginning and an end to all life—and to all human endeavors.

Species evolve and die off. Empires rise, then break apart. Businesses grow, then fold. There are no exceptions. I'm OK with all that. Yet it pains me to bear witness to the sixth great extinction, where we humans are directly responsible for the extirpation of so many wonderful creatures and invaluable indigenous cultures. It saddens me to observe the plight of our own species; we appear to be incapable of solving our problems.

I saw the birth of my first grandchild in 2013, and I worry about the future she faces. When I was born, the human population was 2.5 billion. When she will be just thirty-eight years old, the population will hit 9 billion. If everyone consumed the way an average American does, humans would be using up more than four planets' worth of resources. Hardly "sustainable."

The reason for this crisis is very simple. There are too many of us consuming too much stuff, and we demand that it be as cheap and disposable

OPPOSITE: *Plastic, single-use, water bottles baled and off to the recycler. Sixty percent of Patagonia's fabrics are made using recycled polyester and much of that comes from recycled PET bottles.* Rick Ridgeway

NEXT SPREAD: *Anne Gilbert Chase puts her head down against the blowing spindrift of Hyalite Canyon, Montana, wearing our Pluma Jacket featuring a 100% recycled nylon shell fabric. Our mission is to build the best, most innovative, and most durable products with an ironclad lifetime guarantee. All our products are field-tested. 2016.* Jason Thompson

as possible. (Have you looked at the junk in one of those airline mail-order catalogs recently? Does the world really need a special tool for cutting bananas?) No wonder we don't want to face up to the cause of our problems: It's us! We are no longer called "citizens." Economists, government, and Wall Street call us "consumers." We "destroy, waste, squander, use up," and that's just Webster's definition. The sad truth is that the world economy revolves around our consumption. The stock markets rise and dip according to consumer confidence.

And while we work harder and harder to get more of what we don't need, we lay waste to the natural world. Dr. Peter Senge, author and MIT lecturer, says, "We are sleepwalking into disaster, going faster and faster to get to where no one wants to be."

Can we even imagine what an economy would look like that wouldn't destroy the home planet? A responsible economy?

Patagonia has worked for some twenty-plus years to try to behave more responsibly. In 1991, Patagonia was growing at a rate of 50 percent a year, and we hit the wall in the midst of the savings-and-loan crisis. The bank reduced our credit line twice in several months, and the company ended up borrowing from friends to meet payroll and laying off 20 percent of our workforce on July 31, 1997. That's a day I still refer to as Black Wednesday.

We learned the hard way about living within our means. We had exceeded our resources and limitations. We had become dependent, like the world economy, on growth we could not sustain. I even thought about selling the company. But if I hadn't stayed in business, I never would have realized the parallel between Patagonia's unsustainable push for growth and that of our whole industrial economy.

After that day in 1991, we added a third point to our mission statement. It now reads, "Build the best product, cause no unnecessary harm, and use business to inspire and implement solutions to the environmental crisis."

Making things in a more responsible way is a good start, and many companies like ours have started doing that, but in the end, we will not have a

OPPOSITE: *We ran the "Don't Buy This Jacket" ad about our partnership with customers to take mutual responsibility for the full life of our products. We added the concepts of reducing consumption, repairing and reusing the garment, and finally recycling it and named the partnership Worn Wear.*

DON'T BUY THIS JACKET

It's Black Friday, the day in the year retail turns from red to black and starts to make real money. But Black Friday, and the culture of consumption it reflects, puts the economy of natural systems that support all life firmly in the red. We're now using the resources of one-and-a-half planets on our one and only planet.

Because Patagonia wants to be in business for a good long time—and leave a world inhabitable for our kids—we want to do the opposite of every other business today. We ask you to buy less and to reflect before you spend a dime on this jacket or anything else.

Environmental bankruptcy, as with corporate bankruptcy, can happen very slowly, then all of a sudden. This is what we face unless we slow down, then reverse the damage. We're running short on fresh water, topsoil, fisheries, wetlands—all our planet's natural systems and resources that support business, and life, including our own.

The environmental cost of everything we make is astonishing. Consider the R2® Jacket shown, one of our best sellers. To make it

COMMON THREADS INITIATIVE

REDUCE
WE make useful gear that lasts
a long time
YOU don't buy what you don't need

REPAIR
WE help you repair your Patagonia gear
YOU pledge to fix what's broken

REUSE
WE help find a home for
Patagonia gear you no longer need
YOU sell or pass it on

RECYCLE
WE will take back your Patagonia
gear that is worn out
YOU pledge to keep your stuff out of
the landfill and incinerator

REIMAGINE
TOGETHER we reimagine a world where
we take only what nature can replace

required 135 liters of water, enough to meet the daily needs (three glasses a day) of 45 people. Its journey from its origin as 60% recycled polyester to our Reno warehouse generated nearly 20 pounds of carbon dioxide, 24 times the weight of the finished product. This jacket left behind, on its way to Reno, two-thirds its weight in waste.

And this is a 60% recycled polyester jacket, knit and sewn to a high standard; it is exceptionally durable, so you won't have to replace it as often. And when it comes to the end of its useful life we'll take it back to recycle into a product of equal value. But, as is true of all the things we can make and you can buy, this jacket comes with an environmental cost higher than its price.

There is much to be done and plenty for us all to do. Don't buy what you don't need. Think twice before you buy anything. Go to patagonia.com/CommonThreads or scan the QR code below. Take the Common Threads Initiative pledge, and join us in the fifth "R," to reimagine a world where we take only what nature can replace.

ABOVE: *Senior product designer Christian Regester develops an early prototype at our in-house sewing room. "Perfection is achieved, not when there is nothing more to add, but when there is nothing left to take away." – Antoine de Saint-Exupéry.* Kyle Sparks

OPPOSITE: *Our wetsuits are made of natural rubber—as opposed to petroleum-based neoprene—gathered on* Havea *rubber farms like this one in Sri Lanka. 2016.* Tim Davis

Recycling down at a facility in France. Tim Davis

"sustainable economy" unless we consume less. Economists tell us that would cause the economy to crash.

I think we at Patagonia are mandated by our mission statement to face the question of growth, both by bringing it up and by looking at our own situation as a business fully ensnared in the global industrial economy. I personally don't have the answer, but in the back of my simple brain a few words come to the fore, words that have guided my life and Patagonia's life as a company: quality, innovation, responsibility, simplicity.

I recently read a book about forty companies that have been in business for over 200 years. I thought if those companies could exist that long, maybe they have some guiding principles that a responsible economy should follow. The common traits they all had were quality, innovation, and restrained growth. Coming from a background of making the very best, lifesaving tools for the mountains, we applied the same philosophy to clothing. We have been

A wool recycling facility in Italy. Jeff Johnson

innovators using technology not for the sake of inventing new products, but to replace old, polluting, and inefficient products and methods with cleaner, simpler, and more appropriate technology. Every garment we make, for example, can be recycled now, unthinkable ten years ago.

We are working with other clothing manufacturers on measuring the environmental impact of textile manufacturing and which will be, in the end, public-facing. You will be able to see the impact and history of a pair of jeans by pointing your smartphone at the bar code on their label. By choosing to consume more responsibly, perhaps we can relearn how to be citizens again and be part of the civil democracy.

I have always believed that a design is perfected not when you can't add more but when you can't take anything away. An illustrator becomes an artist when he or she can evoke the same feeling with simpler line and form. Simplicity is the way to perfection. As a mountain climber, it pleases me to see the

ABOVE: *The Worn Wear repair shop in our New York SoHo store. All our stores have staff trained to make on-site repairs. To make it even easier for customers to fix their broken but still usable Patagonia gear, we built Worn Wear repair trucks that tour the country making on-site repairs. We now have two vehicles in the United States and two in Europe.* Colin McCarthy

OPPOSITE: *Worn Wear is actually a business model for how a company can create a partnership with its customers to take mutual responsibility for the footprint of all the stuff we humans consume.*

1%
for the planet.

Patagonia has been giving 1% of sales to grassroots environmental groups working to preserve and restore the natural world since 1985. As of spring 2016, it amounts to some $76 million in cash and in-kind services. Wanting to encourage other companies to do the same, in 2002, Patagonia founder Yvon Chouinard got together with Craig Mathews, former owner of Blue Ribbon Flies, to create 1% for the Planet, a nonprofit organization that has since enjoyed huge success. Today, 1% for the Planet has more than 1,100 environmentally concerned member companies in more than 40 countries giving 1% of their sales directly to thousands of nonprofits around the globe. That's more than $130 million to drive big, positive environmental change. While 1% may not sound like much, it sure adds up.

1% FOR THE PLANET

The target of a large-scale ski resort development in the heart of British Columbia's Purcell Mountains, the Jumbo Valley remains undeveloped thanks to stubborn resistance from First Nations, local activists and the efforts of Wildsight, a conservation group funded in part by members of 1% for the Planet. **Photo: Steve Ogle** © 2016 Patagonia, Inc.

new generations of climbers soloing and climbing free routes on El Capitan in Yosemite that took us multiple days, fixed ropes, and many pitons to climb.

I enjoy manual labor and love using good tools that leverage the efficiency of my efforts. But not a tool or machine that takes away the pleasure of the labor. (I think of that banana cutter, which replaces a good tool: my knife.) I think the simple life really begins with owning less stuff.

We are questioning what Patagonia can do, as a company making some of this stuff, to lead us into the next, more responsible economy. After we grew too fast in the 1990s, we tried not growing at all. That resulted in stagnation and frustrated customers who often could not buy what they needed from us. You do not need a zero-growth economy. (In the same way, you don't have to stop people from having babies in order to stabilize the population: People die, babies are born; you need a balance between the two.) What we are reaching toward is an economy that does not rely on insatiable consumerism as its engine, but an economy that stops harmful practices and replaces them with either new, more efficient practices or older practices that worked just fine. An economy with less duplication of consumer goods, less throw-away-and-close-your-eyes. We don't know exactly how this will play out. But we do know that now is the time for all corporations to think about it and act.

I hope Patagonia can find a way to make decisions about growth based on being here for the next 200 years—and not damaging the planet further in the process. As my granddaughter grows up, I'll do my best to see that, just as I did and her parents did, she has a life in nature that she loves. And that she will want to protect it.

PREVIOUS SPREAD: *1% for the Planet was launched by Yvon and Craig Mathews with the mandate that businesses would give 1 percent of sales to a vetted list of environmental groups.* Photo: Steve Ogle

OPPOSITE: *Fitz Caldwell rocks it. Laguna Torre, El Chaltén, Argentina.* Rebecca Caldwell

Do Good

First published in Let My People Go Surfing: The Education of a Reluctant Businessman *by Yvon Chouinard, Penguin Books, updated edition 2016*

"The day is coming when a single carrot, freshly observed, will set off a revolution"
– Paul Cezanne

Doing the least amount of harm in making our products is commendable, but doing less harm doesn't mean the same as doing good. Growing cotton organically on fields that should really be used to grow food for a hungry planet should not be defined as beneficial for the planet or society.

I feel pretty good about our efforts so far in causing less harm in our supply chain. But have those efforts just been offset by our growth, by us using up even more resources to make even more clothes that many of us don't really need?

Can we get beyond being the "elephant in the room": ourselves? Is there a way to produce our products in such a way that truly would be good for people and the planet?

A few years ago I was talking to a person who had started a successful organic baby food company. She was looking for advice on how she could go further in being more responsible in her business. I said to not be satisfied with merely being organic. "What kind of organic carrots are you using?" I asked. "Where are they grown? Are they grown in large factory farms in the desert that irrigate with fossil water? Are the workers paid a living wage?" These are all questions that when answered responsibly, will lead to causing less harm in

OPPOSITE: *Wes Jackson checks out a Kernza root. Wauhob Prairie, Salina, Kansas.* Jim Richardson

her supply chain. But I didn't know how to tell her to go further than where we were currently stuck ourselves. Now I do.

Among the multitude of threats facing life on Earth there is none more threatening than global climate change. We have put at risk the very factors that make our planet habitable and unique from all other planets.

All the work we do at Patagonia to be a more responsible company is for naught unless we can be a part of the solution to this problem. As David Brower has said, "there is no business to be done on a dead planet." Society's feeble attempts to lower our CO_2 emissions in our use of fossil fuels—endlessly working on symptoms rather than causes—is getting us nowhere. Any slight gains we make toward sustainability are negated by increased growth and consumption.

It is not enough to be satisfied to set a goal of not allowing our CO_2 levels to go above 350 parts per million (we are already passing 400 ppm). We have fiddled for so long without doing anything substantial that we now have to get the levels down to what they were before the Industrial Revolution. The acid absorbed by our oceans is so high that it will take a thousand years to get back to where pH levels are beneficial to life.

How can we do this? We need a revolution and I've always believed that the only revolution that we would likely have would be in agriculture.

I am convinced that if we're going to solve the environmental crisis, we humans can't continue on our current path. Business as usual isn't going to cut it—that's how we got where we are today. And nowhere is the crisis more pressing than in food production, the world's largest industry. The modern "green revolution," with all its technology and chemicals, has failed us.

Research has proven that the green revolution in agriculture with its reliance on GMO seeds, chemical fertilizer, insecticides, and unsustainable use of water has temporarily allowed us to feed more people but it is not sustainable. It comes at the cost of destroying topsoil; poisoning the sky, land, and water; displacing the small farmer; and adding carbon emissions—and in the end it produces less food per acre than more natural farming. Industrial agriculture continues to be the existing paradigm because of massive government subsidies to farmers and the fossil-fuel industry.

OPPOSITE: *A Patagonia anti-GMO ad. 2001.* Photo: Topher Donahue

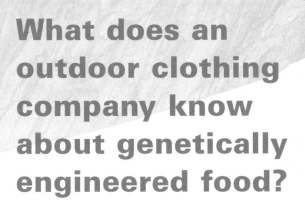

What does an outdoor clothing company know about genetically engineered food?

Not enough, and neither do you.

Even the scientists working on genetic engineering admit they don't know the full story. But despite the fact that we know so little about the impacts, a salmon has already been engineered that grows at twice the rate of normal salmon, a strain of corn has been created with pesticide in every cell, and trees have been engineered with less lignin to break down more easily in the pulping process. What will be the impact on our health, and the health of the ecosystem, once these new species make it out into the wild or into our food supply? No one knows.

Let's not repeat the mistakes we've made in the past with such inadequately tested technologies as DDT and nuclear energy. We don't know enough about the dangers of genetic engineering. Let's find out all the risks before we turn genetically modified organisms loose on the world, or continue to eat them in our food.

Modern food production is one of the main culprits in the destruction of our planet. With 50 percent of the world's habitable land and 70 percent of its water used for pasture and farming, it's doubtful there's any other industry with such deep and widespread impact. And so far, we've done a pretty lousy job of

――――

… we could reverse the trends of global warming simply by changing the way we farm and ranch.

――――

managing ourselves when it comes to agriculture. In the United States alone, we use an estimated 1 billion pounds of pesticides every year. Atrazine, a widely used herbicide and suspected endocrine disruptor, is now present in 94 percent of US drinking water tested by the USDA. Half the world's topsoil has been lost in the last 150 years. Nutrient runoff causes dead zones to blossom in the Gulf of Mexico and in oceans around the world. Biodiversity has plummeted since industrial, monocrop farming, supported by machinery and chemicals, became the norm.

For decades farmers and ranchers have watched land that was once rich and productive grow barren. Modern agriculture, with its promise of increasing production through the use of its plows, monocropping, synthetic fertilizers, insecticides, and pesticides has damaged, eroded, and depleted the soil, forcing farmers into a cycle of dependence, where they can no longer grow their crops without increasing the use of the very techniques that degraded their land in the first place.

The traditional assumption has been that once land is degraded it is degraded forever. But some farmers have found that not only is restoration possible, but it can happen very quickly. By ditching the plow and the spray plane, and using techniques such as cover-cropping, composting, crop rotation, and holistic grazing, farmers can create productive healthy soils within just a couple of years. These soils require less water, produce higher yields during drought, and generally cost less to farm than their modern agriculture counterparts.

It turns out that healthy soils also sequester carbon—a lot of carbon. Cover crops and regenerative grazing techniques increase photosynthesis, which sucks CO_2 out of the air and sinks it in the ground, the switch from chemicals to compost feeds the bacteria and fungi that aid the process and nondisruptive no-till systems keep the carbon locked in. Estimates vary, but even the low end of the spectrum suggests that a global switch to regenerative land husbandry would sequester our total annual emissions back underground. Which means we could reverse the trends of global warming simply by changing the way we farm and ranch.

Scientists at the University of California at Berkeley have done a carbon experiment on a small number of ranches in California. They spread a half-inch layer of compost on rangeland and found that it boosted the soil carbon-sequestration capacity to one half ton to three tons of carbon per hectare per year for each of the eight years the have been testing. [http://alumni.berkeley.edu/california-magazine/just-in/2015-03-10/new-global-warming-remedy-turning-rangelands-carbon-sucking] If this one-time thin application of compost were applied to a quarter of California's rangeland, the soil would absorb three-quarters of California's greenhouse gas emissions.

So what if this idea of sequestering carbon through regenerative agriculture doesn't turn out to be the solution to global climate change? What will we have lost by trying? The dead zones in our oceans will be smaller from less fossil-fuel fertilizer runoff. We will have hurt the stock prices of the large chemical, GMO seed companies, and the giant green revolution agribusinesses. Probably the cost of fast foods will go up from loss of subsidies to the large commodity farms. Will we have gained anything?

We will have given jobs to millions of unemployed young people in meaningful work producing higher quality, more nutritious, locally grown foods. We will have produced more vegetables per hectare using less chemical inputs and water, and gone beyond organic to restorative agriculture. A way to farm that builds topsoil.

That is a pretty big deal. But we have a lot of work to do to get there—and I want to be part of that revolution

In 2013, we started a new company under the name Patagonia Provisions. A food company with the same values as our clothing company. Knowing that we have to produce 50 percent more food by 2050 just to feed this hungry world, we saw an opportunity to help guide the food revolution we will need to do that.

We've put together a small "seal team" of plant geneticists, fisheries biologists, farmers, fishermen, and chefs with a goal of producing the highest quality food.

STRAWBERRIES

A 2012 study by Stanford University found little difference in nutrition between organic and conventionally farmed food other than that there were fewer pesticides in organics. A more recent (2018) study from Inserm—the French equivalent of US National Institutes of Health—found that people who frequently ate organic food were 25 percent less likely to develop any kind of cancer than people who ate organic food infrequently or not at all.

So an organic strawberry from the supermarket is less toxic but isn't nutritionally any better than a conventionally grown one. Chances are that that "organic" strawberry was grown hydroponically without soil or in a field using synthetic soil amendments and this fruit is usually tasteless.

A regenerative and organically grown strawberry has no toxins and is grown in soil using cover crops and compost. This repairs the multitude of micronutrients and minerals that are essential for human health—and the fruit tastes better. The best tasting and probably the most nutritious are wild strawberries.

Claire and Malinda Chouinard picking wild strawberries along the banks of the Cascapédia River, Quebec. Yvon Chouinard

We all know that the type of soil, the climate, and exposure to the sun, etc., greatly affects the quality of wine grapes. Why wouldn't that also be true for vegetables and grains? One of the reasons why it can't be said that an organic carrot is always X percent more nutritious than an industrially grown carrot is that it makes a difference where those carrots are grown. Going beyond organic might also mean growing carrots where they should be grown to optimize their overall quality and do it in such a way that we grow topsoil too.

And I believe that revolution starts, to paraphrase David Brower, by "turning around and taking a step forward." In other words, we need to go back to the old ways of farming, with organic practices, biodynamics, and crop rotation leading the way. Farmers in Brazil used green manures and legume cover crops to double their yields of corn and wheat. Scientists at the Washington State Bread Lab and the Land Institute in Kansas are rediscovering perennial wheat and other heritage grains that require less water and little topsoil disruption. A recent study by Technische Universitat Munchen showed that organic farms emit around 20 percent less greenhouse gasses per yield unit than conventional farms. The Rodale Institute found that organically managed soils can actually sequester more carbon than they release. They found that if all cropland were converted to the regenerative model, it would absorb 40 percent of annual CO_2 releases, and if ranching lands were to do the same, those lands would absorb an additional 71 percent. As we confront global climate change, increasing drought, and a diminishing supply of fossil fuels, it's clearly time to rethink our agricultural practices.

We need to go back to the old ways of fishing, too, with ancient, selective-harvest techniques. In the case of salmon, where healthy, sustainable populations mingle with endangered stocks on the high seas, we can choose to harvest from areas where we know exactly which fish we're catching. We can work to take down dams, stop open-water fish farms, and wean ourselves from destructive hatchery practices. Free-flowing rivers with naturally abundant salmon runs will produce more fish at lower cost, and preserve the riparian ecology at the same time.

OPPOSITE: *Cara club wheat is the product of a cooperative natural wheat-breeding effort to combine high grain yields and flour quality with resistance to multiple fungal diseases. Cara also scored high on evaluations for milling and baking. Skagit Valley, Washington.* Kevin Morse

We need to go back to the old ways of raising animals for food as well. Long before industrial feed lots, growth hormones, and antibiotics came to dominate the livestock industry, there were simpler, healthier ways to produce meat for the table. Free-range, organic livestock produces better, more nutritious meat, creates fewer greenhouse gasses, and allows animals to live a more natural, dignified life. In some cases, such as freely roaming bison, for example, the animals themselves actually contribute to the recovery of wild ecosystems.

If we go back to these old ways, we win on three levels: First, we produce food that tastes better and is better for us. Second, we reduce unemployment—a lot of the conflict around the world has, as its source, the lack of meaningful work for generations of people displaced by technology. And finally, organic agriculture and responsible harvest and husbandry represent our best shot at saving the planet.

Now, what does a clothing company know about food? That's a question I hear a lot, and it's a good one. And I can honestly say that when we started Provisions, the answer was, Next to nothing. But I like to remember that when we started Patagonia more than forty years ago, the question was, What do a bunch of climbers know about clothing? And the answer was the same.

But over the years, we've developed an ethic of how we approach sourcing, making, and selling things, and my goal is to apply this ethic to food. And that means, once again, rolling up our sleeves, learning all we can, and getting to work. We didn't know anything about making fleece out of recycled pop bottles, or organic cotton, or Merino wool or humanely harvested down until we dove into them, either.

With Provisions, it's an especially daunting task, and we don't expect to change the food industry overnight. But I think, if we get it right, we can help start the ball rolling toward a new-old way of producing what we eat.

It's really our only hope.

This is the most important project the company has ever tackled. We might even save the world.

OPPOSITE: *Buffalo on a wet spring prairie on the Cheyenne River Buffalo Ranch, South Dakota.* Jill O'Brien

NEXT SPREAD: *The Earth from space.* Photo courtesy of NASA

We're in business to save our home planet.

Patagonia Mission Statement, October 2018

Our Values

We begin with the premise that all life on Earth is facing a critical time, during which survivability will be the issue that increasingly dominates public concern. Where survivability is not the issue, the quality of human experience of life may be, as well as the decline in health of the natural world as reflected in the loss of biodiversity, cultural diversity, and the planet's life support systems.

The root causes of this situation include basic values embodied in our economic system, including the values of the corporate world. Primary among the problematic corporate values are the primacy of expansion and short-term profit over such other considerations as quality, sustainability, environmental and human health, and successful communities. The fundamental goal of this corporation is to operate in such a manner that we are fully aware of the above conditions, and attempt to reorder the hierarchy of corporate values, while producing products that enhance both human and environmental conditions.

To help achieve these changes, we will make our operating decisions based on the following list of values. They are not presented in order of importance. All are equally important. They represent an "ecology" of values that must be emphasized in economic activity that can mitigate the environmental and social crisis of our times.

- All decisions of the company are made in the context of the environmental crisis. We must strive to do no harm. Wherever possible, our acts should serve to decrease the problem. Our activities in this area will be under constant evaluation and reassessment as we seek constant improvement.

- Maximum attention is given to product quality, as defined by durability, minimum use of natural resources (including materials, raw energy, and transport), multifunctionalism, nonobsolescence, and the kind of beauty that emerges from absolute suitability to task. Concern over transitory fashion trends is specifically not a corporate value.

- The board and management recognize that successful communities are part of a sustainable environment. We consider ourselves to be an integral part of communities that also include our employees, the communities in which we live, our suppliers, and customers. We recognize our responsibilities to all these relationships and make our decisions with their general benefit in mind. It is our policy to employ people who share the fundamental values of this corporation, while representing cultural and ethnic diversity.

- Without giving its achievement primacy, we seek to profit on our activities. However, growth and expansion are values not basic to this corporation.

- To help mitigate any negative environmental consequences of our business activity, we impose on ourselves an annual tax of 1 percent of our gross sales, or 10 percent of profits, whichever is greater. All proceeds of this tax are granted to local community and environmental activism.

- At all levels of operation—board, management, and staff—Patagonia encourages proactive stances that reflect our values. These include activities that influence the larger corporate community to also adjust its values and behavior, and that support, through activism and financially, grassroots and national campaigners who work to solve the current environmental and social crisis.

- In our internal operations, top management will work as a group, and with maximum transparency. This includes an "open book" policy that enables employees easy access to decisions, within normal boundaries of personal privacy and "trade secrecy." At all levels of corporate activity, we encourage open communications, a collaborative atmosphere, and maximum simplicity, while we simultaneously seek dynamism and innovation.

First presented at a 1992 Patagonia board meeting.

Index

Page numbers in italics indicate photographs.

OPPOSITE: *"After a long day of blacksmithing with my Little Giant power hammer."* Tom Frost